Praise for *The Bus*

"[An] honest portrait of NFL life."

—*Sports Illustrated*

"Wojciechowski . . . brings out all Bettis's best qualities in this enjoyable sports autobiography. Accessible, entertaining reading for football fans."

—*Booklist*

"Writing in an easygoing, honest voice, Bettis gives readers a good look at the inside stories of college recruiting, professional contracts, and the agony of NFL injuries."

—*Publishers Weekly*

"Genuinely charming . . . a must-read for fans."

—*Kirkus Reviews*

"Bettis's tale of youthful behavioral struggles in Detroit followed by college greatness at Notre Dame and his subsequently eventful pro career will doubtlessly rope in committed football fans."

—*Bookpage*

"Perfectly riveting . . . It will enjoy a lengthy shelf life."

—*Sunday Tribune Review* (Greensburg, PA)

"Fans get to know all about one of the NFL's most beloved players."

—*Bookshelf*

ALSO BY JEROME BETTIS

Driving Home

THE BUS

MY LIFE IN AND OUT OF A HELMET

JEROME BETTIS

and

GENE WOJCIECHOWSKI

Broadway Books
New York

Published in the United States by Broadway Books, an imprint of The Doubleday
Publishing Group, a division of Random House, Inc., New York.
www.broadwaybooks.com

A hardcover edition of this book was originally published in 2007 by Doubleday.

BROADWAY BOOKS and its logo, a letter B bisected on the diagonal,
are trademarks of Random House, Inc.

Book design by Michael Collica

Library of Congress Cataloging-in-Publication Data
Bettis, Jerome.
The Bus : my life in and out of a helmet / Jerome Bettis and Gene Wojciechowski.
p.   cm.
Includes bibliographical references.
(alk. paper)
1. Bettis, Jerome. 2. Football players—United States—Biography.
I. Wojciechowski, Gene. II. Title.

GV939.B48A3   2007
796.332092—dc22
[B]
2007019214

ISBN 978-0-7679-2666-9

PRINTED IN THE UNITED STATES OF AMERICA

1 3 5 7 9 10 8 6 4 2

First Paperback Edition

I dedicate this book to the man who taught me what it means to be a father, a husband, and a man—my dad.

My father was a giant of a man to me, not because of his size, but because of his stature. From my friends on my block, to the biggest builders in town, Mr. Bettis had a reputation as tough, but fair. He did everything by the book, and that's the way he raised me, my brother, and my sister.

My dad was not the toughest guy in the world, but he was tough when he needed to be. He was also kind when kindness was required, and generous when generosity was in order.

My father was the best father in the world. He was my hero. Whenever somebody asks who inspired me, my answer is always the same: my father. Whether it was working two jobs, or building us a skating rink in the backyard, Dad did what he had to do for us.

I am a father now and I'm just beginning to understand the whys behind everything he did for us. I know I have big shoes to fill, but I learned from the best. My only regret is that he didn't get the chance to see his grandchildren grow up. But he did a great job raising us and the apple does not fall far from the tree—so his grandchildren will be fine.

Dad, you will live in my heart forever. I love you.

—JB
2007

CONTENTS

First Quarter

❖ 1 ❖

January 15, 2006
AFC Divisional Playoff
Pittsburgh Steelers v. Indianapolis Colts
RCA Dome
Indianapolis, Ind.

Steelers offensive coordinator Ken Whisenhunt sat nervously in the visiting team coaches booth of the RCA Dome. A once ear-splitting sellout crowd of 57,449 was now strangely subdued, as if their mouths had been duct-taped shut. Only eighty seconds stood between the Steelers and a second consecutive trip to the AFC Championship game. Pittsburgh led, 21–18, and had the ball on the Colts' 2-yard line.

The reality of the situation had become depressingly clear to the hometown fans. Not only did the Steelers have four downs to cover just 2 yards for the game-clinching score, but the mass transit system known as Jerome "The Bus" Bettis was jogging toward the Pittsburgh huddle. It was over. The Colts, favored by as many as ten points by the Las Vegas wise guys, were going to lose. It would take the Colts the football equivalent of Pittsburgh's fabled 1972 Immaculate Reception, to save them.

Whisenhunt discussed the Steelers' options with head coach Bill Cowher. There were two choices:

Quarterback Ben Roethlisberger could take three snaps and then take a knee three consecutive times, forcing the Colts to use each of their remaining timeouts. Then the Steelers could kick a chip-shot field goal on fourth down, meaning Colts quarterback Peyton Manning would have about a minute, maybe less, to attempt a touchdown drive with no timeouts remaining against the AFC's No. 1 defense.

Or they could do what they had done for years: Give the ball to Bettis.

Whisenhunt knew if the Steelers scored to move ahead by ten the Colts couldn't possibly recover. Whisenhunt recommended the Steelers board the Bus.

"You give the ball to Jerome because Jerome doesn't fumble," he told Cowher and the other offensive assistants. "We're OK because Jerome doesn't fumble."

Cowher agreed.

Whisenhunt called for a goal-line formation. The play was a no-brainer: Counter 38 Power. Bettis could run it with his eyes squeezed shut. Nobody in Steelers history has run that play better than Bettis. Of his 10,000-plus yards gained in a Pittsburgh uniform, it would be fair to say that at least a third of those yards had come on Counter 38 Power.

The Steelers offense took the field. The safest rushing play in the team's Old Testament–thick playbook had been called.

In a nearby broadcast booth, the team of WBGG-AM radio play-by-play announcer Bill Hillgrove, who had spent twelve years as "The Voice of the Steelers," and analyst Tunch Ilkin, a former Pittsburgh All-Pro offensive tackle, told their listeners on the forty-seven-station, three-state-wide Steelers network that the game was done. The last eighty seconds? A formality, nothing more.

As the Steelers broke the huddle, Hillgrove described the action.

Hillgrove: Now the ball's at the 2-yard line. It's gone over on downs to Pittsburgh. They have a first and goal and they've got Jerome Bettis in that lineup.
Ilkin: For all you fantasy football players out there that have Jerome you've got to be very excited right now.
Hillgrove: Wouldn't it be nice for him to get his second touchdown of the game? Here's the give to Jerome. He has it and—
Ilkin: Oh! Fumble! Fumble! He picked it up–oh, no!

Hillgrove: The ball is fumbled . . . and the Colts pick it up! Look out!

Ilkin: Oh, no! My gosh! Oh, my gosh!

Hillgrove: Nick Harper has it—

Ilkin: Oh, my gosh! Somebody's got to tackle him!

Hillgrove: Big Ben tackles him. He tackles him at the 42-yard line.

Ilkin: Oh, my gosh!

Hillgrove: Jerome Bettis, who rarely fumbles, fumbles at the goal line. Nick Harper picks it up and the Colts are still alive with 1:01 to go!

Ilkin: Oh, my gosh! Oh, my gosh! All you got to do is fall on the ball! What a turn of events! OK, now you got 1:01 left, right? The Colts got the ball on the 42-yard line. The game is not over. Cancel the reservations to Denver. We got to finish this one out here. Unbelievable! I just can't believe what I just saw. The Steelers hand the ball off to Jerome with 1:20. All you gotta do is take three in a row quarterback sneaks. . . . The Steelers are lucky that that ball isn't run in for a touchdown by Harper. If it wasn't for Ben Roethlisberger making a shoestring tackle the game's over the other way.

Whisenhunt and the other assistants were in shock. Bettis fumble? How was that possible? Bettis hadn't fumbled once in the entire 2005 season. He'd only fumbled ten times in his last six seasons, only forty-one times in 3,479 regular season carries.

A disturbing thought flashed through Whisenhunt's mind: What if that was the last carry of Bettis's career? Imagine that: The final carry in the glorious thirteen-year career of Jerome Bettis would cost the Steelers a chance to reach the AFC Championship and—if they were to beat the Denver Broncos—to play Super Bowl XL in Bettis's hometown of Detroit.

Whisenhunt wasn't the only one thinking Bettis's career might have come to an inglorious end. In Miami Lakes, Florida, Bettis's former NFL teammate Tim Lester had watched the ball pop free and bounce into Harper's hands.

"No, my boy can't go out like that," thought Lester, who was Bettis's fullback in Los Angeles, St. Louis, and Pittsburgh. "It can't end this way."

In El Paso, Texas, Bettis's former high school coach Bob Dozier also stared at the television screen in disbelief. "Wow, this can't be," he thought. "This kid's done too much to deserve this."

And at Cupha's bar on Pittsburgh's South Side, Steelers fan Terry O'Neill, forty-nine, saw the play and immediately went into cardiac arrest. Two firemen from Company No. 22, who just happened to be in the bar watching the game, rushed to O'Neill's aid and revived him.

The RCA Dome crowd was so loud that the players' eardrums begged for mercy. Manning had sixty-one seconds, three timeouts, and the conference's highest-scoring offense at his disposal. He needed 25 to 30 yards to move into feasible field goal range, 58 yards to win the game outright.

Ilkin, in need of a hug, later asked sideline reporter Craig Wolfley for an update.

"Well, guys, I'm just standing here, just watching Jerome Bettis," said Wolfley. "I've been watching him the last minute or two, and for such an unbelievable career, for such a great leader for the Steelers, this has got to be one of those moments that you just can't believe. It's like a nightmarish moment. He was on his knee, and just the look on his face just said everything about what he was feeling at this time."

No, it didn't. It couldn't.

For thirteen years I had left bits and pieces of myself on NFL football fields from Pittsburgh to San Francisco, all for the chance—just the *chance*—to play in a Super Bowl. That's 13,662 yards, and who knows how many punishing hits, just for the opportunity to reach the pinnacle of my profession. And this one, Super Bowl XL, was going to be in the city where I was born and raised, the city where I carried my first football, where I played my high school ball, where my parents still lived, where I still had deep, strong roots.

Now, in only a few seconds' time, my last chance at realizing my ultimate football dream was in serious jeopardy. And it was my fault. All my fault.

All playoff games are special, but this one meant more to us because about six weeks earlier we had gotten our asses beat by the Colts. And I mean beat—26–7 at the RCA Dome. Now we had a rematch.

Before the game, everybody was talking trash. While we were going through our pregame warm-ups in the end zone, some of the Colts fans started yapping at us. I let them yap, but then I told them, "I'll be back to see you soon, *real* soon."

I don't usually mouth off to fans, but I felt so good I couldn't contain myself. I wanted them to know I'd be in the end zone again, but I'd have a football in my hands and a touchdown on the scoreboard.

From the opening snap we unleashed everything we had and led, 14–0, at the end of the first quarter. The Colts fans behind our bench were jawing at me, and I was jawing back.

"Aw, you wasn't expecting this, were you?" I said. "Uh-huh. What a difference a day makes."

I was playing with them, but there wasn't much they could say back. They were frustrated with their team, and we were the ones responsible for the frustration.

Then, late in the third quarter, I dove into the end zone on a 1-yard touchdown run to put us ahead, 21–3. I'd warned those Colts fans I'd visit them again.

I let out a huge scream. You could see the dejection in the fans' faces. They didn't expect us to come in there and dominate the game.

Oh, I was going crazy. It was so sweet. Then the Colts scored early in the fourth quarter, but we were still up, 21–10. No problem.

Back and forth it went until Troy Polamalu intercepted a Manning pass near midfield with 5:33 left in the game. I was thinking to myself, "OK, we can seal the deal. This is my time now. Time to pound the ball, get the tough yards, squeeze the life out of the clock and the Colts."

I started to run onto the field, but then the officials told us that Colts coach Tony Dungy was challenging the call. Huh? What was there to challenge? Manning threw it. Troy intercepted it. Our ball.

Except that referee Pete Morelli looked at the replay and said—and I still can't believe this—that Troy didn't have possession of the ball. Incomplete pass. Whoa, what was going on here?

The NFL would later say Morelli made a mistake, that the interception shouldn't have been overturned. But that didn't help us then.

I went back to the sideline and watched nervously as Manning hit a

9-yard pass, a 20-yard pass, a 24-yard pass. Bam, bam, bam. Then Edgerrin James scored on a 3-yard run. Then Manning hit Reggie Wayne for the two-point conversion. It was, 21–18, and here we go.

Later, with 1:27 left and the ball at the Colts' 12, Joey Porter sacked Manning for a 10-yard loss on fourth down. I watched the whole thing from the sideline and it was such a perfect moment. Time for me to go to work.

But first I had to do some bragging. Like I said, I hardly ever popped off during a game, but I couldn't help myself this time. I ran out on the field and when I saw Colts defensive tackle Corey Simon, I just went off on him.

"We shocked the world!" I said. "Yeah, I knew you wasn't ready for this. Y'all didn't think we had anything coming in."

I saw Colts linebacker Cato June and I started lipping off to him too.

"Yeah, y'all came in talking all that talk . . . thought it was going to be that same old stuff. Uh-uh."

This was totally not me. I was rubbing it in their faces.

So we got in the huddle and I knew I was getting the ball. I told myself, "OK, Bus, it's on now." I was ready to punch it in. Ben called the play: Counter 38 Power.

This was our money play. We called it, the bread and butter play. In fact, we ran that play so much over the years that our offensive line coach, Russ Grimm, would look at me from the sidelines and start moving his right hand over his left palm, like he was buttering a slice of bread. Time for Counter 38 Power.

Ben took the snap. I took the handoff.

The way the play was supposed to work was like this: I take a jab step to the left, then go to the right and get the ball from Ben. My right guard blocks down, the right tackle blocks down. My left guard, Alan Faneca, pulls around and kicks out the defender, and I run inside his block.

But on that play, Faneca decided to turn up a little bit early. He thought he saw a hole inside and decided to turn up that way. Faneca had been to five Pro Bowls and was one of the best in the business. If he thought he saw a hole, then that was fine by me.

The problem was, with him turning upfield early, I got no kick-out block on the linebacker, and that linebacker, Gary Brackett, was just sitting there waiting for me. So I decided to try to squeeze inside him. I knew I could still score, but I had to cut back inside. I'd made the same move thousands of times in my career.

So I sort of turned my body sideways and Brackett shot over and delivered a perfect hit. I've got gigantic hands and it just about takes a sledgehammer to get the ball out of my hold. But Brackett's helmet hit the ball flush. An absolutely perfect hit. In fact, if you look at the replay, it's not like I was being careless with it. I still had my hand cupped over where the ball used to be.

I felt the ball pop out, but I couldn't see it. Brackett had me by the knees and I was falling backward toward the goal line. I was trying to find the ball on the turf. I figured it was somewhere near my feet. It's weird: In that split second that I was falling I thought, "Well, at the very worst they'll recover the fumble on the 3-yard line and they'll still have to drive 97 yards for the win."

Just as I was about to hit the ground I saw the ball. It wasn't on the turf—it was still floating in the air! Then I saw Nick Harper, who played cornerback, grab it after the ball bounced off the turf at the 7 and I'm thinking, "Oh, my God. Oh, my God. I don't believe I just fumbled the football. I cannot believe I just fumbled the football."

At first, everything was in slow motion. It was like that movie *The Untouchables,* when the baby carriage is rolling down the train station steps and a gunfight breaks out. When I finally saw the ball in the air my mind was screaming, "No-ooooooo!" But I couldn't stop what was happening. I was completely helpless.

Then I saw Harper break free, and suddenly the only things in slow motion were the guys chasing him. We had our goal-line unit—a lot of 300-pounders—in the game, so the chances of somebody catching him from behind weren't good. I saw Kendall Simmons, our 315-pound guard, chasing after him. I saw our fullback, Dan Kreider, doing the same thing. And I saw Ben in the distance. And me? I was on my butt, and by myself (most of the Colts defenders had sprinted off to try to block for Harper). I was a lonely, lonely soul.

Ben kept backpedaling and got in position to force Harper to make a move. Harper hesitated, and Ben, as he was falling backward, stuck his right arm between Harper's legs. Then he grabbed Harper's right foot and Harper fell down. I wanted to vote Ben the AFC Defensive Player of the Year.

If Harper had stutter-stepped and burst back to the outside, I'm not sure Ben would have tackled him. Or if Harper's wife hadn't stabbed him in the left knee the day before our game (I guess they had a fight, huh?), maybe he would have been able to run faster. Instead, he had three stiches in his left leg, and maybe that was the difference.

I don't know what it was—fate . . . destiny . . . a domestic incident— but Ben tackled him.

That was Ben's first and only tackle of the entire season (OK, according to the official stats, our tight end Jerame Tuman got an assist on the play, too). And that one tackle kept Harper from scoring the game-winning touchdown.

As relieved as I was that Ben tackled him, there was no sense of joy on my part. I had fumbled the football. I was devastated, distraught, and pissed off.

And here was the other thing: I woke up the crowd. When we were lined up at the 2, and the ball was hiked, the sound of the crowd was on mute. But when I got up and started walking off the field, it was like the mute button had been turned off. That place has never been that loud. It was deafening.

It was the lowest feeling in the world walking over to the sideline after the play. For starters, I had just been mouthing off to the Colts, mouthing off to the fans behind my bench, and mouthing off to the fans in the end zone. And what did I do? I fumbled the ball and let down all of my teammates. I wanted to dig a hole and jump in.

All I could think was, "To play as good a game as we played, and to lose, would just be a travesty." It was the lowest point of my career. The absolute lowest. No question.

I got to the sideline and I took a knee. I kind of put my head down for a second. I'd always told the younger players to stay positive when they made a mistake, to keep their heads up, not to sink down into the depths. But here I was with my head down and I was sinking into the depths. So I told myself, "Keep your head up. Gotta stay strong."

I knew the TV cameras had to be on me the whole time. You know how those directors are: They want to see you suffer. I was suffering, all right.

I don't think any of my teammates came near me after the play. Maybe backup quarterback Tommy Maddox, but that's it. I was a leper, and I knew it, too. As a veteran you know better than to make a mistake, especially a mistake like a fumble, and then try to join a group of your teammates. Before you knew it they would be trying to ease away from you. In about a minute and a half you'd realize they were all gone.

I'd played enough games in thirteen years to know what usually happened next. If you made a mistake, a boneheaded play like I did, the other team would almost always capitalize on it. Even worse, the guy trying to take advantage of my mistake was Peyton Manning. So I had one of the best quarterbacks in the league, on arguably the best team in the league, and they had the ball with plenty of time. I thought it was over.

The Colts started marching down the field. Manning found Reggie Wayne for a 22-yard completion. The ball was on our 36-yard line. Then he hit Marvin Harrison for an 8-yard gain. Now it was on our 28. There were thirty-one seconds left in regulation.

Manning missed Wayne on a pass. Twenty-five seconds left.

Now it was third and 2. A thought entered my mind: "Have I played my last play?"

I can't explain it, but a calm came over me. I said to myself, "Lord, if that was my last play, I'm comfortable with it. You gave me so much enjoyment out of this sport, so if it was my last play, I'm OK with it."

And then I kind of smiled and walked down the sideline to get a closer look at the action. If Manning was going to end my career, I wanted to see it.

Manning got in the shotgun, dropped back, and threw to Wayne, who looked like he might be open in the corner of the end zone. Suddenly I wasn't so calm anymore. I thought my heart was going to burst from my chest.

But Wayne couldn't make the catch. Fourth down.

Out came the Colts' field goal unit and kicker Mike Vanderjagt. I just knew Vanderjagt would make the 46-yarder and we'd go into overtime. After that, anything could happen. And all because I couldn't hold on to the damn football.

Nothing had ever come easy for me. But this was just another fistfight with adversity. My life had been full of them.

Gladys Bettis is on what she calls Grandma Duty. The matriarch of the Bettis family has four grandchildren in all, and today is her day to look after at least one of them in her suburban Detroit home—the home that Jerome bought her and Johnnie Jr. when he turned pro.

Her cell phone rings. Someone is calling on the house line too. Her granddaughter is crying because she doesn't want to get changed. It's bedlam, and Gladys loves every second of the noise.

On February 16, 1972, Gladys and Johnnie Jr., welcomed their third child into the world: Jerome Abram Bettis. They brought him home to a modest house in a modest, proud neighborhood that didn't stay that way.

Between interruptions from her granddaughter, Gladys tells the story.

"It was a really good neighborhood, but as the kids started getting older . . . I won't say the neighborhood changed, but it was like the people in the neighborhood changed. They didn't seem to have any respect for each other. The children started picking on other children. And maybe the wrong kind of people were moving into the neighborhood.

"I remember Jerome became a safety patrol boy. He was trying to help children across the street, that's what he did. But some older kids started messing with Jerome, tried to hurt him.

"When I found out, I tracked those kids down and I said, 'Don't you

touch him. I'll kill you. Don't even look at him.' I was a fearsome mother. We scared the fire out of them.

"When our children got to be teenagers, I didn't think I was naïve about our surroundings. But I guess I didn't see the things that the kids saw. Jerome was always saying the neighborhood was so tough. I didn't see the problems."

I grew up in a ghetto. I didn't realize it at the time because I was a kid, and kids are like refrigerator magnets: They stick to wherever you put them. But that's where we lived. It wasn't the worst ghetto on the west side of Detroit, but it was in the team photo.

10384 Aurora Street. That was our address. Near Plymouth and Wyoming, a little less than a half hour from downtown Detroit. Anybody who grew up in the Motor City knows the area.

My parents—Johnnie and Gladys Bettis—bought the two-story, three-bedroom bungalow in 1969. It cost $24,000, which was all the money in the world to them, and they needed a thirty-year mortgage to afford the monthly payments.

Martha Stewart was never going to visit our neighborhood. As the years passed, the neighborhood got beat up even more. It went downhill before our eyes. There was an old lady who lived next door to us. Her name was Miss Washington. She was a sweet old lady. She died when I was about eight or nine. By the time I was thirteen or fourteen, that sweet old lady's home was a crack house. And by the time I left for college, the house on the other side of us was a crack house, too.

Our area had slowly turned into a ghetto, but it was still our home. If somebody from outside of Detroit came to our neighborhood, they would have taken one look at it and said, "Wooo, get me *out* of here."

A lot of people on our block didn't have mothers and fathers. We were one of the few families on the block that had a mom and dad. On our block, with the neighborhood guys, the guys in our crew that we ran with, there were probably three families that had moms and dads, including ours. That's just the way it was. There wasn't anything strange about it—at least, not to us.

The neighborhood didn't start out as a ghetto. I know my mother and father took pride in their house. Lots of people did back then. But, year by year, little by little, the neighborhood began to deteriorate, began to show rust marks, if you know what I mean, but it was still our home.

The house was very small. My parents had the master bedroom upstairs, my brother and I shared a room with two little beds, and my sister had her own room across the hall from us on the main floor. Kimberly is the eldest, two years older than my brother Johnny III, and six years older than me. And just so you know, I was named after my grandfather and uncle on my mother's side. The good news is that I was a boy. Had I been a girl, my mom was going to name me Greneda, which she made up on her own. Whew.

We all lived on top of each other, so you'd try to carve out a little space for yourself. John and I had a TV in our room, so that became the place where we could escape from everybody. The TV had a clothes hanger for an antenna and you usually had to beat the top of the thing with your fist to *maybe* get a picture. It was a color TV . . . sometimes. Most of the time the picture was black and white, or just black. That TV teased us for years.

In our house there weren't a lot of rules, but God help you if you broke one of them. When we were growing up, my brother and I weren't allowed to bring girls in the house. Later, it was changed to no girls in our room. Good grades in school were always expected. And we were never supposed to fight or rough house inside.

So naturally we had fights and rassled inside the house. That's what brothers do, though John usually started it. My mother used to tell us to stop, but we weren't scared of our mother. We'd stop for a minute or two, and then as soon as she left the room we'd start going at it again.

My mother was the disciplinarian to a certain degree; she was the lightweight disciplinarian. When she had to do the heavy lifting, that's when she brought in my dad. She handled all the small skirmishes and smaller issues. But whenever something was a major issue, she called upstairs and it was trouble.

My dad worked two jobs—he worked for the City of Detroit as an electrical inspector, and he taught electrical wiring at night school—so he was either at work or he was upstairs in his room trying to get some sleep. When you're a kid you don't realize a lot of things. I thought everybody's dad worked as hard as mine did. If he was upstairs, that meant he needed to relax and rest. It was like the law of our house that he wasn't supposed to be disturbed. And if he was disturbed, there was going to be trouble.

If my mom really got mad at us, she'd stand at the bottom of the stairs and yell to my dad, "Junior, you better get your sons!" And then we'd hear my dad get out of bed.

"John! Jerome! Come to the stairs!"

We'd rush to the foot of the stairs.

"If I have to come down there, both of you are in big trouble," he'd say.

And that would end the monkey business. Usually. Sometimes we'd go at it again and, uh-oh, you heard him walking down the stairs. If he came down the stairs there was going to be a double-whuppin'. One whuppin' for doing something wrong, and another whuppin' for him having to come downstairs in the first place. You never wanted to hear those stairs creaking under his weight.

My parents weren't like these new-age parents, the kind who want to reason with their kids. There were none of those—what do you call them?—time-outs. We got "Blue Thunder."

Blue Thunder was the name we gave the leather belt my dad kept in the hall closet. We called it that because my father really liked the movie *Blue Thunder*, which was about a police helicopter or something. All I know is that when he started swinging that belt, it was like listening to those helicopter blades swirling around. I can't remember who came up with the belt name, me or my brother, but it was one of us. It's always the suppressed, not the suppresor, that give the names. Oh, yeah, we got beat. No question. We always tried to hide Blue Thunder, but my father would always find it.

My parents were loving, caring, and fair. But they were also tough. I had a friend who lived across the street and he used to take change out of his mother's purse. I tried sneaking some change out of my mom's purse once, but I got caught. "We're not raising any thieves in this house," my mom said.

So to teach me a lesson, whenever anything was missing in the house, my mother or father would put me up against the wall and pat me down, like they were the police frisking a criminal. I hated that. But they were trying to make a point—and they did.

When we were growing up, I was a huge Dallas Cowboys fan and my brother was a big Pittsburgh Steelers fan. There was a preseason game and Rafael Septien kicked the winning field goal against the Steelers. That meant I won a bet between me and my brother. I was supposed to get his box of change, about $1.50 or so.

But he wouldn't give me the money. In fact, he took *my* box of change. When I told my mother about it all she said was, "That's what you get for gambling. Don't gamble."

Don't gamble? The only lesson I learned was not to gamble with my big brother unless I could back it up when it was time to collect.

When I was a kid I didn't appreciate the fact that my dad had to work two jobs to support our family. Or that my mom had to get a job when I got a little older. All I knew was that we couldn't cook anything until my mom and dad got home from work. We had a rule in the house that we couldn't turn on the stove unless one of my parents was there. And my mom didn't get home from work until about 3:30. So we had to make do by making sugar or syrup sandwiches. But that's how my mother and father were: They didn't want anything to happen to us.

Our first family car was a green station wagon. Then we swapped that out for a Chevrolet Celebrity. They don't even make those anymore. And my dad had an old Chevy Nova, but it didn't run all the time. In fact, it became a permanent fixture in the backyard. It became a monument. And we became a one-car family.

I didn't have any concept of the outside world. We had family in Buffalo, New York, so we would travel there. We tried to go somewhere each year, but Detroit was all I really knew. A more typical trip was driving out to the suburbs. They had nicer grocery stores out there, so we'd take an hour road trip to the Meijer grocery store. That was the way we'd escape the ghetto.

I was born in 1972, four years after the riots in Detroit. My parents told me about those riots, how African-Americans burned down all of their own stores and, in retrospect, how stupid it was. All the little stores that we had owned and operated, we burned down.

My grandmother used to live near Twelfth Street. Back in the sixties, Twelfth Street was a major thoroughfare for Detroit, but the stores there were burned to the ground. As a result, some of the white store owners never came back and the black store owners couldn't recover. So really, it did everybody a disservice because we burned down the establishments, the local businesses that we needed for day-to-day life.

But I wasn't aware of the racial divide then because I didn't come in contact with the other side, so to speak. I only knew one side. So if you only knew one side, you assumed that was the norm. You didn't see white and black intermingling. You just didn't see it.

I didn't have any real contact with white kids until fourth grade. That's when my mom and dad scraped up enough money to send my brother and me to private school. It was different because there were white kids in the class, though some of them were the teachers' kids, so that kind of didn't count. The majority of the teachers were white, but they were cool.

Fifth grade is when my business savvy took control. Fifth grade is when I started my own business, of sorts.

I went into the candy business. When we would take those road trips to Meijer—and Meijer was Wal-Mart before there was a Wal-Mart (forty registers, just huge, sold everything from clothes, to bikes, to groceries)—that's when I went to work.

Do you remember what it was like when you went shopping with your folks? With us, it was like a ritual: We'd go through the first couple of aisles with our parents. Then we'd kind of get lost. So, boom, we'd take off and disappear to the other shopping departments. When it came time for them to check out, we'd hear our names on the public address system: "Jerome and John Bettis come to Register 26 for checkout."

But what you wanted to do was check in with them *before* the PA announcement. We had to try to time it so that they didn't get on the microphone. If they got on the mic, it was bad news.

I had my own secret routine. When we first pulled into the parking lot, I'd linger a little bit behind and make sure the back door of the Celebrity was still unlocked. And after I took off from my parents in the store, I would go to one of the furthest checkout lines and I would steal a bunch of gum. I would take the gum outside and put it in the car. I'd pull out the backseat, put all the gum in the opening, and then close it back up.

When we got home, I would wait, wait, wait and then slip outside and collect my inventory, my product.

My dad had an old briefcase in the basement. It was broken, which is why he let me have it. But it was still usable as long as you didn't put too much stuff in it. If you put too much stuff in there, it wouldn't open.

So rather than use it to carry my schoolbooks, I used it for my product. I would take my briefcase—just like a businessman—and go to work. I was a salesman. I would go to school, set up shop, and sell pieces of gum for 10 cents apiece. It was a very profitable business considering my overhead was zero.

Of course, it wasn't so profitable for Meijer. The problem was, we didn't go to Meijer but every two weeks. So you can imagine what stocking up was like. I had to have enough inventory to last a long time, so I used to hide enormous amounts of gum in the backseat of the Celebrity.

I had everything down to a shoplifting science: While my parents were shopping, I would jam some gum in my pockets, run out to the car, reload, run to the car, reload. I'd make three or four trips.

Eventually I took on a partner. That's what savvy businesspeople do. I took on a partner because I needed another salesman. He did a good job and he was extra muscle, too. He was a big kid. Me? I was nearsighted, wore glasses, ate syrup sandwiches for lunch, and looked like a nerd. That's what my mother always said—that I was a nerd just like my dad.

Anyway, it turned out we needed the muscle because we had a competitor. Somebody else was trying to get into the candy business against us. He could have been legitimate—actually buying his product—but if he was, his profit margin wasn't as high as ours.

Well, instead of letting the economic marketplace decide which one of us would succeed, we chose a less, uh, complicated way to settle things. We ended his business.

One day we waited until he was out of class. Then we found out where he stored his candy, stole all his inventory, and hid it. It was very Teamsters. That didn't work out too well because he ended up ratting us out. He wasn't absolutely sure it was us, but that didn't matter.

We had to go to the principal's office and there was a big ol' stink when he found out what we were doing. Sheesh, it was a bad deal.

Blue Thunder didn't make an appearance because my folks never found out about it. (Until now. Sorry, Mom.)

After the gum scandal, we kind of made a truce with the other kid who sold candy. And it was at this point that I made another business decision: I was getting out of the gum racket. I was going to sell Transformers.

Transformers were a big deal back then. A Transformer was a semi truck cab or other car that could transform itself into a robot, that sort of thing. But they were expensive and they were hard to get.

Once again, I had to depend on our road trips to Meijer. And because we only went there every two weeks, I basically had to make my business a retail order business. You'd order what you wanted, and depending on the availability of the Transformer, I'd try to get it for you in seven to ten days and at a discounted cost.

This is when the big bucks started rolling in. I went from selling gum for ten cents a stick, to selling Transformers for fifteen to twenty dollars, depending on the one you wanted. If you wanted Optimus Prime, who was the leader of the good guys—the Autobots from the Transformer Universe—he was going to be expensive.

Optimus Prime . . . the Decepticons (they were the Autobots' enemies) . . . the evil Unicon—I remember all this stuff. This was a big business. You have to know your best sellers.

Poor Meijer. That store took a beating and I owe the store manager a huge apology. Of course, I took a beating not long after I started my new business.

It all happened because my mother couldn't keep track of her winter gloves. We were leaving Meijer one night and my mother couldn't find one of her gloves. She couldn't remember if she had left it in the store or in the car.

"Look under the backseat," she told me.

I nearly fainted. Lord, have mercy. All my Transformer product was back there.

"Uh, Ma, they ain't under the seat," I said nervously.

"You didn't even look," she said. "Now look under that seat, Jerome."

Before I could pretend to search for the missing glove, I think my brother reached back and pulled the seat out. I can't even remember for sure because I was in shock. Whoo. That was a bad moment. Needless to say, the business got shut down that day.

My mom stared at all those Transformers and I knew I'd be standing in my underwear when we got home.

"What do I do with this stuff?" she said. "If I take it back in there, they're going to carry my son off to the police."

Believe me, the police sounded good compared to what happened when I got home. Blue Thunder came out of the closet and my dad beat the living daylights out of me. Sheesh. Nobody wanted to watch that. It was an ugly scene. And I deserved it.

All that work, all that whuppin', and I didn't have anything to show for it.

I knew better than to steal those things. My parents were always preaching the difference between right and wrong. But I was stubborn, and sometimes stubborn kids do dumb things.

Had you asked my parents, they would have said Kimberly is most like my dad, that John is most like my mom, and I'm somewhere in between. My mom is a sweetheart. She loves people and could get one of those Buckingham Palace guards to smile if she tried. She has that sort of effect on people. All she ever truly wanted to be was a wife and a mother. She always saw the honor in that. And she's good at it.

As in most families, my mom was the voice of reason. She was the hands-on person with us. Obviously my dad wasn't as hands on; he was upstairs a lot. My dad was pretty reserved, though he actually became a little more chatty as he got older. But there wasn't any doubt that my father was more conservative than my mother.

One Easter my mother took us to the store to get our annual Easter suits. She said we could pick out whatever we wanted. My brother chose a candy-apple-red three-piece suit. That was a bit much for me, so I picked a dark blue, pinstriped three-piece suit.

When we got home, my dad couldn't believe what John was going to wear to Easter.

"Gladys, why did you buy him a candy-red suit?" he said.

"Because he liked it," she said.

My dad just shook his head. Bright red wasn't his style. I guess I was the same way.

Growing up, it always seemed that my dad was kind of tired. He usually was working those two jobs, except in the summer, when he wasn't teaching night school.

One day I decided to take him on. Big mistake.

Here's the thing, I was a late bloomer. If you look at my childhood photos, I'm the kid wearing the white dress shirts and the chemical engineering–style glasses. Those were some big ol' glasses, but you've got to understand that you're looking at a snapshot from a different era. The glasses might look hilarious now, but back then they were relatively cool—

you know, as far as glasses could be cool. And yeah, I carried a briefcase to elementary school. But that was me showing my business savvy.

But one of the defining moments that led me to challenge my father came when I was thirteen. That's the year I outgrew my brother, the same brother who had always beat up on me. He stayed short, but I didn't. I grew up and out.

One day we were playing cards in the basement with some friends and my brother decided he didn't like what was happening. We were betting again and he was losing (I guess I hadn't learned my lesson.) So he took all the cards out and started flicking them toward the ground.

"Pick up the cards," I said.

"I ain't picking up the cards," he said.

"Pick them up."

"No."

We started to wrestle and I kind of mushed his face into the floor of the basement. And that basement floor was dirty too. I kept mushing his face, and he started crying. That was the exact moment that the sibling power shifted. That was when he realized he couldn't physically dominate me anymore.

So a year later I decided that if I could take on my brother and win, I could take on my father and do the same thing. I was fourteen, starting to lift weights, and was a big kid for my age, somewhere between 180 and 190 pounds. Back then they used to call me Baby Huey.

Wrestling was a big deal on TV at the time, so I challenged my dad to a wrestling match in front of our house. I told everyone in the neighborhood about the big match. It was like I was Vince McMahon, the wrestling promoter. I talked it up, talked it up, talked it up. I told everyone it was for the "championship." I even made a championship belt out of cardboard.

So the big day came and the whole neighborhood was gathered around our yard. I came out of the house wearing a robe and my homemade championship belt. I made a big deal about taking off the belt and placing it on the porch. I was ready to rumble.

What a match: fourteen-year-old Baby Huey v. Dad, the 270-pound quiet man.

We locked up and my father was laughing, smiling, sort of going along with the whole thing. We broke off, locked up again, then pushed off each other—just like on TV. It was fun.

Then it wasn't.

I went to lock up again and my father disappeared. He dropped down, lifted me up in the air, and body slammed me to the ground. Boom! I was seeing stars: the Big Dipper, the Little Dipper . . . the whole galaxy. It was horrible, just horrible. There wasn't any air left in my lungs.

I staggered up, but I was stumbling all around. My mother ran out, grabbed me, and yelled at my dad, "Leave my baby alone!" Meanwhile, all of our neighbors were laughing so hard they were crying.

My dad didn't say a word. Instead, he walked to the porch, picked up my championship belt, and disappeared inside the house. And you know what? I never got that cardboard belt back. He kept it.

I was crushed. But I had a newfound respect for my father. I had the *ultimate* respect for him. I didn't realize that him outweighing me by ninety pounds would make such a big difference. I hadn't taken physics yet. If I had taken that class, I would have known better.

My dad didn't say a whole lot, but he taught lessons through his actions. He worked hard. He disciplined hard. And in his own way, he cared hard. He's always been my hero because he never complained, never made excuses. He just did what he had to do.

I'll give you an example: He and my mother were big on us getting an education. My dad was a natural when it came to electrical engineering, but he never got his degree. The same with my mom. They had had other priorities and responsibilities, beginning with us.

If I was a geek back then, it was because of the emphasis on school. They were paying for our private school and it cost a pretty penny. They were scraping up everything they had to get us there. It was one of those things where they'd be late for the mortgage or late paying another bill because they wanted to make sure the school tuition was paid on time. So they were very, very tough in terms of our grades. You had to take care of business, which meant there was less time for me to be with the fellas in the neighborhood.

We weren't poor, but we didn't have any Swiss bank accounts, either. We made those maple syrup sandwiches for lunch. Sometimes we made sugar sandwiches, or sugar and cheese sandwiches. Delicious.

Because my dad worked for the city, people would sometimes give him extra tickets to a Tigers game or a Red Wings game. But bowling was our sport of choice. In fact, for a long time it was my only sport.

My mother kind of kept us as a self-contained unit and we did a lot of stuff together as a family, as opposed to us kids just doing our own thing. I started bowling when I was seven. Every Saturday morning we'd go to Central City Lanes for Coke and Bowl. It was called that because after you bowled your games, you got a Coke and a hot dog. My mother was an instructor there for the little kids.

By the time I was twelve, I was on one of the junior bowling tournament teams. It was a five-man team and we traveled to tournaments all over the Midwest. My average was about 160 or 170, which was pretty good. I had my own bowling shirt, my own bowling ball, bowling shoes, and bowling bag. I threw a big ol' hook.

I'd see the kids walking home from their peewee football practices—the team in our neighborhood was called the Steelers if you can believe that—carrying their helmets and shoulder pads, but football meant nothing to me. It wasn't something I ever asked my mom about. When they played on Saturdays, I was busy bowling. And when NFL games were being played on Sundays, we were bowling in tournaments. Football? I never gave it a thought.

It wasn't until eighth grade that I started to get interested in sports besides bowling. I played quarterback on our Detroit Urban Lutheran flag football team. I was the biggest kid out there, but I was also the fastest. It was very low key, nothing like tackle football. I basically just ran around until I scored.

Some kids dream of being an NFL player. Not me. You don't aspire to go from flag football to pro football. I wasn't even in a big hurry to play tackle football. I was starting to get involved in track and field, as well as basketball. Football was just something else to try.

When I was thirteen, my Uncle Leroy, who is my mother's brother, saw me playing football on the block. He was a high school coach and he told my mom, "You need to let him play football. He can *play* football."

My mom was against it. "He can get hurt," she said. "He ain't going to play football."

My mother grew up in a family of eight brothers. They would use her as a tackling dummy. They took her dolls and pretended they were footballs. She despised the game, all because of her brothers. She called it "the hateful game of football."

But my uncle persisted. "Gladys," he said, "you need to let him play football."

I didn't really care one way or the other. My motivation was more practical. By then some of the teachers at our private middle school wanted us to start thinking about admissions tests for private high schools in the area. My parents were using all they had to send us to middle school, how were they going to afford private high schools? Plus, my sister was leaving for college that fall, and I knew my brother wanted to go to college, too. I figured they weren't going to have any money left to send me. I was always the third one, so everything got tighter by the time it got around to me.

I wanted to go to college, but I knew it was going to be tough for my family to afford the bill. That meant I could try for an academic scholarship, but I figured I probably wouldn't have a lot of college choices. Or I could try to play sports and get a scholarship that way. I'd give football the first shot.

So, that's how football started. In the beginning, it was a necessity rather than a love for the game. It was a means to an end, rather than, "God, I love playing football." I didn't love football. I barely knew it.

I didn't grow up with football posters in my room. I dreamed of becoming a pro bowler, as in bowling lanes. My favorite athletes were Hall of Fame bowlers Earl Anthony and Marshall Holman. I also collected baseball cards for a little while. I could name all the Tigers on that '84 World Series team: Lance Parrish, Alan Trammell, Sweet Lou Whitaker, Kirk Gibson, Jack Morris. I can go on. The Lions? I couldn't name anybody on those teams.

Of course, that changed. By my freshman year at Henry Ford High School, I'd decided I wanted to go to Oklahoma for college, even though I didn't even know where the state of Oklahoma was. I liked OU's football team. They were winning. The Boz (Brian Bosworth) was there. So was Coach Barry Switzer.

I was a linebacker and I was going to play fullback too. Boz was a linebacker and a big deal there, so I figured I'd be the same. The funny part about it is that I hadn't even played a down of tackle football yet. Here I was talking about going to one of the premier college football programs in the country, and I wasn't even sure how to put thigh pads in my football pants.

Uncle Leroy is the one who thought Henry Ford High was the best school for what I wanted to do. But because it wasn't in my parents' district, I had to stay with my Aunt Gloria, who lived literally about twenty steps from the school property.

What a mess it all became. I tested into the school's Alpha Program, which was for gifted students. But the principal hated the head football coach, and the football coach hated the principal. I got caught in the middle because I wanted to play football *and* be in the Alpha Program.

Then later that year, a friend and I were the victims of mistaken identity, where some kids thought we had done something we hadn't. They started fighting my friend, I came to his rescue, and all of a sudden all hell broke loose. It was crazy, stupid stuff.

These kids started showing up at my chemistry class to try to fight me. They were waiting for me after school—and I'm talking about seven, eight kids. One against one, I had a chance. One against eight—and that's the way it would have been— I had no chance. They were going to beat me down. They were going to jump on me. It was an ugly deal and I decided it wasn't worth having to fight somebody every day.

Also, this was the beginning of the era where more kids had guns. I have to admit, my friend and I thought about bringing a gun to school, just to try to scare these other kids. One of my friends' father had a gun and we could have gotten it whenever we needed it. We were in the 'hood, so access to a gun was possible.

But in the end we decided bringing a gun would only intensify the situation. So I said, "Screw it, I'm transferring." I was better off going back to my neighborhood high school.

The thing is, I had had a good season at Henry Ford. I started on the junior varsity as a linebacker and played a little bit as a fullback. We played on Mondays. Then I got called up to the varsity team as a backup. So I was playing on Mondays and Fridays. And we had a good team. Henry Ford was a powerhouse that year.

After I transferred to Mackenzie High School, I went to see the football coach, Bob Dozier. I knocked on the door and heard a gruff, "Come in."

Coach Dozier was in his office doing paperwork and sort of had his head down when I walked in.

"Coach," I said nervously, "my name is Jerome Bettis and I want to play football for you."

I guess Coach was used to little ninth graders asking him if they could be on the team. He wouldn't want to hurt their feelings, so he'd always tell them to try out for the jayvee squad.

I wasn't a little ninth grader. I was about five foot ten, 195 pounds.

Coach Dozier would later tell a reporter that I looked like "a young Superman" that day.

When Coach finally looked up from his paperwork, he took one look at me and said, "Hell, yes, you can play for me." Then he asked me what position I played, and I told him linebacker and fullback.

"Well," he said, "we got two seniors at running back, but we're gonna find a place for you."

And he did. I played tight end and nose guard, but not before some more drama in my life.

Coach Dozier had a preseason conditioning program. On the first day of conditioning drills, we were supposed to run quarter-miles around the track. As I was running the first quarter mile, I passed out. Boom! Shut down.

They took me to the hospital, examined me, put me on some breathing machines, and then the doctor gave my mother the diagnosis: asthma.

I knew something about asthma because my brother was asthmatic. When I was younger, he'd wake up in the middle of the night and he'd be struggling to breathe, almost turning purple. Even though I knew better, I'd start laughing at him, sort of taunting him. It was my way of getting back at him for all the times he had kicked my butt in fights. He'd try to tell me to go get Momma, but I would just stand there going, "Hah, hah, hah." I didn't realize at the time that he could have died.

Asthma isn't very complicated: It causes a restriction of the airways. You can't breathe. It's the worst thing in the world. It's like somebody is putting a plastic bag over your head and they're choking you.

As the doctor was telling me about my asthma, I'm thinking, "Wow, my football career is over before it even got going." But I was lucky because my mom and dad knew how to manage the asthma because of my brother's situation. So instead of discouraging me, they encouraged me to keep playing sports. Although my mother wasn't big on football, she didn't want that to stop me from doing anything. As long as I took my pills and had my inhaler, they said I could play football.

What I didn't know was that I was born with asthma. I had had a little attack when I was one, but didn't suffer another episode until that day on the track. My mom just never told me about the first attack because there was never a problem until that day. And after that, I never had another attack while I was in high school, though my mom always came to our games with an extra inhaler, just in case.

Slowly but surely football became more important to me. I was five ten, about 220 pounds when I was a sophomore. I was so fast that nobody could block me at the nose guard position. I was becoming a beast.

I sort of had a football revelation when I went to Reggie McKenzie's All-Pro Football clinic during my junior year. McKenzie was born in Detroit, played at Michigan, blocked for O. J. Simpson during the Juice's glory years with the Buffalo Bills, and returned to the community to give something back. In 1974 he started his free clinic, which wasn't much more than some plastic cones and a handful of footballs. Now it's a Detroit tradition. Reggie's programs, both athletic and academic, touch the lives of about fifteen hundred kids each year.

I was one of those kids. Pepper Johnson, who was born in Detroit, played at Mackenzie, Ohio State, and then with the New York Giants, was the camp director. Keith Byars, who was a star with the Philadelphia Eagles and played his college ball at Ohio State, coached the running backs. And Cris Carter, another Eagles star and Ohio State grad, coached the wide receivers.

This was a pretty big deal. There were players from all the different Detroit high schools. Your rivals might be in the same drill line as you, or right next to you. It got my competitive juices flowing because I got a chance to compete against those guys before the season started. I got a chance to see someone's face. It was like, "Oh, you're No. 21 . . . You're No. 2 . . . You're the guy who was killing us last year." So I got a chance to interact with these guys and the competitiveness went up another level.

This was also the first time I saw professional athletes and heard their stories. The camp organizers would bring in nonathletes too: a guy in a wheelchair who told his story about choosing the wrong path, taking drugs, and getting paralyzed after someone shot him; a judge who told us he never wanted to see us in his courtroom because he didn't want to put us in jail. I listened, and there was part of me that was affected by their stories. But there was also part of me that thought I was bulletproof, that nothing like that would ever happen to me.

It was an eye-opening experience on all sorts of different levels. I remember when Reggie talked to all the players at the end of the three-day camp. He wanted to know who was going to be the next Reggie

McKenzie, the next Pepper Johnson. Who was going to be the next kid to come out of Detroit and play Division I football?

I walked up to him, sort of pulled him around, and said, "Me."

Reggie later told a *Detroit News* reporter that that was the first time in his thirty-two years of running the clinic that somebody had said that to him.

That camp had a huge effect on me. It inspired me. I realized football could have a significant impact on my life, if I took it seriously. And I took it seriously, especially when I saw Pepper drive up to the camp in a Jaguar. That caught my attention real fast.

I've always had a soft spot for nice cars. And like most kids in my neighborhood, I wanted the finer things in life: the latest Jordans, the coolest leather jackets, some money in my pocket. But my parents wouldn't give me those sort of things. They said kids were getting killed over a pair of gym shoes. Instead, they'd buy me the knock-off version of the cool jacket, the cool shoes, but it just wasn't the same. So I resorted to other means to get some of the cool things.

When I was sixteen, Coach Dozier called my mother and asked if he could come over to the house. He wanted to talk to my parents about something important.

One of the girls who kept the statistics for our football team had told Coach Dozier that I was selling drugs and that I had asked some other kids at Mackenzie to help me. When he told my mom (my dad was at work), she was shocked.

When she confronted me about it, I went into defense mode. I told my mother that it was a terrible lie, that I couldn't believe someone would spread that sort of rumor. I told her Coach Dozier had gotten some bad information.

But Dozier was right, I was selling drugs. Not a lot of drugs, and not for long, but I did sell them. My first reaction was to deny, deny, deny. My parents believed me. Or maybe they just wanted to believe me.

Coach Dozier had told my mom that I was, "a million-dollar baby," and that I could go far in football. "But," he told her, "this could ruin his career."

My mom was dumbfounded by it all. Someone was accusing her baby of selling drugs. On top of that, that same someone was telling her that I could be a football star. My mom had never thought of me in those terms. She was grooming me for an academic scholarship. The possibility of me earning an athletic scholarship had never entered her mind.

She didn't know what to do. She trusted Coach Dozier. And she trusted me. But as much as she wanted to believe my denials, I think she knew something wasn't right.

"Jerome," she said, "you are going to ruin your life."

My mom had seen me looking out the front window as kids in my neighborhood drove by in their nice cars. She had a mother's sixth sense of what I was thinking. So she told me, "Jerome, you're going to have to stop doing this. One of these days you're going to be able to buy one of these Mustangs on your own. You can own one of these cars. These kids—if the police stop them, they'll take those cars away. Son, don't look at them. Don't do what they're doing."

I can explain what I did, but I can't justify it. I've kept it to myself for so long because there was part of me that was uncomfortable about it. In fact, it wasn't until years later that I could actually admit to my own parents that I had sold drugs, and why I had lied about it. But now I want people, especially kids, to understand that I made a mistake, a big one, but that I learned from that mistake.

In our neighborhood—and I know this came as a shock to my parents—selling drugs was the norm. A lot of people did it. That doesn't make it right, but in the context of where I grew up, it happened a lot.

When you sell drugs you learn very, very fast how dangerous it is, how cutthroat, even deadly, the business can become. We carried guns to protect ourselves. It became a way of life having a gun. You didn't even think twice about it.

During that time I led a double life. My mother and father knew one Jerome—the National Honor Society member (and sergeant at arms), the kid who had his mouth washed out with soap on a rope because he cussed one time—but the streets knew a different Jerome. It got to the point where I would get up, dress for school, go to my friend's house, change into my $100 pair of basketball shoes and $400 leather jacket that I had stashed in his closet, and then go to Mackenzie. After school, I'd stop by my friend's house and switch back to my original shoes and jacket. My parents never knew.

Yes, I was raised by loving parents who taught me the difference between right and wrong. And inside that house, I was safe. But you still had to leave that house. And outside that house was the real world. And the real world, at least, in our neighborhood, was tough.

By the time I was sixteen, there were crack houses on our street. Some of the guys I had looked up to as a kid were now crackheads. One of the big neighborhood crack dealers was found dead. Someone had shot and burned him to death.

I saw a girl get shot. We were at the local roller rink and as we were trying to leave, someone started shooting from the outside. This girl fell back in—about five steps from where I was standing—and she had a hole in her chest. It was terrible. She ended up dying. Had I walked out thirty seconds earlier that could have been me.

One of my partners got shot a couple of times. Dude died, and we were close. One of my other partners is still in jail for selling drugs. For life. My cousin is in jail for life for killing somebody. Most of the guys I hung out with are in jail. One of the younger guys on the block killed himself. A couple of them are doing well. But just a couple.

There was no code of the streets or anything like that. You just tried to live day to day. You adapted. I was never a guy who would seek out a fight, but I was comfortable if I was put in that situation.

Guns? We had them. Handguns. Rifles, whatever. I held them all. It doesn't feel crazy, or cold, or anything like that, when you hold a gun. It's just like grabbing a telephone, except that you know you can't kill somebody with a telephone. That's the difference. You know the danger when you pick up a gun.

I was fortunate. I never had to pull the trigger and shoot at anybody. But I would have used a gun had it been a life and death situation. Survival.

That's what it was all about back then. Somehow you became numb to your surroundings. If someone got shot to death, you're first thought wasn't, "Damn, he's dead." The first response was, "What happened? Was it a shootout?"

It's hard to explain the mentality of a ghetto, mostly because it's hard for a lot of people to truly understand what it's like there. In our neighborhood, selling drugs was considered an opportunity to earn cash and to better yourself. A lot of kids wanted to emulate these drug dealers. They wanted the big chains, the fancy cars, all of that. And it became a cycle.

Some kids want to grow up and be a lawyer because someone they admire is a lawyer. Or they want to be an engineer because their dad is an engineer. In our neighborhood, we didn't see a lot of lawyers or engineers, but we did see drug dealers, and some kids wanted to do what the neighborhood drug dealer did. To them, he was successful and they wanted to follow in his footsteps.

The guys I hung out with, we had always called ourselves the ABP: the Aurora Boulevard Posse. It wasn't exactly a gang, it was more like boys in the 'hood. To a degree, that crew shaped you as a person. Call it peer pressure, or whatever, but sometimes you'd do things you didn't necessarily want to do. You had to choose sides, and in the neighborhood, that side was with the guys you grew up with. If one of our guys had a problem, then we all responded to it. If one of our guys got beat on, then we all were going to look for the person who did it to retaliate.

As I got older, the retaliation became different and the threat became different. It wasn't fistfights anymore, it was guns and knives. Every confrontation, every altercation became that much bigger because there was the possibility of death.

I thought I had built up an immunity to it all—the guns, the drugs, the violence—but that was before I experienced a moment that changed my life forever.

It happened one night while we were hanging out on the street corner, which we did quite a bit, and out of nowhere, we started hearing gunshots. Whoever was doing the shooting, they were shooting at us. It was the scariest thing in the world . . . the scariest thing in the world.

We scattered, at top speed, I might add. We started running every which way. Some guys ran through busy intersections without even looking. When we finally hooked up later that night, we saw that one of our friends got his biceps muscle shot off. They blew the whole biceps off his arm. Whoo, that was a wake-up call. I decided that the life I was leading was going to end badly if I didn't change.

Looking back at my own situation, I let the environment shape my decisions as a young man. You don't want to do that, but it's difficult to ignore the negative influences of your surroundings. In retrospect, I should have been stronger.

What I did—sell drugs, carry guns—was wrong, and if someone asked, I'd tell them to measure the consequences of their acts. That's how you get a true understanding of whether it's the right thing to do. Everything you do in life is gauged by the potential consequences. I could have gone to jail. I could have been killed. But back then, I failed to think about those consequences.

It's a sobering thought when I realize how my actions as a sixteen-year-old could have affected me as a thirty-four-year-old man. No college. No pros. No nothing.

I'm not proud of what I did, but I am proud that I had the strength to finally distance myself from those negative influences. I wasn't a bad kid, but I had done some bad things. My parents helped me, of course. So did one of my Mackenzie teammates, Jahmal Dokes.

Jahmal was from the 'hood, but he was an only child and, compared to us, he got spoiled a little bit, in terms of getting a car and material things like that. But he had a confidence about him, and he was funny. And the guy wasn't allergic to work. He played football, but he also worked a bunch of different jobs to make money.

Jahmal would come by the house and we'd hang out. Slowly, I started to spend less time on the streets with those friends who were selling drugs. Instead, Jahmal and I would chill on the porch, or get in his car and just drive. I had found a friend outside of my ABP crew.

"His brother John kind of introduced me to Jerome. We both went out for football and started to hang out a little bit more. I would go to his house after football practice. If you know Mrs. B, well, his mother loved to cook. And I loved to eat, so I was an instant hit in the Bettis household.

"Each year we'd go through those hot summer days in Detroit, and each year we did more and more together. We had those summer football practices and afterward, I'd hang out at his house for a night or he'd hang out at my house for a night. Jerome was very strong in academics and I wasn't that strong. So he taught me stuff about academics and I think I helped teach him a work ethic.

"I did whatever it took to save some money: dishwashing jobs, short-order cook, whatever. In fact, I got Jerome one of his first jobs. It was at Charley's Crab; he was a dishwasher and I was a bakery cook. He worked about a month as a dish dog until he couldn't take it anymore.

"When it wasn't football season I tried to keep myself occupied. When I did go out, I tried to go out with guys who would

have positive influences on my life. There's no shortage of knuck-leheads not doing right, so I wanted to stay away from those sit-uations. So maybe that helped Jerome. But really, we each brought a positive energy to the friendship.

"By the time we were juniors or seniors, John and Kim were out of the house and it was just Jerome. So I was over there a lot. It was like we were brothers.

"At Mackenzie I was the starting short-side cornerback and the third-string running back. He was the starting linebacker and running back. He was something like five foot eleven, 240, ran a 4.4 40. He was a grown man by then.

"One day in practice we were running goal-line plays. Jerome was on offense and they were killing us. Our defensive coach started yelling at us. 'You guys are scared of tackling Bettis! Who's going to stand up and tackle Bettis? Who's going to be a man?'

"When they lined up to run the next play, there wasn't a wide receiver on my side. They were in a tight formation. So when they ran the play—it was an inside dive off the guard and center—I ran right over there and put my five six, 150-pound body in that hole. It was me and another linebacker filling that hole.

"Jerome hit me and I saw stars . . . and he scored. He crushed both of us: me and the linebacker. It wasn't a delightful feeling. That shit hurt. I didn't try that again. That was enough for me. Coach couldn't hype me on doing that again."

—*Jahmal Dokes*

Jahmal was there the night—it was at a girl's Sweet 16 party—that I decided I was going to tear it up on the dance floor. Everybody was doing the Cabbage Patch Dance and I was jammin'. I dropped down to do a split or something . . . and I ripped my pants from the rooty to the tooty. I had to put my coat around my waist because it was an ugly, ugly sight.

Somehow I survived it all. The fine line between ending up in the backseat of a police car or ending up on the front page of the sports sec-tion was probably as thin as Blue Thunder. But I made it. Barely.

I was lucky, simple as that. That could have been me who got shot at the skating rink, or who had his biceps blown off by a bullet. But it wasn't. I don't have an explanation for it, other than that I was beginning to make smarter decisions.

And remember those Ford Mustangs I loved? During my senior year at Mackenzie, my mother won a couple hundred bucks playing Bingo and bought me a car: a 1979 Mustang, stick shift, decent condition. It was doo-doo brown. I loved that beater.

But my mother was right. She said one day I'd own a Mustang. She kept her promise. Now it was time for me to make her proud.

✦ 3 ✦

Bob Dozier has had a busy night. He's deep-fried two Thanksgiving turkeys and a basket of wing dings. His wife is out buying a couple more turkeys to deep fry on the big day.

"This is a good time to talk," he says from his home in El Paso, Texas.

The sixty-one-year-old Dozier retired in 2002. During his long career as Mackenzie High School's football coach, he had three players go on to win Super Bowls: Pepper Johnson, Gilbert Brown (who once blocked for Bettis at Mackenzie), and Bettis.

"I'll tell you a story, just to show you how willing Jerome was to cooperate with things.

"During his junior year of high school, late in the year, I had to fire our starting quarterback. Had to kick him off the team because he lied to me about missing practice. The kid had gone to a Michael Jackson concert, and his mom even helped with the lie. So I had to fire him. This was on a Wednesday. We played Friday.

"So I told Jerome, 'You're going to play quarterback this week. We've got two days to get you in shape.'

"He said, 'What, Coach?'

"Remember, Jerome was a big kid, probably five ten and a half, 220 . . . 225 by then. But he was such a good athlete. Walter Smith was in the same backfield, so I taught Jerome the option. I taught him how to ride the fullback, but I told him to either give it to Walter or just keep *it himself. I didn't want him to pitch it. I taught him two rollout passes; neither one was deeper than 8 yards.*

"So he went out there against Detroit Northern and hit two passes for 37 yards, ran for about 120 yards, scored one touchdown, and did it running the option for the first time.

"Jerome was so physical, just a vicious tackler. We played Ann Arbor Pioneer when he was a senior. Pioneer was located right across the street from Michigan Stadium, and they had one of the top teams in the state. But Jerome was having a hell of a game at linebacker.

"At halftime I was coming out of our locker room when Pioneer's coach, Chuck Lori, came up to me. Chuck and me were friends, but he said, 'Dozier, you're gonna go to jail here in Ann Arbor.'

"I said, 'Jail? What are you talking about?'

"He said, 'If you don't get that Jerome Bettis out of the game before he kills somebody today, you're gonna go to jail up here.'

"One of the things I used to do as a coach was take my seniors out to dinner. A lot of these kids were going to get recruited, so I wanted to try to help them.

"With Jerome and Walter Smith—he played in the same backfield as Jerome and ended up going to Michigan—I took those guys out to dinner and I told them Mackenzie was an unreal environment. Mackenzie was 90 percent black, maybe more, and about 10 percent white. I told them, 'Wherever you go to college, you're going to be in the minority. You have to learn to handle that. You might be in a lecture hall with two hundred people, but only two or three of them will be black. But we've had other guys be successful. If those guys can do it, you can do it.'

"We also had guys who came back home. Coming from Mackenzie, from the neighborhood, there were guys who couldn't handle the culture shock. But Jerome handled it.

"What did Clint Eastwood used to say in the movies? 'Make my day.' Jerome made my day—several of my days. It was a joy and a pleasure coaching that young man."

✦   ◆   ✦

One day I came home from school—this was after my junior season—and there was a letter waiting for me. It was from the University of

Oklahoma. It messed me up because the Sooners were my favorite team. There was just something about Switzer, the Boz, and that program that I thought was cool. I just looked at the envelope with the OU logo on it, smiled, and said, "Ahhhhh."

By then I was playing linebacker and fullback and trying to make a name for myself. I wanted those big-time colleges to notice-me. And they did. I didn't give them any choice.

Every game, every week . . . it was crazy. I went ballistic. I came out of nowhere. Every week I had 100 yards rushing and a ton of tackles. Everyone was like, "Whoa, where'd this kid come from?" Remember, I was the bowler, the geek, the kid with glasses. Now I didn't wear glasses, didn't bowl on weekends anymore. I weighed 230 pounds and had fallen in love with football.

My Oklahoma smile didn't last long. About the time I got that letter, Oklahoma had been put on NCAA probation or was headed there. They had all sorts of problems: players accused of rape, guns in the dorm, players on the cover of *Sports Illustrated* wearing those orange jail jumpsuits. That's when my dad told me, "They're on probation. You can't go."

I pleaded with him to reconsider. I said they'd be off probation by my sophomore year in college.

"Nope, you're not going," he said.

You didn't argue with my dad. Once he made up his mind, that was it. It was a sad, sad day in my house. I cried. I wasn't going to be a Sooner.

My first recruiting letter was from Oklahoma, but it wasn't my last. The letters started pouring in from everywhere. The fun part was to look at the letterheads. Alabama had that crimson helmet. All these different letterheads from all these big-time schools. It was sweet. And confusing.

Since my father had eliminated Oklahoma for me, that left one school as the leader in my mind: University of Michigan.

Michigan was the powerhouse school in our state, in the Big Ten Conference, in the country. Michigan State? They had their fans, but if you grow up in Michigan, especially in Detroit, which is just down the freeway from the Ann Arbor campus, you know everything about the maize and blue.

The legendary Bo Schembechler was the coach back then. And

they ran the ball. They had little Jamie Morris. Morris was as tough as nails.

I wasn't a huge Michigan fan. I wasn't a huge fan of any team, except maybe Oklahoma—and even then I couldn't have told you a lot about Oklahoma's players or football history. I had just started watching college football on a regular basis, so I didn't have any real allegiances besides the Sooners, and I knew they were out of the question. But Michigan was close, familiar, and nationally known.

Notre Dame? Notre Dame wasn't even on the radar. I got letters from them, but at first I didn't even know what Notre Dame was. I thought Notre Dame was in Europe somewhere. I knew about the Hunchback of Notre Dame, but that was about it.

In fact, it wasn't until late in my junior year at Mackenzie, 1988, that I started to notice Notre Dame on TV. They were ranked No. 1 in the country, beat Penn State, then ended the regular season by beating No. 2 USC at the LA Coliseum. Then they won the national championship by beating West Virginia in the Fiesta Bowl.

Just before my senior season at Mackenzie, Coach Dozier picked me and a couple of other teammates to go to the Michigan football camp. It was the first time I'd ever set foot on the campus and, my goodness, it was huge. You had to pay your own way, but going was a big deal. If you were a blue-chip recruit, you went to the Michigan camp.

During the camp, Coach Schembechler made it pretty clear he wanted me to come to Michigan. "You're a Michigan Man," he kept saying. And when I was named the No. 1 camper, they gave me a big trophy and he signed a hat for me. I left there thinking, "I'm going to Michigan."

The preseason rankings had me as the No. 2–rated player in the state, which was good, but not good enough. The truth is, I took it as an insult.

I was listed behind Mill Coleman—Mill "The Thrill," that's what he was called back then—a little quarterback from Harrison High School. He ended up going to Michigan State and played wide receiver. He had a nice college career and played some pro ball. Now he's an assistant coach at Harrison.

Nothing against Coleman, but I wanted that No. 1 ranking. It became a huge goal of mine.

Meanwhile, my father and I slowly whittled down the list of potential schools. At the time, I wanted to study engineering. My father was an electrical engineer without the formal education. So I wanted to become an electrical engineer.

My father did all the homework on each of the universities and then presented the information to me. We had the rankings of the respective engineering schools and then we incorporated those numbers into our other overall ratings. It was a very analytical approach. We ended up with six schools: Michigan, Stanford, USC, Notre Dame (yeah, I finally realized the school was in South Bend, Indiana, not in Europe), Colorado, and Tennessee. Colorado and Tennessee were the longshots.

Of course, that didn't keep the other schools from calling. Alabama and Clemson must have called a million times. I'd be on the phone with a recruiter and the call waiting would click in.

"Who's that?" the first recruiter would say.

"It's Alabama," I'd say.

"Which coach from Alabama?" he'd say.

I'd tell him.

"Oh, you don't want to talk to him. He's a liar."

It got to the point where I'd stop telling them about the other schools that were recruiting me. It was ridiculous.

By the end of my senior season I was the No. 1 player in the state and considered one of the best high school players in the country. I had averaged 15.7 tackles, rushed for 1,355 yards (11 yards per carry), and scored 14 touchdowns. Michigan was recruiting me hard and I was leaning that way.

But then Michigan screwed it up.

It started when Schembechler called it quits after the 1989 regular season. Schembechler had never had a losing season at Michigan and he was the winningest active coach in Division I-A, but he had had some heart problems, so he decided to concentrate on his duties as athletic director.

In early December, Schembechler went to see a recruit in Akron, Ohio—Buchtel High School tailback Ricky Powers. Then a few days or so later, he resigned as football coach.

Here I was, in Bo's own backyard—the No. 1 player in the state—and he couldn't even give me a call, a heads-up that he was going to retire? But he had time to go to Ohio and see Ricky Powers? That's when I knew where I really stood with Michigan.

Powers was the No. 1 kid they wanted. Michigan was giving me a lot of lip service, but the proof is always in the pudding. They were telling me I was a Michigan Man and the guy they wanted, but I couldn't even get a phone call from the head coach? Not even a "We like you, but I'm calling it quits and Gary Moeller is going to take over. He'll get in touch with you." But I got nothing. Absolutely nothing. And I was just down the road from Ann Arbor.

When I read about Schembechler's visit to Ohio, I was really disappointed. In my mind, Michigan lost a lot of ground, all because nobody had the courtesy to pick up a phone.

At the time, I thought I was a better linebacker than fullback. And I loved playing linebacker. Loved it. People have never realized that linebacker was my first true football love.

In our last game against Pioneer in my junior year, oh, my goodness, I felt phenomenal. I was laying them out that game. I knocked one kid straight out of the game. He was a running back. He tried to cut up and I put him to sleep. They had to come and get him. The next kid came in and I was laying hat on him too.

But Coach Dozier suggested I start seriously thinking about becoming a fullback rather than a linebacker in college.

"You're five ten and a half," he said. "The prototypical linebacker the pros want is six one, six two. You're probably a little too short. But you're the perfect size for fullback. You've got exceptional speed. You fit the prototype for a fullback."

Coach Dozier made a lot of sense, but I didn't want to be one of those fullbacks who spent his career blocking for somebody else. I liked running the ball too. So I reexamined my list of college finalists. Instead of looking at their linebacking position, I concentrated on how they used the fullback in their offense.

Colorado and USC used their fullbacks to a certain extent. But Notre Dame was the one that really incorporated the fullback entirely into their offense. Michigan was more of a tailback-oriented attack.

In January I started taking my official recruiting visits. One to USC, one to Michigan, one to Notre Dame. I canceled the other three because I got sick, or because I lost interest.

USC was cool, and January in Los Angeles is a lot nicer than January in Ann Arbor or South Bend. But it was a long, long way from home. I wanted my family to be able to see me play, so USC dropped off the list because of geography.

My next trip was to Notre Dame. My mother and father drove down with me and I didn't know what to expect. Rodney Culver, who was a running back from Detroit and later died in that ValuJet crash in 1996, was my Notre Dame player host that weekend.

In the beginning, it was like the other visits: meet the coaches, meet the faculty, meet the admissions people. I think we even watched a video called, "Wake Up the Echoes," which is all about the history of Notre Dame, including the football program.

Then things got interesting.

Even though I had a 3.5-something grade-point average, did well on my SATs, and was a member of the National Honor Society, I was still very unpolished. Not surprisingly, I had a lot of the Detroit street kid in me.

During my visit, several other players (but not Rodney) and I decided to go to a club that was across the state line in Michigan. For some reason—and I never found out how it started—one of the players started wrestling with one of the locals in the parking lot. That's when another local came at me. Well, reverting to my street ways, boom . . . pow, I dropped him, no questions asked. Then the next thing you know, another guy came at me. Boom, he's out.

Before you knew it, there was a melee in the parking lot. I must have hit three guys. Then we heard police sirens in the distance. Everybody started running. We jumped in our car and got the hell out of there. And as we were driving off, I thought to myself, "I like this place."

I know, that's the sickest thing in the world to say after a mini-brawl, but that fight made me feel a lot different about Notre Dame. It was like I was back home on the West Side. The edgy part of me liked the fight, liked the rumblin'. I thought Notre Dame was going to be a stuffy place, but instead we ended up in a fight in a parking lot. It changed my whole perception of the place. I felt like I wasn't so far away from home.

The police never did catch us, and thank goodness Notre Dame head coach Lou Holtz never found out. If he had, I'm not sure he would have offered me a scholarship.

During the four-hour drive back to Detroit it was obvious where my mom wanted me to go. My mom *loved* Notre Dame. My dad, though, was Mr. Picky. He liked it, but his No. 1 priority was always education. Once I narrowed my choices to Michigan and Notre Dame, he stepped back. He said I couldn't make a bad decision either way. But my mom was relentless. Notre Dame. Notre Dame. Notre Dame. You would have thought she was Irish Catholic.

Notre Dame was recruiting me as a fullback. One of their assistants came to Mackenzie to meet with Coach Dozier and me. The assistant had rented a white Cadillac and parked it in the school lot. While he was in talking to us, someone stole another white Cadillac in the same lot. But at first, the assistant heard, "stolen white Cadillac," and thought it was his rental car that had been taken.

Not long after that, Coach Holtz came to see me at my house. So I had to tell my partners in the neighborhood about his visit. When he arrived early in the evening, everybody was sort of out and about—they wanted to see the national championship coach. Coach Holtz pulled up—and we're in the 'hood here—and he saw all these people looking at him. So he said to me, "Hey, I know I'm with you, so I'll be OK. But will the car be OK? The last one almost got stolen."

"Trust me, Coach, the car will be OK," I said. "Don't worry about it."

Coach Holtz was the first coach to come into my 'hood, so he got a big plus for that. He was with Joe Moore, Notre Dame's offensive line coach, and Vinny Cerrato, who was the recruiting coordinator at the time. Now he's the Washington Redskins' vice-president of football operations.

The recruiting pitch was simple and direct. Coach Holtz said he wanted me to play fullback, and that if I signed with Notre Dame he wouldn't recruit another fullback for two years. (And by the way, he kept that promise.)

OK, that sounded good. But then it was time to bargain.

"Coach," I said, "if I come to Notre Dame, can I spat my shoes?"

I liked to tape the top of my cleats, so maybe you'd just see the toes of the cleats. You know, like spats. I did it all the time in high school and I loved the way it looked. Anyway, Culver is the one who said I needed Holtz to agree to it *before* I signed. Otherwise, there was no guarantee he'd remember once I got there.

"Well," said Coach, "put your highlight tape in and let's see."

We played a highlight tape of some of my games. Coach Holtz watched the video and said, "Son, if you play that good, you can come to Notre Dame and tape your shoes."

This was a big deal for me because, as I found out later, Coach Holtz didn't like players to spat their shoes. Notre Dame had a contract with adidas (still does), and the tape covered the stripes on the side of the shoes. So you had to have special permission to spat your shoes. In big games he'd let everybody tape their shoes, but it didn't happen very often.

There was one other item in the negotiations: my jersey number.

I wore No. 36 at Mackenzie. So I asked Coach Holtz if I could wear No. 36 if I came to Notre Dame. He said that Donn Grimm, the younger brother of the great NFL lineman Russ Grimm (the same Russ Grimm who would later become our offensive line coach at Pittsburgh), wore that number. And since Donn was a senior and had been a starting line-backer on the 1988 National Championship team, he didn't think he could give me that number.

"Is there another number you'd want to wear?" he said, explaining that all the running backs wore single-digit numbers.

"Well, I'll wear No. 6."

I picked No. 6 because I had read up on their quarterback Rick Mirer, who wore No. 3. I figured he had No. 3, I'd take No. 6 . . . No. 36. Get it?

Coach Holtz knew it was basically between Notre Dame and Michigan. He also knew that Michigan wanted me as a linebacker. That's when he put the football decision in very simple terms. I'll never forget it. He said, "Son, if you want to run the ball and score touchdowns, come to Notre Dame."

I have to admit, he almost had me right there. But there was still a part of me that couldn't let go of Michigan. So for my final official visit, I went to Ann Arbor.

Everybody made the visit, including my mother, father, brother, and sister. It was a great trip, but I didn't mention anything to Moeller about Powers and Bo. I knew the deal by then. There was nothing to talk about. Powers was their No. 1 guy.

Through the entire process, Michigan wanted me as a linebacker. They were losing a senior linebacker and wanted me to come in and compete for the starting job as a freshman. But after my talk with Coach Dozier, I had decided my long-term interests were best served by playing fullback.

This sort of caught Michigan by surprise. After all, Lloyd Carr, who was the defensive coordinator and linebackers coach at the time, had come to my high school and brought a No. 36 Michigan jersey with my name on the back. It was a nice gesture, but it didn't convince me to become a Michigan Man.

When I told them I didn't want to play linebacker, the coaches stammered for a few moments and then said they'd put me at fullback.

"But you don't really run the fullback," I said.

This wasn't entirely true. They did use Leroy Hoard in short-yardage, goal-line situations, or when they really wanted to pound the ball. But Hoard wasn't a true fullback. Plus, they weren't going to take out their No. 1 recruit, Ricky Powers, and put me in the game to score touchdowns.

But Moeller was persistent and for a little while, I was intrigued by his argument. But the more I thought about it, the more unlikely it sounded. How could they recruit Powers, but then tell me we'd share time?

I didn't like the odds of that happening. In fact, I had a sneaking suspicion that as soon as I got to Michigan they were going to move me to linebacker.

This sort of thing happens all the time. When I was with the Steelers, Hines Ward told me about his college recruitment. Hines was a great high school quarterback in Georgia and wanted to sign with Tennessee. But he was worried that Tennessee was more interested in a high school quarterback from New Orleans, a kid named Peyton Manning. When the UT recruiter said they wouldn't sign Manning if Hines signed first, that's when Hines decided to go elsewhere. Hines was no dummy. Tennessee wasn't going to pass on Manning, no matter how many quarterbacks committed early. So Hines ended up at Georgia and became a star—at wide receiver.

The night before I was supposed to announce my decision, my dad finally asked me, "Where you going to school?" I couldn't tell him because I didn't know. Then my mom asked me the same question. And I gave her the same answer.

Before I went to bed that night I put a Michigan hat and a Notre Dame hat on my dresser. My dad was the one who bought the hats and who told me he'd support whatever decision I made.

"Sleep on it," he said. "It will come to you."

So I said to myself, "When I wake up I'm going to put one of these hats on, and that's where I'm going to school." As my head hit the pillow that night I honestly wasn't sure which school I was picking.

But I got up the next morning, put on the Notre Dame hat, looked in the mirror and then came out for breakfast. My mom was so happy I thought she'd hurt herself smiling. Then I went to school and announced my choice at a big press conference.

In the end, I chose Notre Dame because of how they used the fullback in the offense. Both schools had great academics, great campuses, great alumni networks. My dad was right; I couldn't have made a bad choice. But from a football standpoint, Notre Dame was a better fit.

I'm sure the Michigan coaches weren't thrilled with my decision. Nobody wants to lose a highly ranked, in-state kid, especially one so close, to an out-of-state rival such as Notre Dame.

Shortly after I decided to sign with Notre Dame, I received a bill from Michigan asking me to pay for the meals given to my brother and sister during my official visit. They said it was against NCAA rules for Michigan to pay for those meals.

I told the Michigan people, "Screw you, I'm not paying." It was just too much of a coincidence; me getting that bill right after I committed to Notre Dame. I bet you I wouldn't have received a bill had I signed with Michigan.

I don't know what happened with the bill. I think Coach Dozier ended up paying for it. I know I didn't.

There were a couple of other weird, little twists after I signed with Notre Dame. That summer, Powers and I were teammates in an all-star game. We were two of eighty players invited to the first-ever National High School All-American Football Championship in Reno, Nevada.

They broke the teams down as East v. West. I was on the East roster, along with guys such as Powers (Michigan), Kyle Brady (Penn State), Ruben Brown (Pittsburgh), Andre Hastings (Georgia—he was later a teammate of mine with the Steelers), Bryant Young (Notre Dame), and Mill the Thrill (Michigan State). The West team included Drew Bledsoe (Washington State), Cale Gundy (Oklahoma), and Lake Dawson (Notre Dame). A lot of incredible players were on those rosters.

At halftime we were losing, 21–10, and I was pissed. I didn't come all the way to Reno to get embarrassed. So another player and I asked our head coach, Jim Render of Upper St. Clair (Pennsylvania) High

School, and his assistants, to leave the locker room. And then I ripped into my teammates. I wasn't very diplomatic.

"You fucking guys think you can just show up and win because of who we are," I said. "If you don't want to *play*, then take off your helmet and shoulder pads right now. But I'm going out there with some guys that want to play."

I even called out a couple of players in front of the team and told them they needed to get their acts together. So what happened? We outscored them, 18–0, in the second half, and I scored the game-winning touchdown with 1:09 left to play.

I'll say this for Powers, though: I was impressed. He was as good as advertised.

But here's the really bizarre moment of the summer of 1990: Not long before I was supposed to report to Notre Dame for freshman orientation, I got a job working security for the Detroit Tigers at Tiger Stadium. By then, Schembechler had left Michigan to become the president of the Tigers.

One day I was working security near the main vending areas when Schembechler saw me. I was standing there in my security uniform and I said, "Hey, Coach, how you doin'?"

He walked straight up to me, poked a finger at my chest, and said, "You're a Michigan Man and you know it." And then he walked away.

Schembechler was absolutely serious. He didn't kid about that Michigan Man stuff.

When Coach Schembechler died in November 2006, just a day before the big Ohio State–Michigan game, that's what I remembered first about him: even in death, he found a way to motivate the troops.

The man had a total passion for Michigan football. You were either with him or you were against him. There was no in between. And I had the finger thump to prove it.

Second Quarter

4

Lou Holtz calls on his cell phone from ESPN's worldwide headquarters in Bristol, Connecticut, where he is preparing for his weekly appearances on the network's college football studio show. But he always has time to talk about Bettis.

"The first time I met him was in his house when I was recruiting him. There were a lot of people there, as I recall: his mom, dad, grandparents, aunt, uncle. I don't pay attention to neighborhoods or the size of houses. I'm more interested in what's inside the house than what's outside of it. And the thing I noticed about Jerome was the respect he showed his family. You knew they had a special young man.

"When he came to Notre Dame, he was coming into a pretty good program. We weren't really looking for somebody to turn the program around. The first year I wasn't impressed at all. He had bad ankles, so he hardly played at all as a freshman.

"Going into the Orange Bowl that year, well, I treat the practice schedule like this: The first weekend I give the seniors off. The second weekend is like fall camp, all fundamentals. The third week is full preparation. But I do remember this quite vividly: we went over to the fieldhouse during that first weekend, when it was just the young players. I watched Jerome and went, 'Wow!' All of a sudden I could see his explosiveness and ability. I thought this guy could be really special. He caught my eye like nobody had.

"The great football players are the ones where you walk off the field *after every practice and say, 'Did you see what he did today?' It started to get that way with Jerome. During his sophomore year he was such a good football player that we put him at tailback when we wanted to run the clock a little bit. You put him behind a fullback and two tight ends . . . ain't nobody in the world going to stop him for less than 10 yards.*

"In the bowl game against Florida, he put on a show during that second half. We decided, 'We're going to do the things we do best: give the ball to Jerome.' There's no doubt he has to go down as one of the great players I've ever coached.

"The thing I've always loved about Jerome is his attitude when he walks into a room. It's always, 'There you are, tell me about you.' It isn't, 'Here I am, let me tell you about me.' With all the success he's had, he's still the same Jerome Bettis. He makes a difference in life. That's what I'd always ask our players: 'If you hadn't come into our lives, would you be missed?'

"If Jerome had not come into our lives, come to Notre Dame, come to the NFL, there would have been a lot of people who would have missed him."

Yeah, I'll admit it: I cried like a baby when my folks drove away after helping me move into my dorm room at Notre Dame. Everybody was crying. Me. My mom. My dad. Sheesh, that's all we did was cry.

For the first time in my life I was truly on my own. And I was scared.

A lot of people in Detroit were making a pretty big deal about me going to Notre Dame and I was excited, too. I was excited right up until my family hugged and kissed me goodbye, got back into the van, and started driving away. That's when it hit me. I started walking back to my dorm and I saw the Golden Dome of the Administration Building and it was like, "Whoa, I'm here now."

I didn't have much, maybe a suitcase, a suit that I wore for high school graduation, a box of clothes, and a little radio. Incoming freshmen football players had to report to school (we stayed at Grace Hall for camp) before the upperclassmen players. And we were both on campus weeks before the regular student body arrived. We basically had the place to ourselves.

I knew I was lucky to be at Notre Dame. I was lucky that some of my earlier decisions as a teenager hadn't cost me. Now I wanted to take advantage of that opportunity. I couldn't screw it up. If I did, then I'd end up back in the neighborhood, in that negative environment. I told myself, "I'm not going back there."

Still, I looked like a kid from Detroit. I had the $500 Pelle Pelle leather jacket. It was so cliché in Detroit to wear something like that, but I wore it. I had the big gold chain with an eagle dangling from the end of it. I had the Detroit attitude: kind of flamboyant, a hustler quality.

In Detroit you've got to be somewhat of a hustler, because the odds of getting out of the 'hood weren't in your favor. And I had been hustling from day one, from selling ten-cent candy, to selling Transformers, to selling around the block. No question, it was all part of the survival mode.

I came from a high school that barely had any white students. Now I was at prestigious, world-renowned, predominantly white, Catholic, affluent Notre Dame.

I knew there was going to be little tolerance for a person like me. I also knew if I got in trouble then my great opportunity was going to be lost. I couldn't let that happen, not after all the sacrifices my parents and my relatives had made for me. I wasn't just going to Notre Dame for myself, I was going for my entire family. I couldn't let those people down.

Once I got to Notre Dame, I had to teach myself to suppress the Detroit in me. I had to steer clear of all confrontation in day-to-day life, which is the opposite of how you survive in the 'hood.

I'll give you an example.

Where I grew up, if somebody bumped into you it was a sign of disrespect. It was crazy. You got into fights over someone bumping into you.

But at Notre Dame, if a kid accidentally bumped into another kid in the hallway, it was no big deal. One kid would say, "Excuse me." The other kid would say, "No problem." That was that.

To be honest, I didn't really know what to expect. I didn't have any views about white America because I didn't know anything about it. How can you have a view of something that you're ignorant about? All I knew was my world. And my world was changing fast.

> *"I went off to Tuskegee University in Alabama and Jerome went to Notre Dame in South Bend. I was playing cornerback at a predominantly black southern college in Division II. He was playing at one of the elite schools in the country. Our perspectives were so different, but our experiences were so similar.*
>
> *"We would always talk on Sundays. We had those telephone calling cards and we'd talk every Sunday—and it usually didn't have anything to do with football.*
>
> *"Coming from inner-city Detroit, we had developed such hard exteriors, almost to the point where we didn't appreciate people speaking to us.*
>
> *"But people in the South are very engaging and friendly. They talk to you all the time. So I'd call Jerome and tell him, 'These people down here are crazy. They're always talking to you.'*
>
> *"And he'd say, 'Same thing here. People are speaking to me so much I've got to walk with my head down.'*
>
> *"We still had that Detroit mentality. We were learning that the rest of the world had a totally different outlook and approach. So being in those situations was the key for both of us. We both went to schools with multicultural environments, and because of that we had to grow and mature. It was such an evolution for both us, in terms of being successful outside of our own environment."*
>
> *—Jahmal Dokes*

There were twenty-three of us who reported to freshman camp. Out of those twenty-three, there were five Parade All-Americans. Fourteen of the recruits, myself included, were ranked in the top 100 of almost every recruiting publication. I can't think of any major recruiting analyst who didn't rank our class as the best in the country.

In retrospect, it might have been the best recruiting class in Notre Dame history and maybe among the best in college football history. It was just ridiculous the caliber of players that were in that class.

Five of us—myself, Bryant Young, Aaron Taylor, Tom Carter, and

Jeff Burris—would become first-round picks in the NFL Draft. In all, twelve players in the Notre Dame Class of 1994 would be selected in the draft—nine of us in the third round or higher.

Even Coach Holtz knew he had something special. I remember him telling reporters that this was the most excited he had ever been about a recruiting class. His exact words were, "I just feel this group might be special."

So did we.

Our first meeting with Coach Holtz was in an auditorium. No big deal. Then the upperclassmen reported and we had a full team meeting in the same auditorium. Most of us freshmen sat where we sat for the first meeting: down in the front.

We weren't in those seats for more than a few minutes when some of the seniors stormed up to us.

"Get your ass out of that chair!" one of them said to me. "Your seat is in the back!"

I'm telling you, that was a scary moment. We didn't know the first three rows of the meeting room were for the seniors, that the next four rows were for the juniors, that the next four rows were for the sophomores, and that the freshmen sat waaaaaaaaay at the top.

It was during one of these team meetings that Coach Holtz conducted a hands-on seminar on how to talk to the media. I was one of the freshmen he called up to the front of the auditorium. There was a Minicam for the interview, but no interviewer. That's when Coach Holtz started asking me questions like he was the reporter.

Sheesh, I was so scared. I don't remember anything I said. I had no clue. For one, the entire team watched Coach Holtz do the interview. And, of course, I fumbled and stumbled through the whole thing.

When he was done, Coach Holtz put the mock interview on the big screen and critiqued my answers. It was humiliating at the time, but it might have been one of the best things that ever happened to me. It taught me the importance of speaking well and keeping your poise under pressure.

Before the upperclassmen showed up, us rookies thought we were pretty good. Then the veterans started rolling in and all of a sudden we weren't shit. We were getting our asses handed to us.

I even got a rude awakening from one of my fellow rookies. I was carrying the ball in practice and had my usual run-over-everybody attitude. Jim Flanigan, our big-time freshman linebacker, had his usual crunch-anybody-who-thinks-they-can-run-over-everybody attitude.

Flanigan hit me so hard he separated my shoulder. The guy was a stud. He crunched me up bad. It was like, "This ain't the public school, buddy. It's the big time."

Everything was such a new experience for me: being on my own, being at Notre Dame, being a lowly freshman, being six one (even though I was only five eleven, I listed my height as six one on my freshman info sheet for the school's Sports Information Department because I liked the sound of it). And when school started I had to adjust to my class load (I was an engineering major), the demands of football, and my new roommate.

At Notre Dame there is no jock dorm. So all the athletes are integrated into the general student body, which is the way it should be. I was assigned to Alumni Hall, an all-male dorm built in 1931. It has stone carvings of Knute Rockne, as well as Clashmore Mike (he was the school's Irish terrier mascot, and the main reason why residents of Alumni proudly refer to themselves as "Dawgs"). Some pretty famous ND alums have lived there, including a secretary of agriculture from the Reagan Administration, a U.S. ambassador to Honduras, and the president of Emerson Electric. And, I guess, me.

Because the football players were on campus before the student body, I got to pick which side of my dorm room I wanted. One day I walked in and there was my new roommate, a white kid from Chicago. His dad was a dentist and they were moving all sorts of stuff into the room.

First of all, he had his own personal computer. I was shocked. I'm thinking, "Damn, you got your own computer? You ain't got to go to the library to use a computer? And you've got a printer too?" I thought I was rooming with the richest kid in America.

He had a sound system and the fanciest calculator I'd ever seen. I'd never seen so much technology. I didn't know kids lived like this. And did I mention he was white?

This was the first time I ever had to communicate with a white kid. I didn't know what to say or how to act. I kept telling myself, "This is going to be interesting."

We hit it off fine until he started hanging his shorts and underwear on a nail he had tapped into the bed. He was a long-distance runner and when he got done with his runs at night, he'd drape his sweat-soaked underwear on hangers and then put the hangers on the nail. It blew me away because this was some of the nastiest shit in the world he had hanging up there. It freaked me out because I didn't know what to do about it.

I was still "Detroit Jerome." I was brash and didn't really know how to talk to people without using street tactics. And street tactics dictated using fear.

At home, I would have just said, "You're gonna take this shit down or I'm gonna kick your ass." But I was so scared of getting kicked out of school, that *I* was the one who was paralyzed by fear. I was terrified that I'd say something, he'd react the wrong way, and I'd knock his teeth out.

I know this sounds weird, but I was so conditioned to confront people, that I didn't know how to just *talk* to somebody about a situation.

So I didn't say anything at first. I just stared at that wet, nasty-looking, stinky underwear and fumed. I couldn't believe he didn't put his underwear in a hamper and then wash it.

I let it go for a long, long, long time until one day I just said to him, "You gotta stop that. That's nasty." I think I told him my family was coming to visit and I didn't want them to see his underwear. I was able to finesse it, which was a big step forward for me since finesse was kind of a new word in my vocabulary. I was like a bull-in-a-china-shop kind of guy coming out of high school.

And you know what he said? "Sure, no problem. Sorry about that."

That was it. Wow, it was something so small to him. Meanwhile, I was agonizing over it like it was the most important thing in my life. It doesn't sound like much, but that incident taught me a lesson in handling difference, and how to adapt without using my fists.

When the first depth chart was posted I was listed as the third-string fullback, mostly because I was a freshman and had missed some practice time because of a bruised quadricep muscle. Culver was the starter. Peter Vaas was the running backs coach.

It didn't take long before I realized that the polite, witty, and charming Coach Holtz who came to my house in Detroit was a little different than the Coach Holtz who stepped onto a football field. He was tough. He barked all the time, especially at the quarterbacks. During the passing drills he'd constantly tell them, "Deep, short, intermediate. Deep, short, intermediate." That's how he wanted them to go through their passing progressions.

Except that he didn't realize he was screwing up. Deep, short, *then* intermediate? That didn't make any sense. Even my auntie could figure that out. It should have been, deep, intermediate, short.

But nobody was going to tell him different, especially not a freshman like myself. Instead, we tried not to laugh, which was hard, since one of our freshmen quarterbacks, B. J. Hawkins, could do a perfect imitation of Coach Holtz. Lord, have mercy, B.J. had us crying, we were laughing so hard. We missed those imitations when B.J. later transferred.

Though Coach Holtz yelled at the quarterbacks the most, if anyone screwed up, he'd notice. But those poor quarterbacks got it the worst.

Because of my deal with Coach Holtz, I spatted my shoes every day during training camp. Soon everyone on the team was doing it. Then Coach Holtz walked on the practice field one day and announced that nobody was allowed to tape their shoes.

I couldn't believe it. Coach Holtz had sat in my house and *promised* me I could spat my shoes. He lied to me! I was so mad that I actually thought about transferring.

That's when I heard him pull up in the golf cart he used during practice.

"Bettis, get in here!"

So I got in the cart. He took me to the farthest edge of the practice field and then he said, his voice much softer and apologetic, "I know I said nobody can tape their shoes. But you can—just not today, OK?" So that was our little deal.

Coming from a public school like Mackenzie, I marveled at the football luxuries at Notre Dame. At Mackenzie, Coach Dozier was our coach and trainer. We had to buy our own tape so he could wrap our ankles. At Notre Dame, where it was the crème de la crème of everything . . . the top of the college football food chain, they had an entire staff of trainers.

Jerome with Jahmal Dokes at their high school graduation.
Courtesy of the author

Jerome breaks a tackle against Michigan State.
© *Michael & Susan Bennett/Lighthouse Imaging*

Jerome marries Trameka.
© *Paul Wharton*

Trameka, Jada, Jerome, and Jerome Jr.
© *Paul Wharton*

The Bettis family: John III (brother), Kimberly (sister), Gladys,
Jerome, and John Jr. *Courtesy of the author*

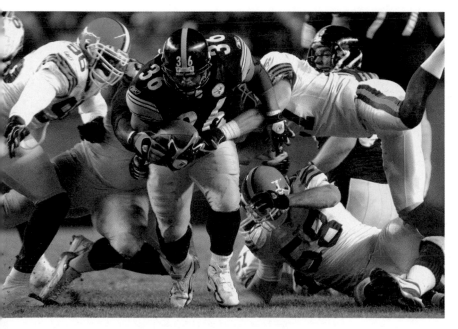

The Browns can't stop The Bus.
© *Michael Fabus*

Jerome with Hines Ward.
© Michael Fabus

Jerome at the Pro Bowl in 1996 with Dermontti Dawson, Levon
Kirkland, Chad Brown, Carnell Lake, and Rod Woodson. *© Michael Fabus*

Touchdown at Heinz Field.
© *Michael Fabus*

Jerome and Coach Hoak.
© *Michael Fabus*

Jerome and Coach Cowher.
© Michael Fabus

Jerome prays with the team pregame.
© Michael Fabus

Jerome and Ben Roethlisberger kissing Lombardi Trophy.
© Michael Fabus

Jerome and Jahmal Dokes after the Super Bowl win in Detroit.

The Bus celebrates winning one for the thumb.

At Mackenzie, we didn't have a stadium or a locker room. We had portable bleachers and PE lockers. At Notre Dame, we played in a stadium designed by the same architects who designed Yankee Stadium. It was the house Rockne built. It oozed history.

At Mackenzie we had to buy our own cleats. You'd buy one pair and they'd have to last you two years. At Notre Dame you'd get a pair of fresh out-of-the-box adidas cleats for grass, a pair for wet grass, a pair for artificial turf, and then a pair of back-up cleats. I'd stare at all the shoes in my locker and I couldn't believe it.

And you should have seen our training table spread. It was incredible. There was every kind of entrée you can imagine, but definitely no syrup sandwiches. I had to ask somebody, "Wow, you mean I can eat *anything?*" They had all these entrées, and ice creams, and side dishes. I almost lost my mind.

We opened the 1990 season at home against Michigan. We were the preseason No. 1 in the country and Michigan was No. 4.

When I first walked into the locker room before the game and saw my helmet sitting there, I was overwhelmed. You see, during training camp your helmet gets beat up, scuffed up from all the head banging. And it was worse for freshmen, since our helmets featured a strip of athletic tape on the front with our names written on it.

But on the Friday night before a home game, the Notre Dame student managers clean the helmets and then apply a coat of gold paint—with actual gold dust in it. When I saw mine sparkling in my locker I was like, "Whoo-hoo-ee. Yes sir, we got the gold, baby."

Helmets mean a lot to a player. You can usually tell how much a guy plays and if he likes to mix it up by the amount of "meat" he has on his helmet. Let's say you're playing a team with white helmets, like Penn State. At the end of the game you'd take your helmet off to see how much white helmet paint—how much meat—was on it. The more meat you had on your helmet, the more it meant you were popping them during the game.

I was so geeked for Michigan that I don't think my cleats touched the ground during warm-ups. We were playing under the lights and Notre Dame Stadium was filled to the brim. My family was there. I was going against the program that had wanted me more as a linebacker than fullback. And their No. 1 recruit, Ricky Powers, was there.

One problem: I didn't play.

I wasn't injured; the coaches just didn't put me in. The only thing that hurt was my heart. I wanted to play against Michigan so much. I wanted some maize and blue meat on my helmet. But I didn't get a sniff.

About the only consolation was that we won, 28–24, and that Powers didn't do anything either.

I made my Notre Dame debut the next week in our win against Michigan State and had my first carry the week after that, against Purdue. I scored my first Notre Dame touchdown against Navy. In fact, I played in eleven of our twelve games that year, mostly on special teams. But as the season went on, I started to get a few carries here and there. I started to get a chance to show what I could do.

We began the season at No. 1, but then we lost to unranked Stanford, dropped to No. 8 in the polls and then slowly worked our way back to the top ranking. Then we lost to Penn State in our last home game, beat USC the following week, and were invited to play No. 1–ranked Colorado in the Orange Bowl.

On the way, I started to make a little name for myself. In early November, in our win against No. 9 Tennessee (Coach Holtz blared "Rocky Top" during our practices until we all wanted to throw up), I laid some big blocks for Ricky Watters. That game sort of put me on the football map. People started to notice me. Up until then, the guys in the dorm would see me after a game and say something like, "Hey, man, saw you on the field." But after this one, they were saying, "Aw, man, great game. You did a great job. You're good."

Our 1990 team was good enough to have won a National Championship. Mike Heldt, Todd Lyght, Watters, and Chris Zorich were our captains, but Raghib "Rocket" Ismail was our star. Coach Holtz loved that kid.

He was a junior that year, and he could do anything: play flanker, return kicks, and punts. He was an electrifying talent.

In one of our last practices before we were supposed to fly to Miami, a Notre Dame administrator informed Coach Holtz that Rocket needed to sign a form to be eligible for the bowl game. But Rocket wasn't at practice that day and nobody knew where he was.

Coach Holtz was beside himself.

"Where's Rocket?" he kept saying. "He's got to sign this thing."

Mind you, Coach Holtz wasn't worried that Rocket had gone AWOL from practice. Nobody *ever* missed practice without there being absolute hell to pay. No, he was worried that Rocket wouldn't be able to sign the form.

Coach Holtz called the team up, which took a while since we were spread all over the practice fields.

"Where the hell is that kid?" Holtz said. "If he doesn't sign this, he isn't eligible to play. This is what I'm gonna do. I'm gonna have everyone leave practice now and you're going to comb the campus, and you're going to find Rocket and make sure he comes here to sign this form."

We couldn't believe it. Coach Holtz called off practice—which he never did—all so we could go look for Rocket?

Let me tell you what would have happened if *I* hadn't shown up for practice. First of all, there wouldn't have been any damn search committee commissioned by Coach Holtz. Oh, goodness, he would have killed me. He would have said, "Hey, Jerome, I wouldn't trade your ass for one iota. I'll tell you what, son, you got all the intangibles. But missing practice? After doing that, I don't know how I can trust you on the field. So I can't let your ass play. If I do, they'll come and get me."

But Coach Holtz had a soft spot for Rocket. Rocket *was* different. He was a great college player, but back then he was a little uncomfortable with all the attention. One time after a game, he hid in a towel hamper and had the managers wheel him out of the locker room. That way he wouldn't have to talk to the media.

Anyway, somebody finally found Rocket. A friend of his had had a death in the family, so Rocket had gone over to help him out. But he did sign the form that day and came to Miami with us.

We lost to Colorado, 10–9, though we could have very easily won that game and made an argument for a share of the national championship with Georgia Tech. At the very least, we would have been the undisputed No. 2. But we had five turnovers, missed an extra point, and had a field goal attempt clang off the upright.

Late in the game, Rocket returned a punt at the 9-yard line (I have no idea why Colorado kicked to him), broke free, and went 91 yards for a touchdown. It was one of the greatest runs you'll ever see. I thought the game was over. We were going to beat Colorado and finish 10–2.

Turns out it was the greatest run that never counted. One of the officials dropped a late penalty flag for clipping and the touchdown was wiped out. Rocket turned pro not long after that game.

That was also the same game I learned about Coach Holtz's loyalty to his seniors. In the second quarter I broke off a nice 18-yard run, took it down to the 3- or 4-yard line and was thinking, "OK, let's punch it in"—with me doing the punching.

Instead, Coach Holtz took me out of the game. I came to the sideline and he said, "All right, son, I'm going to let the seniors win it from here."

Watters scored on a 2-yard run and I didn't carry the ball the rest of the game.

I didn't understand his reasoning. We had been sputtering pretty much the whole game. He put me in, and I helped take us down deep into the red zone. And then he said he wanted the seniors to take it from there?

I was pissed, really pissed. In fact, I think that's what really drove me during that offseason and into the next year. I didn't want him ever to be able to pull me out of a game again.

By the spring of 1991 there wasn't much question that I was going to be the starting fullback. I had had a really good spring practice and was determined to become a factor in our offense. No way was I going to settle for just eighteen carries for the season, which was my total as a freshman. I had given myself a B grade for my freshman season. Now I wanted an A. I even jotted down my goals on a piece of paper: at least 700 yards rushing, lead the team in rushing, be consistent.

During that same spring, the school's Sports Information Department gave each of us a questionnaire to fill out for the 1991 football media guide. I was so serious about my answers.

Nicknames: Bear . . . Detroit Thunder.

I Would Buy a Ticket to Watch This Athlete Perform: Micheal Jordan (yeah, I misspelled his name).

My Football Fantasy Is To: Win the Heisman Trophy.

Favorite Non-Sports Hero: Parents.

My Craziest Ambition: To jump out of an airplane.

Behind My Back, People Say I'm: Not as nice as I seem to be.

I'd Like to Be Stranded on a Desert Island With: Me, myself, and I—to find out what's really inside of me.

If I Could Change One Thing About Myself, I Would: Want to be 2 inches taller.

My Favorite Play: Is when I get the ball in the middle of the line and inflict pain on anyone who tries to tackle me.

Once I'm Finished With College I Hope I'll Have Time To: Travel and do something for my community.

And the one that would come back to haunt me years later in Indianapolis—*My Worst Fear*: Fumbling the football on the goal-line.

I went home that summer a different person. I wasn't exactly Mr. Notre Dame, but I wasn't Detroit Jerome, either. I got back to the neighborhood and I realized I couldn't do a lot of the same things I had done there when I was in high school. I had to be more careful, more responsible. I was still with the boys, but I wasn't *one* of them anymore. Understand the difference? I was a visitor now.

That summer I got a job at General Motors working at their tech plant. I wanted to be an engineer, so every day I drove the doo-doo brown Mustang to 13th and Mile. I wore a shirt and tie and worked at the tech plant, helping out with research and performance tests on the GM engines. That was also the same summer I joined a mentorship program to help underprivileged kids. I guess I was starting to grow up.

At that point in my life, pro football wasn't a consideration. I thought I'd play football at Notre Dame, get my engineering degree, and then get a job. My grades were OK, but I began to realize that engineering was harder than it looked. The classes were *tough*. I held my own, but it was a grind with my football schedule.

When I reported that August for training camp the depth chart had a different look to it. Culver, our team captain, had moved to tailback, which meant fullback was all mine. This was going to be my coming-out season. Then one day during practice, Coach Holtz called us up and asked us to take a knee.

Coach Holtz didn't do this sort of thing very often because it took so long to get everybody together and because it took away from practice time. We were spread over three different fields, so if he was calling the whole team up it meant he had something important to say.

"There's a guy on this football team, he's going to get our ass beat," said Coach Holtz. "He doesn't have a commitment. I can't trust him and, personally, I don't think his ass cares. We're going to lose a national championship because of this guy. He doesn't want to win, thinks he's God's gift, thinks he's the next big thing."

As Coach Holtz was talking, I started looking around at the other players. I was thinking, "Who's going to cost us a national championship? Point him out. I'll talk to him. Commitment? I'll make sure the kid understands commitment."

Then Coach Holtz pointed at me and said, "Jerome Bettis, would you stand up."

I nearly swallowed my tongue. He had been talking about *me*. He crushed me in front of the entire team. I was so hurt.

As I started to stand up it was like everything was in slow motion. His words were just hanging in the air, like smoke. The thoughts in my mind became louder than whatever else he was saying. It was like my mind was yelling at my ears, saying, "Oh my, God, what is happening here?"

When he was done humiliating me, I sort of staggered back toward practice. We were getting ready to do some running back drills when out of the haze I heard that golf cart again. He told me to get in.

I said, "Coach, why'd you do that?"

He said, "I just want to get you going."

Believe me, he didn't need to get me going. But I sort of understood what he was trying to do. He was trying to keep me humble. But, man, there's a fine line between being humbled and being humiliated.

I rushed for 972 yards during that sophomore season, scored 16 touchdowns, and averaged 5.8 yards per carry. One of my teammates, Nick Smith, asked me what the difference was between my freshman and sophomore year. I said, "I was good last year. But this year the whole country knows I'm good."

In the Sugar Bowl upset of Florida (they were ranked No. 3, we were No. 18), I had 150 rushing yards, scored three times on three consecutive runs, and was named the MVP. Before that game, Coach Holtz told us that someone in New Orleans had asked him if he knew the difference between Cheerios and our team. The difference, the guy told Coach, was that the Cheerios belonged in a bowl.

Of course, Coach Holtz loved telling us that story. Anything to get us psyched up. In retrospect, I think he made the whole thing up. But we fell for it.

We didn't win a national championship (we finished 10–3), but it had nothing to do with my level of commitment.

That was a big year for me because I established myself as a fullback who could make a difference. I had 111 yards against Indiana in the season opener, 179 against Stanford, and 178 against USC. I tore their ass up in that game. Afterward, I guess USC Coach Larry Smith said I was the greatest fullback he'd ever seen. And when reporters asked Coach Holtz about me, he said, "I gotta be honest with you, he's better than I thought he would be."

Then I had the huge game in the Sugar Bowl and suddenly everything changed. Now it was a realistic possibility that I might play in the NFL. Before my sophomore season, I hadn't given it any consideration. None. But for the first time I was thinking about a future that might include pro football.

Not long after the Sugar Bowl I saw a TV show where they were debating whether I would petition the NFL to be eligible for the 1991 draft. I thought they were crazy.

First of all, I had only had one good season. Plus, I was having fun being a college kid. I played in the Bookstore Basketball tournament. I met kids from every part of the country and from every backround. I was getting an education. I was even on campus when they were filming the movie, *Rudy*. Life was good.

The only thing I didn't have was a car. The doo-doo brown Mustang couldn't survive the drive to South Bend, so I always borrowed my new roommate's bicycle. I called it my Baby Benz. By the way, thank you, Nathan Uy, for letting me use your bike.

Most of all, I was having fun playing ball. I wasn't ready to get a full-time job, even if that job was in the NFL.

The thing is, I got a little carried away. In early February 1992, about a month or so after we beat Florida, I was part of a group of Notre Dame players who attended the 17th Annual Football Smoker at St. Vincent's Church in Fort Wayne. A lot of people were still asking me if I was going to turn pro.

So I made a promise to the crowd of about twelve hundred Irish fans.

"I assure you I will play football at Notre Dame as a junior and at Notre Dame as a senior," I said. "You can bank on that."

The crowd went nuts and a reporter from the *Fort Wayne News-Sentinel* wrote down every word I said. The newspaper headline read: Notre Dame's Bettis Says He Won't Leave for NFL.

By the time the 1992 season started I was being mentioned as a Heisman Trophy candidate, along with our co-captain, Rick Mirer, who had decided to stay for his senior year. Mirer, I could understand. With him as our quarterback, we had scored a then-school record 426 points in 1991, which worked out to 35.5 points per regular season game.

Me? I was a fullback. Fullbacks didn't win Heismans. There wasn't even a place for us on the All-American teams.

To be honest, I thought we were going to win the 1992 national championship. I even said so on the players survey we had to fill out for the media guide.

That was the same questionnaire that asked what I'd never heard of before coming to Notre Dame. I wrote, "Touchdown Jesus, but now it's my best friend." Another question said, *I'd like to ask Lou Holtz* . . . and I wrote, "If he could give me the Heisman."

We had a complete team: great defense, great offense, great coach. Most of our really big games—Michigan, Stanford, Boston College, and Penn State—were at home. And we had a lot of experience. I couldn't find a serious weakness.

We opened the season ranked No. 3 in the polls and killed Northwestern at Soldier Field in Chicago. Then, in a game where we got booed in the final minute by our own home crowd, we tied Michigan, 17–17.

Everybody thought Coach Holtz was trying to run out the clock for the tie. But what really happened was that on our final drive (we got the ball back at our own 14 with 1:05 left), he forgot the clock started after a penalty.

We had been flagged for an illegal formation on the second play of the drive and Coach Holtz assumed that the clock would start at the next snap. But there had been a rule change that year and the clock started right after the penalty. Mirer was talking strategy with Coach on the sideline and we wasted about fifteen seconds. A couple of incomplete passes later, the game was finished, but not the controversy.

We got booed, but it wasn't like we did anything wrong as players. Coach Holtz took the blame for the botched clock management. But at least we were still unbeaten.

After two more wins we played No. 19 Stanford at home. What a nightmare. Bill Walsh, who had been the color analyst for our games on NBC the season before, was back as head coach. He knew our personnel, our coaching staff, our tendencies.

But as good as a coach as Walsh was, there's no way we should have lost that game. We were up, 16–0, but then just handed them the win.

I fumbled on each of our first two possessions in the second half. Stanford's safety—maybe you've heard of him: John Lynch—caused one of the fumbles. Lynch also broke one of Lake Dawson's ribs. And he also ended what might have been the winning drive when he intercepted Mirer's pass in the end zone late in the fourth quarter.

Walsh was so happy after the game that he cried. We wanted to do the same thing, but for different reasons. That loss ended our hopes of a national championship and was one of the lowest days of my college career. Not only that, but I injured my ankle in that game.

After that, we ran the table, though I didn't start in four of our last five games because of my bum ankle. But my ankle was fine for our regular season finale against USC (89 yards, 1 touchdown).

By then, my parents were getting calls from players agents all the time. Even with the injury, I still had gained 825 yards and scored 12 touchdowns. It wasn't the season I was hoping for, but it wasn't bad.

Ten months earlier in Fort Wayne I had promised I'd be back for my senior year. I wish I could say I was misquoted, but I wasn't. "Bank on it"—that's what I said. But that was before I hurt my ankle, and before my mother got laid off from her job during my junior season. My dad, as always, was still working two jobs.

Injuries are part of football, but I had to weigh the positives of coming back to Notre Dame versus the negatives of possibly getting injured as a senior. And with my mom not working, I knew it was going to be especially difficult for my family.

My parents made it clear that they didn't want their financial situation to factor into my choice. But deep down I knew that if I turned pro, I'd be able to help them. They had already taken out a loan to get me an insurance policy as a junior. That way if I suffered a career-ending injury I'd receive compensation. It would be a nice check, but nothing like the money I'd get if I were a high pick, got a big signing bonus, and went on to have a nice NFL career.

I didn't have a lot of time to make a decision. Our regular season ended November 28 and the NFL deadline to declare for the draft was January 6. In between, we had final exams and a January 1 Cotton Bowl game against Texas A&M.

Thanks to me trying to show off as a freshman (and getting crushed by Flanigan), my shoulder always made a clicking sound when I moved it a certain way. So before we left for Dallas, the team doctor of the Detroit Lions gave me a physical. There were a few nervous moments, but the shoulder checked out clean.

The experts all said I'd be a first-round pick if I came out early. ESPN's Mel Kiper Jr. said I was all but guaranteed to go anywhere between the tenth and fifteenth pick. That caught my attention.

But it wasn't until we crushed A&M to finish the season 10–1–1, that I made up my mind (I had scored three times in the game). Coach Holtz met with me and my mother and father, and said that normally he'd recommend that a junior come back for his senior year. He had told cornerback Tommy Carter, who also was thinking about declaring, that it would be a mistake for him to leave early. But with me, he said that I had done all that I could do at Notre Dame.

It was unbelievably cool of him to say that, and it basically confirmed my decision that it was time to go. In fact, when our team was in Dallas for the Cotton Bowl, I had told Coach Holtz that I was leaning toward leaving.

Some people said that if I came back I'd be one of the leading Heisman candidates in 1993. But they had said the same thing about Mirer in 1992, and he didn't even finish in the top ten of the Heisman voting (neither did I). Instead, Gino Torretta won the Heisman that year and our Reggie Brooks, who wasn't on anybody's preseason Heisman list, finished fifth. So I wasn't going to come back because I *might* win a twenty-five-pound trophy.

I loved almost everything about Notre Dame, but on January 5—the day before Coach Holtz's fifty-sixth birthday—I officially announced that I was leaving. I left Notre Dame as the fourteenth-leading rusher in school history to that date and sixth in career rushing touchdowns. Our teams finished 29–7–1 and won two bowl games. But those were just numbers. More important, I left as a better and more mature person.

I knew I was going to miss the place and the people. Coach Holtz was tough, but he had been honest with me. I liked playing for him because he always had a plan.

Joe Moore was the longtime offensive line coach who recruited me to Notre Dame. That was my guy. He was a crusty old hoot, but he was something else. He's the guy who came up with one of my nicknames—and it wasn't The Bus. "The Bus" was first given to me by somebody on the Notre Dame student newspaper staff, *The Observer*, though it didn't really catch on until years later. Instead, I was known as Big Daddy at Notre Dame. Coach Moore used to have a little saying: "He's as big as a truck and quick as a Caddy, that's why they call him, 'Big Daddy.' "

Coach Moore was probably the only guy on the entire coaching staff who wasn't scared of Coach Holtz. He didn't care what Coach Holtz said. If Coach Holtz tried to get involved with Coach Moore's linemen, Joe would say in his gravelly voice, "Get your head out of there. I got it. I got it." No matter what Coach Holtz said, Coach Moore would always say, "I got it. I got it."

Coach Moore was fired in 1996 by Bob Davie, who had taken over for Coach Holtz. It was so sad, and the worst part about it is that Coach Moore was the one who helped convince Coach Holtz to hire Davie.

I was disappointed and angered that Davie fired him. It was the wrong thing to do—and a jury agreed. Coach Moore, who was sixty-four at the time, won an age-discrimination lawsuit against Notre Dame. In 2003 he died of lung cancer.

I knew I was going to miss those coaches, my teammates, and the little things, like running out of the tunnel at Notre Dame Stadium or tapping the signs when we'd leave the locker room for the field. There was one sign that had the ND logo and a leprechaun on it. Tap, tap, tap. Then you'd slap the Play Like A Champion Today sign as you went by. You'd think those signs would have bruise marks by now.

But it was time to leave. Coach Holtz was right; I'd done everything I could as a Notre Dame football player.

5

Mel Kiper Jr., who turned the NFL Draft into a cottage industry, answers his phone at his suburban Baltimore home with his usual gushing enthusiasm. Does the guy ever have a bad day?

Kiper began writing about the draft in 1981 while a student at Essex Community College in Maryland. ESPN hired him and his hair three years later for the network's expanded coverage of the draft. A legend was born.

His encyclopedic knowledge of even the most obscure NFL prospects is scary. But Kiper politely asks if he can put the phone down while he finds his original assessment of Bettis, which was published in his pre–1993 NFL Draft Report.

"Got it," Kiper says. "I'll read it to you."

So he starts to read:

" *'Jerome Bettis.*

" *'5–11¼, 248 pounds, 4.62 40*

" *'Overall Top 150 ranking on draft board: 4th.*

" *'Projected: 10th pick, Los Angeles Rams.*

" *'Combine note: Didn't work out.*

" *'Subscribers to any of my reports over the last few years know how high I have been on this pile-driving runner. In my opinion, he's in the All-World category when it comes to doing everything a club could ask in a big back . . . Bettis doesn't absorb hits, he delivers the blows. On film, I've actually seen defensive backs run away from the area just to avoid a collision.*

" 'With most power backs, you don't see so much versatility. That's not the case here. He's a superlative receiver, able to make the tough catch 30 yards down the field. As a blocker, you won't come across many who do their job any better. He thrives on contact, yet plays within himself on most occasions.

" 'Great football player. Destined for a stellar career in the NFL. The only thing that could hold him back is a little excess weight once he gets into his mid-to-late 20s.' "

Kiper pauses to consider what he wrote thirteen years earlier.

"You know," he says, "I wasn't off by much, was I?"

Nothing can really prepare you for the NFL Draft. You become a commodity, a product, and everybody—scouts, player personnel directors, general managers, owners, coaches, assistant coaches, and the media—spend almost four months comparison shopping and deciding if they want to purchase you.

After I decided on an agent (Lamont Smith, who's based in Denver), we put together a pre-draft plan. Because I was still nursing an ankle injury, and because Lamont thought I'd go in the top ten, we decided it wasn't in my best interests to work out at the NFL Combine, which was held in Indianapolis in February.

I still attended the Combine, which meant I underwent physicals, had Polaroids taken of my body, did interviews with teams and the media, completed personality tests, and took the Wonderlic exam. I'd never had so many X-rays taken, never answered so many stupid questions, and never felt more like an item at an auction house than I did at the NFL Combine.

I understood why the teams did it. They were getting ready to make huge financial investments in us, and they wanted to know what they might get for their money. But some of the stuff, especially the personality test and the Wonderlic, was just stupid. Did they want a football player or a scientist?

I met with the San Francisco 49ers, who were looking for a replacement for Tom Rathman at fullback. I met with a handful of teams, including Los Angeles Rams Coach Chuck Knox.

Some things you never forget, and I'll never forget what Knox asked me at the Combine. He said, "Do you want to run the football?"

"I'd love to run the football," I said.

"Good," he said. "Because we're not looking at you as a fullback. We're looking at you as a tailback."

I smiled so hard, I almost pulled a muscle. I was thinking to myself, "Hey, tailbacks make a whole lot more money than fullbacks. Yeah, I think I can play tailback."

I didn't work out at the Combine, but I did work out for NFL coaches and scouts in early March at Notre Dame. Tampa Bay's Sam Wyche was there. So was Chicago's Dave Wannstedt, Cincinnati's Dave Shula and Cleveland's Marty Schottenheimer. And Rams running backs coach Chick Harris was also at the Loftus Center for our Pro Day.

It seemed like a lot of the coaches were there to see me and Brooks, especially since Mirer and linebacker Demetrius DuBose had decided to work out later in the month. That was fine with me.

Not long before the April 24 draft, the Phoenix Cardinals flew me out to Arizona to meet head coach Joe Bugel. The Cardinals had the No. 4 pick and desperately needed a running back. We had a good meeting and I thought that was where I'd end up.

Georgia's Garrison Hearst was supposed to be the first running back taken, even though doctors had discovered that he had been playing with a tear in his ACL. The thing is, he had played great on that knee, so maybe it wasn't such a big deal.

The draft was held in New York at the Marriott Marquis in Times Square. I was suited and booted for draft day. I spent about $700 on a Marzotto suit and some serious money on a pair of brown Ballys. I knew I was looking *clean*.

Lamont, my family, and I sat in the waiting room with the other players and their families and agents. I was a little nervous, but not too bad.

New England had the first pick and took Washington State's Drew Bledsoe, my old high school all-star game opponent from Reno about four years earlier. Then my ND teammate, Mirer, went No. 2 to Seattle.

Phoenix traded up to No. 3 with the New York Jets and took Hearst. I guess Bugel didn't like me as much as I thought. As it turned out, Hearst blew out his knee during his rookie season and Bugel lost his job.

The minute the Cardinals took Hearst I was almost certain the Rams would take me. Almost. There were rumors that the Indianapolis Colts, who already had some Notre Dame running backs, were trying to trade up from No. 16 to get me. And my father kept teasing me, telling me that the Colts were about to make a deal. I did not want to go to Indianapolis.

The Rams wanted a running back almost as bad as the Cardinals. In fact, the word circulating around the ballroom that day was that the Rams had tried to move up so *they* could take Hearst. But Phoenix beat them to the trade.

The Jets took Florida State linebacker Marvin Jones with the fourth pick, followed by Alabama defensive end John Copeland to Cincinnati, Alabama defensive end Eric Curry to Tampa Bay, USC wide receiver Curtis Conway to Chicago, Louisiana Tech offensive tackle Willie Roaf to New Orleans, Washington offensive tackle Lincoln Kennedy to Atlanta and, with the 10th pick in the 1993 NFL Draft, the Rams selected Jerome Abram Bettis.

When the phone rang in the Green Room, I said, "Coach, is that you?" And, thank goodness, it was Coach Knox and not Colts Coach Ted Marchibroda. A few moments later, Rams owner Georgia Frontiere called me and said, "Welcome to the team. Glad to have you." Then I heard my name called and it was time to go out and let Commissioner Paul Tagliabue and America get a look at my Marzotto and Ballys.

I was going to a big-market, warm-weather team that had finished 6–10 in 1992 and was going to be coached by a guy who loved to run the ball (the offense was nicknamed Ground Chuck). They already had a 1,000-yard rusher on the roster—Cleveland Gary—but he had a tendency to fumble and he hadn't signed a new contract yet.

At the press conference at Rams headquarters I said it was an honor and privilege to have a chance to play for Knox. Knox had coached Matt Snell, Emerson Boozer, Mel Farr, Steve Owens, Lawrence McCutcheon, Joe Cribbs, Curt Warner, and John L. Williams—and helped turn all of them into NFL stars.

"He will definitely get the football," said Knox, who had called Reggie McKenzie weeks earlier to get a scouting report on me. "And we only have one football."

After the draft and mini-camp sessions, it was time to get down to business. The contract negotiations dragged on and soon I was a hold-out. I relocated to Denver and worked out as Lamont and the Rams tried to agree on a contract.

Meanwhile, my trainer had me doing some wild stuff. We did a hike up a mountain. It took two hours to get up there, but only forty-five minutes to get down. There almost wasn't a contract to negotiate because I nearly busted my ass four of five times coming down that mountain.

Lamont was smart; he didn't give me all the details of the negotiations. Instead, he would say, "We're closer today." He kept it vague. He wanted me out of the loop.

Lamont knew that if he told me the Rams had just offered a $4.5-million deal, I would have reached for the first pen I could find. Four-and-a-half-million dollars? Are you kidding me? I would have said, "Why am I not in camp? They're going to give me all of that money just to play football?" Hell, I had been playing for free all these years. That $4.5 million would have sounded good to me.

I went to Lamont's office every day and he'd give me an update. As a deal got closer he told me I needed to pack a suitcase, just in case. It was like he was giving me a two-minute travel warning.

Finally, Lamont called and said the deal was done: five years, $4.625 million, including a $2-million signing bonus and incentives that could push the package over the $5-million mark. It didn't seem possible. I couldn't fathom the word, *million*. It was like a foreign language—one I was more than happy to learn.

So after missing the three-week conditioning camp, then a pre-advance camp, then the first five days of actual training camp, I finally reported to the Rams' facilities at Cal State Fullerton on July 23. Of course, it's not like the Rams gave me the red-carpet treatment. I had to get my own ride from the Orange County airport when I got there. But that was OK. I couldn't wait to get on the field. I was in total football mode. It was like, "The deal's done? OK, let's go to camp."

I got my old jersey number back, 36. And it's funny the things you remember, but the equipment guy gave me a pair of cleats and they were hard. It was like, "Man, I hope I don't have to wear these things all the time."

Everything just felt a little different, a little out of sorts. I was kind of nervous going out for that first practice. It's like I was the new kid at school.

Once things settled down a little bit, I spent some of that bonus money. The first thing I did was buy my mom and dad a house. It was the greatest feeling in the world to be able to give back to the ones who had given so much of themselves for me. That was like a dream come true for me.

My dad was the worst negotiator in the world. Sheesh. When my parents found the house they liked (it's just off the No. 2 fairway of the Detroit Golf Club), my father wanted to offer *more* than the asking price. Barry Sanders's wife was our realtor and she kept telling my dad to settle down.

After I bought the house, my parents sent me a video of them in their new place. It felt so good to be able to put a smile on their faces. And then I put a smile on my own face and bought the car I'd been wanting to buy since I was in high school: a silver Mercedes SL 500. I think it cost me about $90,000.

From the doo-doo brown 1979 Mustang, to the brand new 1993 Mercedes. It was all so weird. But good weird.

I rented a condo in Fullerton, which was close to our practice facilities in Anaheim. Fullerton wasn't exactly Newport Beach, but it was close to work. And I was there to work.

Every player remembers his Welcome-to-the-NFL hit. Mine came in practice at training camp. We were running a goal-line play when veteran linebacker Chris Martin cracked my ass. It was the Jim Flanigan hit times two. He almost knocked me to Catalina Island.

Knox had me playing tailback and fullback, which was tough, especially for a rookie, because the plays were new, and the responsibilities were different for each position. For the most part, I was playing fullback. But then a couple of our other tailbacks suffered injuries, and with Cleveland Gary still a no-show, Knox had to move me to tailback.

From what I had read, the Rams wanted to trade Gary to the Dallas Cowboys. He had rushed for more than a 1,000 yards in 1992, but Knox wasn't crazy about him. The Rams only offered him a $35,000 raise during the offseason, so it was pretty obvious they were looking to move him.

But in early August I hurt my right ankle during practice, spent almost four hours undergoing tests, and was told I'd have to miss about two weeks of playing time. I was on crutches and my ankle was put in a removable splint. My injury killed a deal the Cowboys had with the Rams: Gary for a second-year wide receiver from Jackson State named Jimmy Smith.

Smith didn't play in 1993 because of complications from an appendectomy and was cut by the Cowboys before the 1994 season. The Jacksonville Jaguars signed him and all he did was become the all-time leading receiver in franchise history. When he retired after the 2005 season, Smith was the seventh-leading receiver in NFL history, and eleventh in receiving yards.

And if I hadn't hurt my right ankle he would have been an LA Ram.

Instead, the Rams re-signed Gary after his holdout. He wasn't happy about me or my contract, especially after he had led the team in rushing and receiving the previous year.

I understood his situation, but he had no reason to be mad at me. I wasn't the one who drafted me. I wasn't the enemy.

When he did show up, it was obvious I wasn't on his Christmas list. I didn't have a problem with him, but even though he tried not to show it, I could tell he had a problem with me. I was a threat to him, and because of that he never went out of his way to help me with anything. Here he was, sort of the elder statesman of the Rams running backs, and he didn't want to help a guy who was learning a new position. It made the learning curve steeper for me, but it also taught me a valuable lesson: For the rest of my career, I was always—*always*—the first guy who wanted to meet a new player when they came to the team. And whenever my team drafted a running back, I'd go out of my way to offer any help I could. I never wanted a player to feel the same way Gary made me feel, like he was against me. That's not what a teammate does.

My ankle injury kept me out of most of the exhibition games, but I was ready for the season opener against the Green Bay Packers at Milwaukee. Gary started and I didn't play until midway through the third quarter. Knox seemed to like how I played (five carries, 24 yards), but we lost, 36–6.

I'm sure Gary wasn't thrilled about sharing tailback time with me, but those are the breaks. I was just doing my job.

The next week in our home opener against Pittsburgh, I scored my first NFL touchdown and played the entire second half. Gary got hurt, so I made my first pro start the following week in the Meadowlands against the New York Giants.

When I was growing up, Lawrence Taylor was one of my favorite players. I was a linebacker; he was a linebacker. So this was a sentimental game for me, what with being on the same field as LT. In fact, I still have a photo from that Giants game, where he's hanging on to my leg and can't bring me down.

Gary started against the Houston Oilers in Week 4, but I played. I almost wish I hadn't. There was a goal-line play where we were going to block the point of attack, but not block one of the linebackers. That linebacker, Al Smith, happened to be the guy assigned to me.

Even as our quarterback, Jim Everett, was calling the play, I was thinking, "This doesn't sound like a very smart blocking scheme." I mean, since when do you design a play to leave a linebacker unblocked?

Lo and behold I got the ball, and just as soon as I hit the end zone—*pow!*—Smith cracked me. He hit me on my helmet so hard that it went into my neck and made a huge gash. I've still got the scar. Without a doubt, it was the hardest hit I took in my entire NFL career.

I still scored, but I left the field not knowing the difference between Houston and Dallas. Whoa, was I woozy.

The next week I rushed for 102 yards against New Orleans and Knox named me the starter for good.

I might have been a rookie, but I was a talker in my early days. You couldn't shut me up. I'd tell the other team's defense, "I hope you're ready for a long day, baby." Or, "I'll be back." Or, "Next time I come your way, you gonna be ready to quit?"

The vets, even the guys on my own team, didn't know what to make of me. Jackie Slater, our All-Pro offensive tackle, told reporters that opposing players would come up to him during a game and say, "That big son of a gun is crazy."

So I started at Atlanta against the Falcons, separated my shoulder the next week at home against Detroit, and then three weeks later had to deal with a baseball-sized lump on my hip. It was just a big, ugly knot back there. But I wasn't going to miss a game because of that thing. And I kept quiet about the separated shoulder because I didn't want other teams to target it.

Thanks to an offensive line that included Slater, Irv Eatman, and Leo Goeas, and my fullback Tim Lester, I rushed for 133 yards against San Francisco, 115 against Phoenix, and 212 against New Orleans, which was the most by a rookie since Bo Jackson had a 221-yard game in 1987.

With three games left in the regular season, I had 1,103 yards and a good chance of winning the NFL rushing title. Rookies don't do that sort of thing.

By then we were eliminated from playoff contention, but the team sort of rallied around this idea of me winning the rushing title. It became a goal for the offensive linemen and our fullbacks.

The problem was, the great Emmitt Smith of the Cowboys cranked it up late in the season. In Week 17 we played Cleveland, which was a big deal for me since my hero Pepper Johnson was on the Browns. He tagged me all day and each time he'd say, "Not this time, little brother . . . Not this time, little bro."

He was right. I only gained 56 yards on sixteen carries. The only consolation is that the Hall of Famer Jim Brown sought me out after the game, shook my hand, said he liked my running style, and told me to keep my head above water.

Going into our final games, Smith was 35 yards ahead of me in the rushing race. But Emmitt had a big game (168 yards) in overtime against the Giants, so it was going to take a miracle—204 yards—for me to pass him. So before our game against the Bears, I said, "That's OK, I'm going to make these guys pay anyway."

Knox and our offense did everything they could to help me. I rushed a team-record 39 times, but the Bears didn't want to be part of history, Chris Zorich, a teammate of mine at Notre Dame, played defensive tackle for the Bears. Everytime he tackled me, he said, "You're not going to make it against us."

The Bears held me to 146 yards, 57 yards behind Smith. But at least we won the game.

What a strange, strange season. I finished with 1,429 yards, which was the sixth highest total for a rookie running back in NFL history. Only Eric Dickerson, Earl Campbell, Barry Sanders, George Rogers, and Ottis Anderson—not bad company—had had better first seasons. I was voted the Associated Press Offensive Rookie of the Year, finishing far ahead of my two Notre Dame teammates, Mirer and Brooks. And I was selected to the Pro Bowl (and brought Tim Lester to Honolulu with me).

But we lost more games in my first eleven games as a Ram than I did during my entire three years at Notre Dame. It was the first time I had ever had success by playing on a losing team. I felt like I did everything I could do, but we still finished 5–11 and in last place in the NFC West Division.

Everett, who had the second-lowest quarterback rating in the conference, was traded to the Saints after the season. The worst thing you can call a player is soft, and Everett was as soft as puppy fur. I liked Jim, but it was obvious that a lot of the veterans never trusted him after his infamous "phantom sack," where he just collapsed to the turf even though nobody touched him, in the 1989 NFC Championship game against the 49ers. The Rams had to trade him. By then, Everett was nothing from a team standpoint. Nobody was going to follow him.

Even weirder was the relationship between Gary and me. I wouldn't say we ended up as friends, but he finally opened up and said what I figured all along: he was more mad at the Rams than at me. Still, he made things harder for me, and probably for himself, than they needed to be.

There were also some rumors of Knox getting fired, or just calling it quits. I didn't want him to go. I had just gotten there, so I wanted him to stay and get the program turned around and start winning games.

And just to make things a little more stressful, there were reports in the paper that Frontiere was thinking about moving the franchise to Baltimore or St. Louis, two old-time NFL cities that had lost their teams to Indianapolis and Phoenix, respectively.

Baltimore or St. Louis? I was a twenty-one-year-old NFL player living in Southern California. There was no beach in St. Louis, no Hollywood scene in Baltimore. I'm not saying I was Mr. Celebrity, but there was definitely a social scene. We'd go out to the clubs and I'd see Prince over there or Eddie Murphy over here. I'd see Magic, Arsenio Hall, rappers. I met them all. We weren't going to see any of those folks in Baltimore.

I was smart enough to understand that pro football, not partying, was my career. I had a good time, but the LA glitz and glamour was sort of a fantasyland. It was a great fantasyland, but you had to be careful about mixing business with too much pleasure.

But Frontiere wasn't too interested in our social lives. I'm not even sure she was too interested in football.

During our charter flight to New Orleans that season, Frontiere walked to the back of the plane to talk to some of the players. She saw Everett, said, "Hi, Jimmy," and gave him a big hug. Then she looked around and said, "Oh, all these new faces."

Hey, I was a new face, but a lot of the other guys sitting there were three-, four-year veterans. But she didn't have a clue who any of them were. And never did.

She was also horrible about being on time. My first year there we waited about two hours before she showed up for the team picture. We were standing there in full uniform, just waiting and waiting. And this was after practice, so it was on our time. There were some angry players that day. They were lucky. The next year she didn't show up at all.

After I played in the Pro Bowl and got back to my condo, my mom called.

"Whattya doing these days?" she said.

"I ain't doing nothing," I said.

"Well, then I want you to come on home."

Huh? Home, as in Detroit? I mean, I was living it up in LA. I was Rookie of the Year. I wasn't in college anymore, where you would come home for the summer.

Then my father got on the phone.

"We want you to come home," he said.

So I came home. I couldn't tell my folks no. I probably became the first Mercedes-driving, NFL Rookie of the Year to be ordered to live with his parents. I stayed in one of the bedrooms, took out the garbage, did chores. I wasn't the Rookie of the Year anymore; I was the third child. And you know what? It might have been the best thing that ever happened to me.

In LA, everybody would have been telling me, "You the man . . . You the man . . . You the man." And maybe I would have started to believe it. Maybe I would have started to become a different person. That Hollywood scene could take up-and-coming stars and chew them up. That doesn't happen when you're taking out the garbage at your folks' house in Detroit.

After we shipped Everett to New Orleans, we signed veteran quarterback Chris Miller. With Everett gone I figured we'd be a less one-dimensional team, which meant defenses couldn't load up against me and the run. I even came up with a 1994 personal slogan: 2,000 Yards or Bust.

Only two players, O. J. Simpson and Eric Dickerson, had ever rushed for more than 2,000 yards. But this time I was the starter from the beginning, I wasn't injured, my weight was down to 239 (lower than what I weighed in *high school*), and Knox was talking about giving me more carries. And I thought we'd be a better team. So 2,000 yards seemed possible.

Oh, my goodness, did I do some silly things going into that season. I filmed a Nike commercial where I looked into the camera and delivered the punchline, "You're showing this commercial in Dallas, right?"

You see, I wanted Emmitt to know I was coming after his rushing title. "If someone can get 2,100 yards, they are going to lead the league," I told the Rams beat reporters. "But if they don't get 2,000, they are going to be behind me, I'll tell you that."

I was determined to be a different kind of runner during my second season. As a rookie I had played the position like a fullback. That was my mentality from college. It was all I had ever known. So when I got to the pros I did the same thing: I plowed through people, always looking for someone to hit.

But it didn't take long to realize I couldn't run over everybody in the NFL—and I had the body to prove it. Like I said, during my rookie year I separated my shoulder, bruised my sternum, and had a knot the size of a baseball on the top of my butt. I was so banged up at times that I had to wear a red jersey during practices, just like the quarterbacks. A red jersey means you can't get hit. Nobody likes wearing a red jersey.

I was so physically beat up that I knew I had to tweak my running style. If I didn't, if I kept trying to play the same way, I'd be out of the league in no time. So during that off-season I made a conscious effort to learn how to be a tailback, instead of a fullback playing tailback.

I studied how the great tailbacks survived the game. I paid special attention to the techniques of the smaller backs, like Sanders and Emmitt, and even went back and looked at how Tony Dorsett used to play. Out of necessity, these guys had perfected a series of moves, spins, and shakes to avoid taking the big hits. They were so graceful and intuitive. They were born to be tailbacks.

I was born to inflict bodily harm. So I had to start from scratch and learn how to be an NFL tailback. Believe me, there aren't any instructional books available. But by studying those other guys, I began to understand how to change my body angles, how to make people miss, and how to take advantage of my size without tearing my body up. I'd never be able to duplicate the quickness of Sanders, but I could apply his running principles to my game. People always talked about my nimble feet? Well, that was the off-season I started doing drills for my footwork. The better the footwork, the easier it was to spin, turn, and contort your body to make tacklers miss.

It's all physics. I wanted to use their energy against them. Instead of two trains colliding, I wanted to position myself where they'd glance off me because of my body angle, or better yet, I wanted to use their hit to propel myself in a different direction.

Yeah, I was heavier than a lot of linebackers and every defensive back. But if someone keeps hitting you with a small hammer long enough, it starts to leave marks. I was getting hit flush too many times by the small hammers. So I had to adjust, or else.

Look at Hall of Famer Earl Campbell. I admired him as a player, but I was also very conscious of the fact that Campbell only played eight years in the league. And he only played eight years for a simple reason: He got beat up. So the last thing I wanted to do was get beat up so bad that I became a borderline cripple who wouldn't be able to play with his kids or enjoy the rest of his life. I was very conscious of that scenario.

Don't get me wrong; I wasn't going to become a soft runner. Like I've said, calling him soft is the worst insult you can give another player. You're attacking his character, his manhood. You never want a soft player on your team.

I just wanted to become a more durable player, a player less susceptible to injuries. I was still going to inflict punishment, but I wanted to do it on my terms.

As it turned out, even with my new and improved running style, I didn't become the third player to break the 2,000-yard barrier. I guess I went bust. So did the team.

We finished 4–12 and I rushed for 1,025 yards. Knox got fired and Frontiere decided to move the team to St. Louis because of a sweetheart financial deal with the city.

I hated to see Knox go because he was the reason for my success. But we weren't winning football games, so something had to change. That's when the Rams hired University of Oregon coach Rich Brooks. I didn't know a thing about the guy.

Meanwhile, I made my second consecutive trip to the Pro Bowl and decided that it was time for my Rams salary compensation to be adjusted. Part of my original contract said that if I rushed for 1,200 or more yards twice and was selected to at least one Pro Bowl, the length of the deal would drop from five years to four.

Well, I rushed for more than 1,200 as rookie, would have rushed for more than 1,200 yards in 1994 if we hadn't thrown the ball so much during the second half of the season, and I already had two Pro Bowl appearances. So I was clearly outperforming the contract. Don't get me wrong, I was making a lot of money ($943,700 in 1994), but I thought I had earned the right to discuss a raise.

My agent, Lamont Smith, approached Rams management, who said they would discuss the subject once the team completed its move to St. Louis. That was fine. Check that—it was fine until I got to St. Louis for mini-camp and saw a billboard with a big picture of me on it. They were selling me to St. Louis, but they were dragging their feet about a contract extension and raise. That wasn't so fine with me.

The Rams said they needed more upside to make a deal, meaning they wanted me to agree to a longer extension. So we sent a letter to them with a proposal and never heard back from them. Lamont tried calling. No response.

During mini-camp, Brooks said he was going to install a new offense and defense. Of course, there wasn't enough time during the mini-camp to do this, so he asked the veteran players, myself included, if we'd report to the July training camp earlier than usual. That way, he said, we'd have more time to digest the new system. Of course, everyone said yes.

Now fast forward to just before camp started. Lamont still hadn't heard anything of substance from the Rams front office. So I told Lamont I wasn't reporting to camp unless they called. I knew a new contract was probably dead, but no way was I going to training camp without at least the courtesy of an explanation. I had called the Rams management myself to try to clarify the situation, and couldn't even get a call back. So it wasn't a monetary issue anymore; it was a principle issue—just like when Schembechler and Michigan never called.

When I didn't show up on July 21, the deadline for veterans to report to camp, the Rams called Lamont and wanted to know where I was. I was in Denver, and I was going to stay there until the Friday before the first preseason game against Seattle. That was the last day I could go in and still get credited for a season toward unrestricted free agency.

The Rams fined me $4,000 a day, and Brooks and Rams senior vice-president Jay Zygmunt made it clear to the media there wasn't going to be a new contract. Brooks said it was "a standard rule" not to renegotiate with someone who has three years left on their deal. "If we did that, we'd have people lining up at our door," he said.

Never mind that I was only 175 yards short of turning that five-year deal into a four-year deal. Instead of being reasonable, the Rams and Brooks played hardball. Zygmunt was quoted in the paper as saying he had talked to Lamont, but had "no reason" to call him. "Bettis is supposed to be here," Zygmunt said.

When I finally reported to Maryville University for camp on August 5, there were all sorts of TV cameras waiting for me. I got my playbook, my dorm room key, and a meeting with Brooks. The Rams never did budge on my contract. Instead, they said they'd talk about the possibility of a new deal after the 1995 season.

When I met with Brooks one of the first things he said to me was, "You lied to me. You said you were going to come to camp early."

Lied? Brooks knew why I was holding out. It was in all the papers. I didn't hold out because I didn't want to learn a new offense.

But Brooks held that against me. In the season opener at Green Bay, he pulled me after just seven carries. That was the same Packers team that would end up in the NFC Championship. They had one of the best defenses in the league. It wasn't like I was out there screwing around. The Packers were good. But I gained 4 yards on seven carries, so I was out.

I was livid. It was Brooks's way of punishing me.

Later in the season, in a loss against the Falcons, he pulled me from the lineup late in the third quarter after only nine carries (but 61 yards). We were down, 24–6, so he put in our "Posse" unit (which was usually used on third-down situations) for the rest of the game. We lost, 31–6.

For Brooks, it had become personal and apparently unrectifiable.

I tried to patch things up. I talked to him on more than one occasion and said, "Coach, what can I do to help this team? What can I do to stay on the football field?"

And he said, "Oh, you're doing fine. You're doing a great job."

It didn't make sense. I'm on the bench, but I'm doing a great job? He was selling me a dream. I knew it. He knew it.

I tried to separate the football side of my life from the business side.

But I finally reached the breaking point in our December 3 game against the New York Jets.

I was on the field, playing *in the game*, when I found myself thinking about my situation with the Rams and all the feelings I had about the way I had been treated. And as I was putting it all in perspective, we snapped the ball, and a Jets defender—a guy I should have blocked—breezed through and sacked our quarterback. He sacked him because I didn't know where the hell he came from. And I didn't know because my mind wasn't in the game.

So I did something I had never done in my entire playing career: I pulled myself out of the game. I told our running backs coach Johnny Roland, "I'm done, man." And that was that. I was doing my team a disservice by being on the field.

But it wasn't until we played the Buffalo Bills at home the following week that I truly realized how much my holdout and my struggles on the field had affected my image. Thanks partly to the way Brooks and Rams management had framed my holdout to the public, I was perceived as another greedy, selfish ballplayer. And no question, it didn't help that we weren't winning a lot of games and that my rushing numbers were way down.

During the Bills game, one of our running backs lost his shoe during a play. So I jumped in there to take his place and that's when I heard them: boos. Loud, passionate, and hurtful boos directed at *me*.

I carried the ball one play, gained 3 yards, and then jogged back to the sideline. More boos. I got booed coming in and booed going out.

I was distraught. I couldn't believe it. I was sick. At a home game I got booed! I was used to being booed on the road, but this was a first.

Those boos affected me. When the franchise had first moved from LA to St. Louis, I was sort of the centerpiece of the transition. I was on billboards. The local paper had me on the cover of the preseason football section. I was the first player to get his own local radio show. And my jersey was the best-selling football jersey in town.

But that was before Brooks turned on me, followed later, with Brooks's help, by the St. Louis fans. Say what you want about me, but I always played hard (and often hurt) for that franchise. I had wanted to renegotiate my contract; the Rams didn't. I became the bad guy; the Rams didn't.

There was no question that Brooks made me the scapegoat. We had started the season 4–0, but we simply weren't a good running team.

Brooks wasn't committed to running the ball. He liked zone blocking instead of man-on-man blocking: Zone blocking is passive; man-on-man blocking is how you pound out the yards.

Our offensive line did the best it could, but it suffered from some injuries. And I'll take my share of the blame, but only a share. The bottom line was this: Unlike Knox, Brooks didn't emphasize the run. We didn't have the mentality you needed to run the ball. You just can't click it on and off. You have to be committed to it, and we weren't.

We finished 7–9 and I rushed for only 637 yards on a career-low 183 rushes. During my first seventeen games as a Ram I had eleven 100-yard performances. During my last twenty-six games, zero. It got so ridiculous that I only got twenty-nine carries in the last five games of the season.

After the season, Lamont set up a meeting with the Rams. We met for dinner at a restaurant in San Francisco. It was me, Lamont, Brooks, Zygmunt, and Rams president John Shaw. After some small talk, Lamont got right to the point.

"Look, we all know the situation here," he said. "Nobody's happy and we want permission to seek a trade."

That's when Brooks said, "Oh, no, no, no. Jerome is my kind of back. He's my guy. He's the guy I want to have here."

I was sitting directly across from Brooks and I couldn't believe what I was hearing. *Jerome is my guy? I don't want to trade him?*

Lamont and I looked at each other and we were both thinking the same thing: "Are you kidding me?" The coach who wouldn't play me was now treating me like the No. 1 pick in the draft.

"Do you mean to tell me that you don't want to trade him?" Lamont said.

"No, I don't," said Brooks.

But then Zygmunt spoke up.

"Well, hold on," he said. "The possibility does exist. It's something we have to look at."

I didn't say anything to Brooks, but my look spoke a million words. To Zygmunt's credit, he kept it straight when he acknowledged that the Rams had to consider trading me.

When our meeting at the restaurant ended I didn't say a word to Brooks. We didn't shake hands, either. I was boiling.

At this point the football marriage between Brooks and me was through. Divorce was imminent. I was filing my papers. Irreconcilable differences.

Not long before the 1996 NFL Draft I got a call from Johnny Roland. Roland always kept it straight with me. He always told me what was going on and didn't play the political game.

"We're probably going to draft Lawrence Phillips, the kid from Nebraska," he said. "Would you be interested in playing fullback?"

"Coach," I said, "I'll be honest with you. I'll play fullback, but not in St. Louis."

There was a pause. Roland knew the truth.

"I understand, man," he said. "I appreciate it."

Phillips was an incredible running back. Based on talent alone, he might have been the best running back coming out of college that year. But he had had a number of well-publicized criminal problems.

And despite that, the Rams wanted him instead of me. Wow. That was tough to understand, even tougher to accept. They were basically saying I was a cancer in the locker room, that I was a bad apple. But look at the apple they plucked off the draft tree.

If Brooks had said, "Look, as a coaching staff we've decided you don't fit our system," I could have dealt with that. You don't want me as a player, that's fine. I might not like to hear it, but I can deal with it. But when you start telling people I'm a cancer in the locker room, then we've got a serious problem. Not one guy in our locker room—even the guys who were competing against me for the starting tailback job— would have substantiated what Rams management was saying. It was fiction, that's the sad part.

There was no question my tailback career in St. Louis was done. I mean, they wanted me to play fullback. I had rushed for 3,091 yards during my first three seasons and been to two Pro Bowls, and now they wanted me to block for Lawrence Phillips. Are you kidding me?

Bernie Miklasz of the *St. Louis Post-Dispatch* had written a column late in the season and said, "It would be foolish to give up on Jerome Bettis. He can't be out of gas. Not this soon."

Miklasz had no idea how right he would turn out to be. But even before Roland called, I knew I didn't want to play for the Rams again. No way was I going back to that franchise—period. The Rams probably didn't think I was serious, but I was absolutely prepared to retire before I played one more down for Brooks.

With the Rams no longer an option, there was only one place for me to go: to my second home, Notre Dame. I met with Sam Gaglio, who was the assistant dean at the Mendoza College of Business (I guess I didn't want to be an engineer after all) and told him I was serious about preparing for life without football. I was so mistrustful of Brooks that I was willing to walk away from the Rams after just three seasons.

First, I had to submit another admissions application and then, in a letter to the faculty, I had to detail my reasons for wanting to return to Notre Dame. They don't just let you in because you've got a nice smile—or a pro football career.

I had always been interested in the business world. Remember that 1991 Notre Dame player questionaire I had filled out? One of the questions asked what I'd like to do after football. I had written, "I would like to run my own company." Well, it turned out the company was going to be me.

Once I was readmitted for the 1996 spring semester, I signed up for eighteen hours' worth of classes and started hitting the books. One day I stopped by Coach Holtz's office and we started talking about my situation. It didn't take long for him to get to the point.

"Who was that guy on the field wearing your jersey last year?" Coach Holtz said. "Because I know it wasn't you."

He was right; it wasn't me. Coach Holtz didn't know all the circumstances, but he had seen some of our games, had read my body language and instantly recognized that something had changed. Thanks to Brooks, I had become a very disgruntled guy. I was harboring a lot of ill will. Anybody who knows me—and Coach Holtz had coached me for three years—knows that isn't my personality.

I didn't want to quit playing football. I just didn't want to play for the Rams. I was still working out at Notre Dame, just in case they decided to trade me. But if they didn't, the next thing I carried was going to be a diploma.

Before I left Coach Holtz's office that day, he gave me one piece of advice.

"Come back and be the player you've always been," he said.

Nothing would have made me happier. All I needed was a new place to be that player.

6

The 2006 season marked the forty-fifth year Dick Hoak drew a paycheck from the Steelers—ten years (including one Pro Bowl appearance) as a running back, and the last thirty-five as the team's running backs coach. No other Steelers coach, including Bill Cowher, comes close to that sort of seniority.

During the Cowher-Hoak tenure, no other NFL team rushed for more yards than the Steelers, who surpassed the 30,000-yard barrier during Bettis's last season. Of those 30,000-plus yards, Bettis contributed nearly a third, 10,571.

Sitting in his office at the team's headquarters at the University of Pittsburgh Medical Center (UPMC) Sports Performance Complex, Hoak recalls how the Steelers acquired The Bus.

"It was getting near the draft and we knew things weren't right in St. Louis with Jerome and the Rams. We needed a running back and he was on the market there. So Coach Cowher and Tom Donohoe came to me and Chan Gailey, who was the offensive coordinator at the time, and said, 'Take a look at this guy and tell us what you think of him.'

"We watched a couple tapes, came out of the room, and they said, 'What do you think?' We said, 'Get him.'

"Back then we had our mini-camp at Duquesne. At the time, Jerome was probably 250–255 pounds, or something like that. The first couple of times we gave him the football . . . this kid's feet were amazing for a guy that size. We just sat back there and looked at each other when he *went through a hole and just stepped over things. Guys that big aren't supposed to do that. But he could do it.*

"I don't know why or for what reason St. Louis let him go. They didn't have anybody great at the time. They were struggling a little bit and this guy's a Pro Bowler. I don't know why he wasn't playing. I have no idea.

"We gave up something like a second and a fourth for him. It was a steal."

Lamont called me in April with the best kind of news: the Steelers were doing a background check on me.

I didn't know it at the time, but Steelers coach Bill Cowher had already spoken to Coach Holtz about me. Coach Cowher had been recruited by Coach Holtz at North Carolina State and played for him in 1975. The Steelers also talked to Coach Moore at Notre Dame, Steelers fullback (and my former Rams teammate) Tim Lester, and to Chick Harris, who was my running backs coach during my first two years with the Rams.

At the time, I was in college student mode. I was waist-deep working on my business management degree and trying not to think too much about my football future. The only thing I knew for sure was that I'd never wear a Rams uniform again. And the Rams—even though Brooks had said the exact opposite at our meeting in San Francisco just a couple of months earlier—had decided it was time to trade me.

As the NFL Draft approached, Lamont said there were two teams seriously interested in making a deal: the Steelers and the then Houston Oilers. The compensation packages (draft picks to the Rams, etc.) were basically the same.

"If you could choose, which team would you rather play for?" Lamont said.

The Oilers had the ninth pick in the draft. If they didn't get me, they wanted Ohio State's Eddie George, who had won the Heisman Trophy the previous season. He was a taller, slightly different version of me, but still physical enough to wear down a defense.

The Steelers had the twenty-ninth pick in the draft and were looking to retool their backfield. Bam Morris had been their guy, but that was before he got arrested on two counts of felony drug possession in Texas. His trial was supposed to begin the same day the Steelers opened training camp. Also, the Steelers had decided not to retain fullback John L. Williams.

Oilers coach Jeff Fisher seemed like he'd be a good guy to play for, but I thought the Steelers' system was more suited to big running backs. Through the years guys like Franco Harris, Barry Foster, Tim Worley, and even Morris had done well in that system. The Steelers, who led the NFL in rushing in 1994 and were sixth in 1995, were committed to the running game.

Based on their history and success with big backs, I told Lamont that Pittsburgh would be my first choice.

On draft day the Oilers traded down to the seventeenth pick, and then traded back up to the fourteenth spot and selected George. That was the same day I got a phone call from the Steelers.

"Jerome, this is Coach Cowher," he said in that distinctive Pittsburgh accent of his. "The last time I saw you was during your rookie year, and you guys beat up on us. Ever since then I thought, if you can't beat 'em, then join 'em. Welcome to the Pittsburgh Steelers."

"Thanks, Coach," I said. "Glad to be there."

Actually, I was ecstatic to be there. My business degree from Notre Dame would have to wait, but I was leaving a Rams franchise that had finished last or tied for last in the NFC Western Division in each of my three seasons. In those three years, the Rams had won a total of sixteen games and fired a coach.

Now I was going to a team fresh off an 11–5 record and a Super Bowl appearance. They had an experienced offensive line and the best blocking fullback in the business. It was a team that wanted me, and wanted to run the ball. After my Rams experience, that was important.

It also meant a lot to me when Tom Donohoe, the Steelers director of football operations, dispelled all the Rams propaganda about me being a bad guy in the locker room. When a reporter asked Donohoe if there were any character issues about me, he said, "Absolutely none. When you get a chance to talk to him, you won't talk to a finer young man or a better character guy than Jerome Bettis."

I don't mention that out of ego. But when your reputation gets beat up, like mine did with the Rams, it's nice to hear someone defend you.

The Steelers got me dirt cheap. They only gave up a second-round pick in 1996 (turned out to be University of Washington tight end Ernie Conwell) and a fourth-round pick in 1997 (which the Rams later used in a package to get offensive tackle Orlando Pace). In return, they got a twenty-four-year-old Jerome Bettis and a 1996 third-round pick, which was only thirteen picks lower than the second-round selection they gave up. They used that third-round choice on Arkansas linebacker Steve Conley, who they would have taken in the second round had they kept the pick. So all it really cost the Steelers was a fourth-rounder in 1997. They now call it the Trade of the Decade.

My contract, which carried over from the Rams, was reasonable too: $620,000 in 1996, $710,000 in 1997, and the Rams took the salary cap hit on my signing bonus. But if I rushed for 1,200 or more yards in 1996, I had the option of voiding my deal in 1997 and becoming a free agent.

Of course, Donohoe, being the smart guy he was, wanted to restructure the deal. I would have done the same thing if I were him. But he only offered about a $200,000 raise, which wasn't going to work. That option clause in 1997 was worth more to me than $200,000, especially if I had a big year in 1996.

Donohoe said, "You know, you're not starting in this offense, so you probably won't get the 1,200 yards."

In a way, I thought he was insinuating that the Steelers could make sure I didn't get the 1,200 yards if I was close. But by then I had decided to take my chances. I had decided to bet on me.

As promised, the Rams took Phillips with the No. 6 overall selection. They had the tailback they wanted and I had the new team I needed. And just when I thought it couldn't get any better, it did. I looked at the Steelers 1996 regular season schedule and there it was: Pittsburgh v. St. Louis Rams, November 3, at Three Rivers Stadium. Believe me, I found a pen and circled that date. As an added bonus, we were playing them in Pittsburgh during the preseason too.

Erric Pegram was the starting tailback. I played against him when he was with the Atlanta Falcons, so I knew he was good. You don't put up a 1,000-yard season, which is what he did in 1993, without having some talent. But he was a smaller guy, and I felt it was only a matter of time before Cowher would want a jackhammer instead of a jack rabbit.

I already knew a few of the Steelers—linebacker Greg Lloyd and cornerback Rod Woodson—from my Pro Bowl trips. And Coach Hoak made the transition even easier by not trying to change my running style. He was great to work with because he kept it simple. He was a stickler for providing us with the exact information we needed to succeed (blocking assignments, what defenses we'd see, defensive tendencies, etc.), and then letting us do our jobs.

These were blue collar, low maintenance–type of guys for the most part. But the locker room environment was a little different than what I experienced with the Rams. There was sort of a class hierarchy with the Steelers, as opposed to my time with the Rams, where everybody hung out with everybody else. Didn't matter if you were a vet, on offense or defense, a starter or a backup.

In Pittsburgh, it was very cliquish, though not in a bad, disruptive way. You had sort of your A group: Lloyd, Woodson, safety Darren Perry, safety Carnell Lake. Then you had your B group, the tweeners, the guys who were on the cusp of becoming starters. Then you had your C group, the younger players.

I didn't gravitate toward a specific group because that's not my personality. I like everybody. Plus, I don't believe a team functions as well if you have different groups.

The Steelers, though, were the exception to that rule. We had so many players with great athletic ability that cliques never became an issue.

Lloyd was clearly the team leader. He had a black belt in tae kwon do, so you knew not to mess with him because he was borderline on the edge. He would bring a gun into the locker room (this was before firearms were prohibited), and nobody—OK, maybe Jack Lambert when he played—looked more intimidating or fierce in a Steelers uniform than Lloyd. Greg was a good guy, but if he didn't know you, he didn't talk to you. And because of that, people sometimes thought he was mean-spirited. I know he didn't get along with the media. He used to wear a T-shirt that read, "I Wasn't Hired for My Disposition." He wasn't kidding, either.

Our defense wasn't going to be a problem, not with guys such as Lloyd, Lake, Woodson, and linebackers Chad Brown and Levon Kirkland in the lineup. Most of the questions had to do with our offense, specifically, our quarterback situation.

Jim Miller was our starter, with Kordell Stewart and Mike Tomczak as the backups. Miller was a veteran, but had taken his share of tough hits. Kordell was young and inexperienced. Tomczak was another veteran you could throw in there.

We had a veteran team and there wasn't any question in my mind that we'd make the playoffs. But once we got there, could we keep it going?

I'll admit it: It felt weird putting on that Steelers uniform the first time. I grew up as a Cowboys fan. I hated the Steelers as a kid. My brother, John, on the other hand, was a die-hard Steelers fan. Even though we grew up in Detroit, we never cared about the Lions. The Lions sucked. Always have.

John rarely asked me for anything when it came to football. But this time he couldn't help himself. He said he wanted the first photograph taken of me in a Steelers uniform. So I arranged for the team photographer to take the picture at the first mini-camp. My brother loves that photo. It was the ultimate revenge for him: His little brother, who couldn't stand the Steelers as a kid, wearing a Steelers uniform.

We played the Rams in early August, but it was just a meaningless preseason game, a glorified scrimmage. I rushed for 49 yards on seven carries and then took a seat. The August game meant nothing. The one in November would mean everything.

In my first official regular season game for the Steelers we lost. Jacksonville beat us, 24–9, Lloyd tore a patellar tendon and was gone for the season, and Miller got pulled after completing nine passes for just 83 yards. Miller was our starter during all of training camp, but that didn't mean a thing. When Coach Cowher gave him the hook late in the third quarter, I was thinking, "It's cutthroat around here." Miller, who was making his first NFL start, got yanked and was basically done for the year.

Kordell came in, but his sister had passed away not long before the game, so he didn't play well. In fact, he didn't complete a pass. Then they brought in Tomczak and stayed with him for the rest of the game and the season. But even then we weren't completely settled. Coach Cowher liked to use Kordell in certain red zone and goal-line situations.

Tomczak was close to the end of his career and, at best, was a serviceable starting quarterback. He could make some plays for you. He probably wasn't going to win a game for you, but he could lose one. That's how you separate the good-to-great quarterbacks from the average ones: Can he win a game for you? Can his presence create problems for a defense?

Deep down—just based on his age and physical abilities—I had my doubts about Tomczak.

I split time with Pegram in the opener, but it wasn't long before my carries and my yardage totals increased. We won five in a row and it felt like old times again: 116 yards against Baltimore, 133 against Buffalo (my first-ever Monday Night Football appearance), 115 against Houston (my first Steelers start—Pegram had strained a knee ligament against the Bills), 103 against Kansas City, 109 against Cincinnati (I broke a rib and had to take a painkilling shot during the game).

When Pegram got hurt, I don't know who was more upset, Pegram or Donohoe. I had hit the Ravens for 100-plus yards and then went crazy against Buffalo. And I just kept going. Everytime I hit triple digits, the price of my new contract went up.

By the time our showdown against the Rams arrived, I was third in the league in rushing (698 yards) and there was talk that I could break Barry Foster's Steelers record of 1,690 yards. But I was thinking more about facing Mr. Brooks and the Rams, than I was the team rushing record.

Of course, I didn't make those feelings known. Whenever a reporter asked me about the Rams, I took the high road. I even thanked Rams management for trading me to the Steelers.

But everything—and I mean *everything*—about that game was personal to me. I did a good job of hiding my true feelings until Saturday night, when we were in the team hotel. Lester, who had been released by St. Louis before the 1995 season, was my roommate and he started talking about how we had to beat up the Rams. Before long, I was geeked up too.

We killed them, 42–6, which was the important thing. But I had 129 yards and two touchdowns on just nineteen carries, including a 50-yard scoring run that ranks as one of the favorites of my career. From an individual standpoint, that run brought me the most joy.

Brooks had said he wanted to draft Phillips because the Rams needed a game-breaker type of back. Well, he saw one, but he was in a Steelers uniform. Exactly what Brooks said I couldn't do, I did—and I did it against him.

And ask Rams linebacker Roman Phifer if I was washed up. I ran over him at the goal line.

I wanted to keep playing, but Coach Cowher pulled me out of the game late in the third quarter. I tried to talk him out of it (I was only 47 yards shy of a 1,000-yard season), but he said it was a long year. He was right, but I could have run forever in that game.

I never saw Brooks after the game, though I heard later that he wouldn't give me my due on the 50-yard run. "I could be a breakaway runner through that hole," he told reporters. "Let's be honest. He took it to the house and he did a great job. But you or I could have run through that hole."

Typical Brooks.

Much classier were the postgame hugs that I got from my old Rams and Notre Dame teammate Todd Lyght, as well as St. Louis safety Keith Lyle. Even Phifer came over and gave me a hard time for the hit on the goal line.

Later, I got a surprise visit from Rams co-owner Stan Kroenke. Kroenke came to our locker room after the game and congratulated me on the performance. That was a gesture I'll never forget.

I wasn't really paying attention to Phillips's stats during the game, but several reporters told me afterward that I had outrushed him, 129–6, and had outrushed the entire Rams team by 65 yards. Interesting numbers, but they wouldn't have meant a thing if we hadn't won the game.

Three games later against Miami, I broke the 1,200-yard barrier, which meant, *cha-ching*—I was a free agent. I had gambled on me and won. Better yet, we were 9–3.

But then both the Steelers and I limped into the playoffs. We lost three of our last four regular season games and I sprained my ankle in Game 14 against San Diego. I barely played in our final two regular season games.

But, if nothing else, we were in the playoffs. I hadn't played in a post-season game since my final year at Notre Dame, so I wasn't going to take anything for granted. Who knew if I'd ever get a chance like this again?

I rushed for 102 yards in our blowout win against the Colts in the AFC Wild Card game, but bad news: I tore a muscle in my groin.

I did what I could the next week against New England in the Divisional playoffs, but it was useless; it was a bad one. And my ankle wasn't anywhere close to 100 percent.

I tried to warm up before the game, but it was obvious I couldn't move very well. So right before kickoff I got three shots in my ankle and eight shots in my groin. You've got to do what you've got to do.

Look at your ankle. No fatty areas, right? So you can imagine what those needles felt like. And I'm not sure I would have wished those eight groin shots on Rich Brooks.

It wasn't a pretty sight. My leg was black and blue down to my knee from the internal bleeding caused by the groin tear. And I had to literally hold my testicles up so the doctor could insert that big ol' needle into me.

He kept saying, "You numb yet?"

And I kept saying, "No."

Another shot.

"Numb yet?"

"No."

Another shot. And five more after that. He couldn't find the spot. And even after eight tries he never got it fully numb. That's how deep of a tear it was.

I rushed for 43 yards on thirteen painful carries. That was the game where we played in the fog at Foxboro. Actually, we played like we were in a fog. Tomczack threw for only 110 yards and had two interceptions. Kordell came in and went 0 for 10.

Meanwhile, Patriots running back Curtis Martin killed us. He had 166 yards and New England won, 28–3. Bill Parcells and his Patriots were going to the AFC Championship (and then the Super Bowl), and we were going home, after an 11–7 season, because New England outplayed us, because we couldn't run the ball and the Patriots could.

I'm not blaming Tomczak for the loss, but that was one of those games when you needed your quarterback to win it for you. I was hurt. Our defense was on its heels. We needed a quarterback capable of making big plays.

Tomczak wasn't that kind of quarterback. That's not his fault. Usually we just needed him to manage the game for us. But when we needed him to *win* a game for us, he didn't have that type of talent. Like I said, serviceable.

I was disappointed about the loss, but after three years with the Rams it was nice just to reach double-digit victories and make the playoffs. And did I mention the Rams finished 6–10 and fired Brooks?

The Pro Football Writers of America named me the Comeback Player of the Year and named the Oilers' Eddie George the Rookie of the Year. I also was chosen to play in the Pro Bowl. So the Steelers and Oilers had to be happy with their draft-day deals.

But poor Phillips only had 632 yards for the season and was out of the NFL by late 1999. In 2006 he was convicted on seven counts of assault with a deadly weapon. It's tragic, no question.

Everybody learned some lessons from that 1996 season. Coach Cowher learned that a three-way quarterback competition doesn't work. And I learned not to stand down wind of Coach Cowher when he yelled at you. The man could go into some rages, and when he did, watch out. I never wore one of those plastic eye-guards on my face-mask, but there were times I wish I had when Coach Cowher got near me during one of his spittle-fits.

You could always tell when Coach Cowher was going to yell at somebody. He'd jut his chin and his fingers would flare out just so. And then he'd get into your face. His favorite catch-phrase? "Keep it in perspective," he'd say.

Meanwhile, the Steelers management learned that they should have offered me more than the $200,000 raise they originally suggested before the season. Instead, I rushed for 1,431 yards (and it might have been 1,600 if I hadn't basically missed the last two games), which gave me the option of becoming a free agent. And that's what I did after the Steelers made an initial offer that I thought was too low.

I didn't want to leave Pittsburgh. It's a blue-collar football town. How I played and how I ran was a blue-collar style of football. It was a perfect fit.

Plus, the Steelers were all about tradition, championships, and passionate fans. They were like the Notre Dame of the NFL. If you go to the Pittsburgh International Airport you'll see a life-size mannequin of Franco Harris making the Immaculate Reception. There's even stories about Steelers fans who are buried wearing their black-and-gold pajamas, holding a TV remote, and having their legs covered by a Steelers blanket.

Now that's a city that loves its team.

I consider myself a football history buff, so it didn't take me long to learn about the Steelers. The Steelers had those great uniforms, and those championships, and, of course, Myron Cope, who was part of the team's radio broadcast team for thirty-five years before retiring in June

2005. Cope is the guy who invented the Terrible Towel in 1975, when he asked Steelers fans to bring their gold dish towels to a playoff game against the Baltimore Colts. The Steelers won the game and the Terrible Towels became a Steelers institution. The proceeds from the sale of official Terrible Towels go to Pittsburgh's Allegheny Valley School, which assists the mentally and physically challenged.

Cope is the guy who would say things like, "Yoi!" or "okel-dokel" during the broadcasts. He's also the first guy to call me The Bus on the air. And if Myron said it, it usually stuck.

Of course, it was a total accident that Myron even heard about the nickname, but thank God, he did.

Here's what happened: In our preseason game against the Packers, we stayed in Appleton, Wisconsin. One of my former Notre Dame coaches, Jay Hayes, was on Barry Alvarez's staff at the University of Wisconsin and he made the drive from Madison to Appleton. He was there to visit his brother, Jonathan, who played tight end for the Steelers.

When Jay walked into the hotel lobby with his kids, I just happened to be there.

"Hey, Bussie!" Jay said. That's what he had always called me at Notre Dame—Bussie.

Well, Bill Hillgrove, who was a member of the Steelers broadcast team, was also in the hotel lobby. And he heard Jay call me Bussie. Bill told Myron, and Myron, in that squeaky voice of his, said, "You know, he kind of *looks* like a bus."

Myron called me The Bus during the Packers–Steelers broadcast, and the rest is nickname history.

Pittsburgh was my kind of place. It appreciated players who weren't afraid to get some blood on their jerseys, who didn't care how cold it got on game day, who gave the fans an honest effort, win or lose. I believe I am one of those kind of players.

I knew I was in a strong bargaining position—I was the league's third-leading rusher in 1996—and as a player with a limited shelf life you can't waste that kind of leverage. Deep down I was hoping I could stay in Pittsburgh.

The Steelers offered about $2 million a year. Don't get me wrong, that's a lot of money, but I also knew about the law of supply and demand. There wasn't a big supply of 1,400-yard running backs out there, but there was demand.

Washington Redskins general manager Charley Casserly called and offered a four-year $16-million deal right out of the gate. Uh, hel-loooooooo. That'll do it.

I called Coach Cowher and said, "Coach, I just want to call and thank you for the opportunity that you gave me. I appreciated it. I just want you to know that."

"What's going on?" he said. He was definitely taken by surprise.

"Well, there's this deal on the table for me—four years, $16 million—and I'm going to take it."

There was pause. He knew I wasn't playing him because it was me calling, not an agent. An agent wasn't going to give a damn where I went; my agent wanted me to take the Redskins offer.

"Jerome," he said, "give me twenty-four hours."

"Coach, I don't know if I can give you twenty-four hours, but I'll give you twelve."

"I'll call you back," he said.

The phone rang a little later. It was Coach Cowher.

"Jerome, can you work with us? I can't quite match the offer, but I can come close."

"Coach, if you can come close, you got yourself a running back."

"OK, we're going to get it done."

The Steelers had a history of not re-signing their free agents. But in my case, they were so serious about reaching an agreement that then team president Dan Rooney (he's now the team chairman) became involved in the negotiations. When they offered me a four-year $14.4 million contract and a $4 million signing bonus, I couldn't say no. It's like that line in the movie *Wall Street* where Charlie Sheen's character asks Michael Douglas's Gordon Gekko, "How many yachts can you water-ski behind?"

I could have made more money someplace else (Washington, San Diego, or Arizona), but the only yacht I wanted to be behind was the Steelers. They were the ones who had traded for me. They were the ones who had put the football in my hands.

By rejecting the Redskins deal, I left about $1.5 million on the table. But I knew that I had something sweet in Pittsburgh, and I wanted to take advantage of it. I loved the offense. I had a good offensive line and a great group of teammates. And I didn't know what was on the other side of the street.

The new contract, the biggest in Steelers history, made me the third-highest-paid running back behind Barry Sanders and Emmitt Smith. I also became the first starter to re-sign with the Steelers since free agency began in the league five years earlier. And maybe it was a coincidence, but my annual salary, $3.6 million, matched my jersey number.

"I graduated in the fall of 1995. Everybody had assumed I'd drop out of school and move out to LA when Jerome turned pro and was drafted by the Rams in '93. They thought I was going to leave and be part of his entourage. But I told him, 'Look, I've put three years into this deal and I want to graduate from Tuskegee.' I think he respected that.

"I got my marketing degree and my first job was at Morton International, the salt company, which is based in Chicago. I worked in the branding department—packaging and advertising.

"By January of 1997 I was making about $50,000, plus commissions. I had my company car, my 401K, and I had just gotten engaged to my college sweetheart. Then Jerome came home after the '96 season with the Steelers.

"He said, 'I think I want you to work for me. Pittsburgh is a tremendous opportunity, not only on the field, but off the field as well. I can't process all of those opportunities. This would be a great environment for you to learn. And during the off-season you can work on your MBA. And I promise you this: You'll be able to meet all the people I meet and shake the hands of the people whose hands I shake.'

"So in 1997 I went to work for Jerome Bettis Enterprises. And let me tell you, there was no off-season.

"But he kept his promise."

—Jahmal Dokes

Life was good. So was our football team.

Kordell, who had become one of my closer friends, won the starting quarterback job and everybody was excited to see what he could do. He was still a work in progress because he had never gotten a lot of practice work at QB. Everybody called him "Slash" because we had used him in so many different ways (receiver, runner, even a punter once) that his quarterbacking fundamentals suffered. That wasn't his decision; he had wanted to concentrate solely on being a quarterback. But the team had needed him in other capacities, so that's what he did.

But now the job was his. We had an unproven quarterback with a strong arm (remember his game-winning throw to beat Michigan in 1994?) and the ability to run the ball. He had a huge upside.

Meanwhile, Coach Cowher had told me shortly after I signed my deal that the offense was going to revolve around me and the running game. Smart idea. By playing to our strength it would take some of the pressure off our young quarterback.

One of the first things people say when a guy signs a big contract is, "Is he worth it?" I've seen guys lose their work ethic when they sign a big-money deal. I've seen them lose their aggressiveness and their hunger to excel.

I wasn't going to let that happen with me. I didn't want to give the Steelers, my teammates and coaches, or our fans any reason to say the team didn't get its money's worth out of me. So I rushed for 1,665 yards in 1997, which was 200-plus-yards more than I gained before the new contract. To outperform what I did the previous year was important to me.

But I'd be lying if I said I wasn't a tiny bit disappointed not to play in our final regular season game. All I needed was 26 yards to break the Steelers' single-season rushing record held by Foster. But Coach Cowher wanted me to rest my injured knee, so he deactivated me for the last game. I understood his reasoning, but, man, 26 yards . . .

Once again we reached the playoffs, and once again we were eliminated in our second postseason game. We beat the Patriots in the Divisional Playoff, but lost to John Elway and the Denver Broncos in the AFC Championship. We blew it.

We had crushed Denver late in the regular season at Pittsburgh, and we had done it by running the ball (I had 125 yards that game; Kordell had five TDs, two of them rushing touchdowns). So naturally we had the same game plan for the AFC Championship.

But late in the first half, with us up 14–10, and the Broncos unable to stop our running game, our offensive coordinator Chan Gailey called a pass play that got intercepted in the end zone by Denver cornerback Ray Crockett.

Elway drove the Broncos right down the field and they scored on a TD pass to Howard Griffith with 1:47 left in the half. They held us, got the ball back, and Elway threw another touchdown pass, this one with only thirteen seconds left before halftime. Now they had a 24–14 lead and all the momentum going into the third quarter.

Had we just kept running the ball, we could have worked time off the clock and maybe kicked a field goal or scored a TD ourselves. We should have just kept pounding away (I finished with 104 yards, and could have had more), but we got too cute for our own good.

There's one play I'll never forgive Gailey for calling in that game: a pass play on second and goal from the 5-yard line during the third quarter.

At the very least, I thought we should have tried another run, maybe two, or even three. But we tried a pass, and Kordell threw an interception to linebacker Allen Aldridge in the end zone.

I give the Broncos credit for winning the game, but we were definitely the better team. I was sick to my stomach watching them beat the Packers in Super Bowl XXXII. I mean, sick. I couldn't believe it. That should have been us winning that game.

Looking back, there's no question we likely guaranteed Elway's induction into the Pro Football Hall of Fame. It was Elway's first Super Bowl win in four tries. He won another Super Bowl ring the next year too.

If I were a Hall of Fame voter, I would have cast my ballot for Elway, with or without a Super Bowl championship. If Dan Marino, who never won a Super Bowl, got in, then Elway had to be in Canton as well.

Anyway, the Hall of Fame shouldn't be about winning the Super Bowl. That's what a champion is about, not what a Hall of Famer is about. The Hall of Fame is about being a great player. I mean, how many championships did Gale Sayers and Dick Butkus win with the Chicago Bears? How many did Earl Campbell earn with the Oilers? Zero. But in their era, winning a title wasn't a Hall of Fame prerequisite. In this era it is, and that's a shame. It shouldn't be that way.

When it comes to Hall of Fame voting, a quarterback should be judged the same way you'd judge, say, a defensive tackle. Did he dominate in his era? Did he dominate his position in his era? Did he change the game? Did he influence the way the position was played in the future?

Elway and Marino did all those things.

I played with Elway on the AFC Pro Bowl team that season. In fact, we ended up playing together in four different Pro Bowls. He had one of the strongest arms I've ever seen. He threw it so hard that receivers got what they called, the Elway Cross. That's when the tip of the ball (it sort of forms a cross where the four stitched parts come together) would actually leave an indentation in the skin, like a branding iron. I also heard he'd broken receivers' fingers and torn the webbing between their fingers.

Elway was a legend in Denver and he deserved it. I never thought of myself in those terms. He had been groomed to be a star. I was a kid who bowled in weekend leagues. So our career paths were a lot different.

But I did want to make an impact on my team and in my community. And, being a business major, I also wanted to make smart career moves.

One of the first things I did was become involved with local charities and establish some of my own charitable initiatives. It might sound kind of corny, but who knows where I would have been without Reggie McKenzie's free football camp. That camp had a profound effect on me. So I knew firsthand how the kindness of one person could affect the life of another person.

From a business standpoint, I also wanted to have a firmer grip on how people used my name. I couldn't take credit for the nickname The Bus, but I could control its use. So Jahmal Dokes and I came up with a business strategy to essentially create a Jerome Bettis brand within the NFL brand. It had been done in other sports, especially in the NBA (Michael Jordan, Shaquille O'Neal, etc.), but almost never in the NFL.

When I was with the Rams I trademarked the nickname the Battering Ram. So if somebody wanted to use it on a T-shirt or in an advertisement, they had to get my permission. I did the same thing with The Bus. In fact, a certain unnamed shoe company once started printing shirts and other items with "The Bus" on them. Needless to say, we had to beat up on that company when that happened.

Anyway, Pittsburgh and I were getting along just fine. The city loved the Steelers. And the Steelers loved it back. But Pittsburgh's love was about to be tested.

Third Quarter

7

Hines Ward might not be the most elegant wide receiver in the NFL, but he's the toughest. No receiver is more physical or blocks better than the Super Bowl XL MVP.

His football hero: Bettis.

"I got drafted by the Steelers in '98. Jerome and Kordell were the hottest things going then. I remember thinking, 'Man, I'm getting a chance to play with Jerome Bettis.' For me, it was like being a kid in a candy store.

"I'd watch how he practiced, how he interacted with each teammate. White guys. Black guys. He didn't really belong to a clique. He treated everybody the same.

"So my rookie year I just sat back in awe. I remembered watching him in college, in the Sugar Bowl. He was this big, powerful running back who ran crazy on Florida. I became a big fan of his.

"He just had an aura about him. For me, being a young player, I wanted to do everything I could so my guy didn't get a chance to tackle him. You didn't want to let Jerome down.

"You know what Jerome would do before the game started? He would apologize to you. He'd say, 'If I run up your back, I'm sorry.'

"Well, he did, and trust me, it's very painful. I pride myself as being a tough wide receiver, but when it happened, I just kept pumping my legs. And I prayed.

"It was just amazing to watch him. Those defensive backs, safeties, *linebackers . . . they'd call him fat, slow. But by the fourth quarter, they didn't want to tackle him. They were just bouncing off him. I've seen defensive backs want to get out of his way. And I've seen defensive backs and strong safeties fill the hole and get nothing. It was funny watching those guys get up after hitting him. They'd say, 'Man, I just hit The Bus, and he didn't budge.'*

"Jerome was just so physical. Every play he just rolled down the hill and dusted himself off. It was amazing."

I don't know what happened. One minute we were a single play away from being in the Super Bowl. The next minute we were 7–9, missing the playoffs, and beginning a three-year Steelers nightmare scenario.

It all began in 1998. As usual, we lost some players to free agency, but I still thought we had a decent chance to make some postseason noise. What scared me was our offensive line, which was undergoing a pretty substantial rebuilding job. We also had a new offensive coordinator, Ray Sherman (Gailey had left to become head coach of the Cowboys). And my blocking security blanket, Tim Lester, was put on the Physically Unable to Perform list in August because of his shoulder surgery rehab.

Tim and I had been through a lot together. A fullback and a tailback are like a mini-team within a team. He had always been part of my pregame ritual, a ritual that I followed throughout my NFL career.

We would always listen to Tupac before a game. I played, "Me Against the World." That was my philosophy when I stepped on the field: It was me against the world.

I *had* to listen to that song before I played. It was almost like a superstition. A couple of times I got to the stadium and realized I didn't have the CD. So we had to get somebody to find it for me or buy a new one. I was serious about Tupac.

Tim always led me out to the field before a game. He'd always say, "Ride or die." That was our motto from another Tupac song, "As the World Turns."

I hit where it hurts, I ride or die for my turf.

I'd follow Tim out to warm-ups, just like I'd follow him through the hole during a game. That's a pregame tradition I had with all my full-backs during my career.

I respectfully made it clear to Coach Cowher that I hoped in 1998 we'd run the ball more when we got into the red zone. That was something about Gailey's philosophy that drove me crazy. Under Gailey, we'd get inside the 20-, 10- or even 5-yard line and suddenly forget that we had one of the better running games in the NFL.

So I made my feelings known to Coach Cowher. When in doubt, run the ball. We certainly had enough big running backs to pound the ball. There was me, Richard Huntley, and a rookie from Utah, sixth-round pick Chris Fuamatu-Ma'afala.

Speaking of rookies, 1998 was the year we drafted an LSU lineman named Alan Faneca with the twenty-sixth pick of the first round. And in the third round we got a kid from Georgia—Hines Ward.

We won three of our first four games and six of our first nine, but it didn't take long to realize we weren't nearly as talented as the Steelers of 1997. We had those Ws, but if you looked below the surface, we were in a fragile state.

Nobody could say it publicly at the time, but our offensive line was awful. With so much switching around and so many new faces, the offensive line struggled all season. We just couldn't run the ball on a consistent basis. Plus, it didn't help that I played part of the year with broken ribs.

I had 41 yards in the season opener against Baltimore, but then 131 yards the next week against Chicago. Then 48 against Miami. Then 138 against Seattle. Tennessee, a team that always sold out against the run, held me to 26 and 29 yards in our two meetings. So it was tough.

And none of our recent seasons would have been complete without a quarterback controversy. This time it came late in the year when Kordell got pulled from the game against Tampa Bay. He got so upset that he actually cried, and then he started pointing at Coach Cowher and yelling at him. You can't excuse Kordell's actions, but it was frustration, pure and simple.

The season didn't officially begin to collapse until our Thanksgiving Day game at Detroit. What should have been a personal high point for me—I was going home to play in front of my family and friends—turned into one of the low points of my career.

We were 7–4 when we arrived in Detroit. The Lions had their usual awful record, 4–7 at the time. Since it was the holiday season in my hometown, Coach Cowher was nice enough to let me invite the entire team to my mother's house Wednesday night for Thanksgiving dinner.

My mother cooked four turkeys, a dozen Cornish hens, two or three hams, and lots of desserts. It was a feast.

This was a big trip for me because it was the first time I had ever played as a pro in Detroit. I bought ninety-one tickets for the game and rented a bus to take everyone to the stadium. I wanted it to be a special day for everybody.

It was special, all right, but for the wrong reasons.

Even though the Lions had Sanders—and he was always a threat—I didn't think we were going to lose the game. Even when we were tied at the end of regulation, I thought we'd take care of business.

Coach Cowher sent Carnell Lake and me out to midfield for the coin toss. The winner of the toss got first pick in sudden death overtime. Of course, we wanted the ball.

Phil Luckett was the referee. He started to explain the coin toss procedure, but he was going so fast I don't think he realized what he was saying. He said, "On this side of the coin is tails, on this side of the coin is heads. Call it in the air . . ." And then he flipped the coin in the air.

I called tails. The coin hit the ground and there it was, tails.

I started yelling, "Whoo-hoo, whoo-hoo, whoo-hoo." We were going to get the ball first, and the odds always favored the team who got the ball first in sudden death.

But then Luckett said, "The call is heads."

My brain did a somersault. What? No! The call wasn't heads. I said tails. Tails!

But Luckett said I had called heads. I was in shock. I looked over at Lions' defensive lineman Robert Porcher—I'll never forget this—and the look on his face told it all. He knew Luckett had gotten it wrong. But he just smirked, turned, and took off for the Lions sideline. He didn't want Luckett to change his mind. The whole thing was unbelievable.

Luckett screwed me on the call. Totally screwed me. Porcher heard me call tails. Lake heard me call tails. The only person who got confused was Luckett, who said afterward that I had called "heads—tails."

That's absolutely not what happened. I know what I called, and it wasn't "heads—tails."

Detroit got the ball and beat us with a 42-yard field goal. We lost that game and the next four to finish the season 7–9.

I ran for 1,185 yards that year, but all anyone remembers from that season is the coin flip game. Every Thanksgiving Day I became the butt of the football jokes. The ghost of Thanksgiving past, and all that.

Guys would drop quarters on the ground and ask me, "Hey, Bussie, is that tails?" Even Coach Cowher banned me from doing any more coin tosses. My own coach banned me.

About a week later, at a United Way charity dinner, I saw NFL Commissioner Paul Tagliabue. Tagliabue didn't mention the controversy, but someone else started flipping a coin in front of me. Not funny.

The only good thing about the entire incident was that the NFL instituted what was known as the Bettis Rule. Now the coin flip preference is made before the game, so there isn't any confusion on the field. What they ought to call it is the Luckett Rule. He was the only one confused out there.

What an ugly season. We had gone from the AFC Championship to bogus coin flips to our first losing season since 1991. I knew it was going to be a rebuilding year, but I didn't think we were going to crash and burn like that.

Here's another difference between being on a winning team and a losing one: In 1997 I flew to LA to appear with several other NFL players on *Wheel of Fortune.* I left after our team meetings on Monday night, recorded the show Tuesday (our off day), and flew home in time for our Wednesday workout. No one said a word.

But in 1998 I did the same thing and some fans ripped me for leaving town, even though it was our off day, I had permission from Coach Cowher, and I was doing the show for charity (my The Bus Stops Here Foundation). But that's how it goes when your team isn't doing well. People look for someone or something to blame.

Believe me, being on *Wheel of Fortune* wasn't part of our problem. We never had a chance that year because, in retrospect, we simply didn't have enough talent on the roster. I mean, c'mon, we got eliminated from the playoffs by Cincinnati—and the Steelers almost never lost to the Bengals (12–2 v. Cincy between 1991 and 1998). But we did that year. The Bengals won three games, two of them against us. Embarrassing.

There were a few bright spots, but not many. Hines only caught fifteen passes, but he was an incredible special teams guy, especially on kickoff coverage. Usually you don't see a wide receiver on the kickoff team, and if you do, he usually runs down there fast and slyly works himself out of the way of contact.

But not Hines. Hines is probably the first wide receiver I saw who went in there and made *plays*. You could see his toughness. We didn't know how good a receiver he might become, but nobody questioned his heart or toughness.

Faneca's development was more obvious. By the middle of October he was in the starting lineup and you knew he was going to be good. He had played some significant minutes earlier in the season and had done well, which is rare for a rookie offensive lineman. Those guys usually have to take their licks quite a bit before they figure it out. But he was a natural, which is why he was an easy choice for our team's Rookie of the Year award.

Faneca got better, but we didn't. Incredibly enough, we got worse, finishing 6–10 and missing the playoffs for a second consecutive season.

I should have known it was going to be a bad 1999. First, the Steelers decided not to re-sign Lester, who I thought was the best blocking fullback in the league. Yeah, he was my closest friend on the team, but I would have said the same thing about his blocking skills even if we had hated each other. I even told the Steelers I'd give part of my salary to keep him.

But they had no intention of keeping Tim. It wasn't about money (they never offered him a contract); it was about wanting to give the job to Jon Witman. Witman was a Penn State guy handpicked by another Penn State guy, Coach Hoak.

I didn't have anything against Coach Hoak for wanting him, or against Witman for wanting the job. But Lester and I had been through the fires together. I knew what to expect out of him as a blocker. As a tailback, the biggest thing is knowing what the guy in front of you is going to do in a tight situation. I knew exactly when Lester was going to cut a guy, block him to the inside, block him to the outside. I could tell just by the way he positioned his body. And knowing what he was going to do gave me an extra half-second to make a move.

Without Lester there's no question my rushing numbers wouldn't have been as good as they were. I was angry and told reporters that I'd be "a very, very disgruntled employee" if the Steelers didn't re-sign him. It wasn't a threat, it was just the way I felt about the situation.

I'm loyal, and if you earn my loyalty I'm going to go down swinging with you. And I'm big on principle. I felt Lester was the best guy at his position and without him I was the one at the greatest risk. Why? Because if Witman didn't work out, my numbers were going to go down. And if my numbers went down, so did our chances of winning games. After all, we were a running team. And if we started losing, I was the one who was going to get criticized, not Witman or Hoak. So, yeah, Lester's departure could directly affect me and my performance.

In the end, the Steelers didn't re-sign Lester. And nothing against Witman, but it was tough to say goodbye to Tim.

Two months later I had more troubles. One morning in mid-May, when I was in Los Angeles (no more living at my parents' house) for my off-season workout sessions with training expert Bob Kersee, I woke up with a bad stomachache. I thought it was just something I ate, but that wasn't it, and the pain in my stomach area kept getting worse and worse. I called the Steelers trainer, John Norwig, and he had me contact a doctor at UCLA. I went to the UCLA Medical Center, where the doctor diagnosed me with an inflamed appendix and, bang, I was in the hospital for an appendectomy.

The funny thing is, the Steelers didn't want the media to know about the surgery. So when I went to the hospital, someone told me to register under the name Tex Goldstein. That was my alias. Do I look like a Tex Goldstein?

Word eventually got out, and so did my alias. Before long, some of my teammates were calling me Tex.

Then about a week before training camp I tore some meniscus cartilage in my left knee while working out with Kersee in St. Louis (that's where he was based). I told the Steelers about the injury, had arthroscopic surgery to clean up the meniscus, missed all of training camp, but got myself in good enough shape to be ready for our regular season opener at Cleveland. It was my second arthroscopic knee surgery of the off-season, and my body never felt quite right that entire year.

That 1999 season was also Joey Porter's rookie season. He came into camp and they assigned him Greg Lloyd's old number, 95. That raised some eyebrows with the veterans, who weren't sure anybody, especially a rookie, should be wearing that number.

Lloyd had moved on to the Carolina Panthers, but he was a five-time Pro Bowl player and one of the best linebackers who ever played for the Steelers. So when Porter wore No. 95 during the preseason, we all took a peek to see if he was worthy of it. The thing is, he looked pretty good.

But Porter did a smart thing. Instead of living in Lloyd's shadow, he had the equipment guys change his jersey number to 55. That gave him his own identity.

Of all the seasons I spent in Pittsburgh, the 1999 team was the bottom of the barrel in terms of talent. Rock bottom. It reminded me of my days with the Rams, when you're thinking, "Sheesh, it's going to take us a while to get off the schneid, because we are not a very good football team." It was an ugly deal.

We had lost more guys to free agency, which was normal for the Steelers. They had a business philosophy when it came to players. It was almost as if they had devised some sort of football actuarial tables and determined what the optimum years were for a player at each position. Being thirty years old or older was not a good thing if you were a Steeler. But I was twenty-seven, so I guess I was OK.

Even though we won only six games that year, I wasn't about to give up on the franchise. I knew what we were capable of doing, but it was upsetting and disappointing to see how many players we lost to free agency season after season. In a lot of cases, the Steelers didn't replace those players with similar or better talent.

Despite our struggles, I really enjoyed living in Pittsburgh. I had a Monday night radio show. I had a Wednesday night TV show that usually had higher ratings than Coach Cowher's show (sorry, Coach). I had a deal with the Giant Eagle grocery store chain that sold a Bus-related line of snacks. I had a Web site. I had my charities. And I did some commercials for ESPN, EA Sports, and Ford before the season.

Jahmal even convinced me that we should lease one of those 45-foot Madden Cruiser–kind of buses and rent it to corporations for tailgates and appearances. The bus (sticker price: about $750,000) was wrapped in Steelers colors with my likeness on it. The corporation would pay my charitable foundation for use of the bus and for allowing them to put their company logos on it.

That bus went everywhere—to home and away games all across the country. But I never drove that thing. Are you kidding? I can drive cars and golf carts, that's it. Instead, I hired my mother's oldest brother, Abram "Butch" Bougard (a retired bus driver), to do the driving. Uncle Butch babied that bus like it was his own. I don't think it ever got a scratch on it— and he took that thing all the way out to California and back.

The only place that bus didn't go that year was to the playoffs. We lost seven of our last eight games and had the worst Steelers record since 1988. I ended up with 1,091 yards, but only had two 100-yard games.

Football is a game, but the NFL is a business. That's one of the first lessons you learn when you arrive in the league.

I was almost always able to separate the field from the finance. But during the 2000 season, the final year of my four-year contract, I had to manipulate the system, or else the system was going to manipulate me right out of Pittsburgh.

I had broken the 1,000-yard barrier in 1999, but it wasn't my best season statistically. In fact, my rushing totals had declined in each of the last two seasons. So I knew the coaches (we had a different offensive coordinator for the third year in a row—Kevin Gilbride) had some doubts about me. Plus, we were losing games and I was making a lot of money.

Remember Richard Huntley? Huntley had a chance to sign with the Miami Dolphins, get a $2 million signing bonus, and become a starter. Instead, he signed a three-year $4 million deal (including a signing bonus that was half of what the Dolphins were going to pay him) to stay with the Steelers. His entire three-year contract was about $1 million less than the $3.2 million I was supposed to make in 2000. So from an economic standpoint, he was a very attractive alternative to me.

The coaches, especially Gilbride, loved Huntley. Huntley had gained 567 yards, averaged 6.1 yards per carry, and rushed for five touchdowns in less than 100 carries. It didn't matter that a lot of those yards had come in garbage time or that our offensive line had really struggled the previous two seasons. To the Steelers, Huntley was younger, faster, and cheaper.

Coach Cowher wanted Huntley so bad that he apparently told him the starting tailback job would be his if he didn't sign with Miami. At least, that's what Huntley told the media. In fact, Ed Bouchette, who covers the team for the *Pittsburgh Post-Gazette*, wrote that Huntley told his agent that I was going to be released.

Coach Cowher denied it, but why would Huntley have turned down a starting job with the Dolphins to remain with the Steelers as a backup? It didn't make sense. Even weirder is that the day before they signed Huntley, they agreed to discuss a contract extension with me. They must have thought Huntley was going to go to Miami. When he didn't, I became expendable.

Meanwhile, I had another huge problem: my left knee.

Even though I played the entire season on it in 1999, I knew the knee was never quite right. I couldn't do my usual pre–training camp workout sessions with Kersee because my knee would swell everytime I ran.

No way could I tell the Steelers that my knee was bothering me. If I told them, there's no question they'd cut me and my salary. See you later, Jerome. Thanks for stopping by the booth.

So instead of running, I rode the stationary bike to save some wear and tear on my knee. I came into camp in good shape, but I had a knee that would swell like a balloon if I put too much stress on it. Worse yet, I had to figure out how to hide the injury from the Steelers.

Each year at training camp there was a conditioning test for the players. It was terrible: fourteen 40-yard dashes, and they had to be run in a certain time. In the past, I'd never finished the test because of my asthma. Everybody understood why I couldn't finish, and it was no big deal.

Until this time.

I knew my knee would never survive that test, so I concocted a scheme to spare me those 40-yard dashes. It just so happened that I was putting ice and then heat on my knee to keep the swelling down. But I did it so much that it actually irritated the skin and caused the *back* of the leg to swell.

Now I had an excuse. I went to Coach Cowher and said, "Hey, Coach, what would you rather me do: run the test or practice this afternoon?"

Knowing Coach, I assumed he'd want me there for practice. After all, I had never completed the conditioning test in the four years I had played for the Steelers.

I assumed wrong.

"Run the 40 test," he said.

Uh-oh. I knew something was fishy. If I was their guy, then Coach

Cowher wouldn't have cared if I did the test. But all of a sudden there was a big push for me to finish those 40s.

There was no question they were looking for reasons to cut me. I was twenty-eight, had averaged 327 carries as a Steeler, and was nearing that unspoken thirty-year age limit the organization put on most of its players. It didn't matter that I had rushed for 8,463 yards, the fourth-highest total among active running backs, or that I had been a two-time Steelers MVP.

Instead, management was wondering if I had hit the wall. If so, they were ready to make a move with Huntley. They had re-signed Huntley and, according to Huntley, had promised him first crack at the starting job. And Coach Cowher was telling reporters, "You can't have enough good running backs."

Somebody wasn't telling the truth. At the very least, they were looking for any excuse to take my starting job and then cut me. More than likely, they had already made up their minds.

Well, I was so pissed about having to do the conditioning test that I ran the whole thing with hate in my eyes. I felt they weren't being honest with me. If I was the odd man out, then they should at least say so to my face.

So I ran the test and let the anger be my energy. I never once bent down or put my hands on my knees. Not for one minute. I purposely tried to control my breathing so it wouldn't look like I was gasping for air. Tired? They weren't going to see that from me.

Hate propelled me. I was running off of hate because they were questioning my talent, my heart. So I did their fourteen 40s and when I was done, nobody could believe it. You could see the coaches were surprised that I had completed the test. Not only completed it, but kicked ass in it.

Now there was a new buzz: "Bettis looks really good and he's ready to go."

They thought I was finished. They were being coy about my status, but I turned it around on them by running a lights-out conditioning test. If they didn't want to be honest with me about Huntley, then I sure as hell wasn't going to be honest with them about my knee. I was on *my* side of the fence now, and from my side it looked like the Steelers were trying to set me up for a fall.

This wasn't like the Brooks situation with the Rams. I *knew* Brooks didn't think much of me after the holdout. But as I started putting the pieces together with the Steelers, there was no question what was happening. After all, this wasn't my first rodeo. When a player's salary numbers start getting high, and his age creeps up, and his production hits a plateau or declines, management has to make a decision. The Steelers, it seemed, had made a decision.

In 1999, I had 299 carries and my fourth consecutive, 1,000-yard season with the Steelers. But my knee had been in bad shape. It was never 100 percent during the season.

In 2000 the knee was much stronger, but the cartilage still needed to be cleaned up. When the swelling was down, I could perform at a high level. But I needed to figure out a way I could get off my feet, get some rest, and do it without losing my job. I needed to make a preemptive move.

So early in training camp, during a short-yardage situation, I took a handoff, took some contact, and, bang, went down in a heap. I sort of yelled out, grabbed my knee, and waited for the training staff. Man, did I do a nice job of acting.

The thing is, I wasn't faking that I had an injury. I was just faking that the injury happened on that short-yardage play. I had to fool the coaches and the team's medical department into thinking the injury had occurred on that play. Otherwise, the Steelers would have had their reason to cut me and my salary.

Basically I was playing career poker with some crummy cards. So I had to bluff.

The trainers took me to get an MRI and, sure enough, the doctors said I had some cartilage that needed to be cleaned up. They didn't know it was an injury caused the previous year because I had never mentioned it to them during the off-season. Anyway, the diagnosis was great news because teams aren't allowed to cut a player while he's injured.

I effectively negated any funny business they were trying to pull on me. Plus, if I was on the roster after Week 1, my $3.2 million base salary was guaranteed for the year. And I took the pressure off a head coach who was probably trying to get rid of me.

Some people will read this and say I wasn't being very ethical. I'm fine with that, because to me this wasn't a question of ethics. It was a question of gray areas.

In 1999, I didn't take enough time to fully rehab my knee. I rushed back so I could play in the first game of the season. I wanted to be there for my team, even though I knew it was going to be touch and go with my knee. I should have waited to play, but I didn't.

So I played hurt (a bad knee, as well as broken ribs) and still gave them 1,091 yards. When the knee started acting up again during the off-season, I couldn't risk shutting it down again. If I did, I was probably gone. Out of self-preservation I had to make the system work for me.

In my mind, what I did was justifiable because the original injury occurred while I was playing for the Steelers. And it was still there, in one form or another, when I reported to camp in 2000. I hurt in 1999. I hurt in 2000. All I did was buy myself enough time so they couldn't cut me.

Rather than undergo another arthroscopic surgery—and feel the same way I did after the 1999 procedures—I decided on a more conservative approach: rest. So with the training staff's approval, my practice time was limited. On a game week, I would only practice on Thursday and Friday, sometimes only on Friday.

Saturdays weren't any fun, though. Even with the limited practice schedule, my knee would swell. So every Saturday a team doctor would come in and drain the knee. The needle was as long and as thick as a No. 2 pencil. Think about that for a minute. Then the doctor would stick that needle into the puffy part of my knee and extract all sorts of pus, blood, and little pieces of cartilage.

Yeah, it hurt. Damn right it did. But if I wanted to play, that's what I had to do. Pain is part of the game. It's as much a part of the game as the crowds or the Miller Lite commercials or the TV cameras. If you can't endure pain, you can't play in the NFL.

I let *USA Today's* Jarrett Bell, whom I've known for a long time, use me as the centerpiece for a story he was doing on the toll an NFL season takes on your body. He saw it all. My purple ankle. My bruised butt. The red welts on my back. The scars. The scratches and gashes on my arms and legs. The torn tendons in my thumbs. The ring finger that is missing a chunk of flesh.

He saw me try to get out of bed that morning. It took forever. I told him that sometimes I couldn't walk down the stairs in my house.

Instead, I had to sit on the top step and very, very slowly slide my way down on my butt.

This was the life I had chosen, so I wasn't about to complain. But I don't think the average NFL fan has any idea what it takes to play the game when you're injured. Broken ribs are one of the worst injuries. I know, because one time I broke three ribs, which is a pretty rare thing. Usually you just break one, but I had the trifecta.

You can get an X-ray to detect the breaks. But an X-ray is useless when it comes time for the doctor to inject you with the painkillers necessary to play in a game. It's not like he can look at the X-ray and connect the dots. It doesn't work that way.

No, you have to raise your arm and then he sticks a needle in there, taps on the bone with the needle point to find the exact spot of the fracture, injects the painkiller, and then removes the needle. Then he gets a new needle, inserts the needle, taps on the next rib bone, injects, and then removes. And then he gets another needle, inserts, taps, injects, removes.

And did I mention that you can't move while he's doing this? If you move, and the needle jabs too deep, he could puncture your lung.

Those painkilling shots were a necessary evil. With broken ribs, the chances of them breaking off and puncturing something were very small, so it was an acceptable risk for me. The possibility of me injuring them more was tiny.

But I would never take a painkiller in my knee or hamstrings. Those are parts of the body where you need to feel the pain. If you can't, then a sprained ligament might turn into a torn ligament.

My teammates and coaches never pressured me to take painkilling shots. But there is an unspoken understanding about playing with injuries in the NFL.

A coach and the other players need to know they can count on you. If a guy doesn't take a painkiller, he's labeled as soft. They don't know if they can truly depend on you.

Me and pain had a great relationship. We always found a way to work it out. An injury might hurt like hell, but my threshold for pain was pretty high.

That's why I didn't—and still don't—feel the least bit guilty about falling to the turf during that short-yardage drill in training camp. If they want to say I deceived them, then I'd say they tried to deceive me when it came to Huntley.

What I did was save my butt because I was on the blocks. And I saved their butt too. I kept them from making a bad decision—they just didn't know it at the time.

On one good knee and sheer determination I rushed for 1,341 yards (the fourth highest total of my career and also the fourth-highest yardage by a Steelers running back) on 355 carries. Cheat someone? Does 1,341 yards sound like I cheated the Steelers? And we did that with the twenty-ninth-ranked passing offense in the league. So you know how many guys were in the box.

During that 2000 season I played with a lump the size of a cue ball in my lower left leg. Norwig was worried about a blood clot.

I played with turf toe, which sounds a lot nicer than it is. Basically, someone smashed my toe backward.

I played with bruised ribs. At least, that's what I told myself. They could have been broken, but I never bothered with X-rays.

I played with someone sticking a big needle in my knee every Saturday.

So believe me, the Steelers got their money's worth out of my twenty-eight-year-old body.

The season didn't start well. I only had nine carries for 8 yards against Baltimore in our season-opening loss. But the Ravens' defense was incredible that year. They shut us out and only allowed 165 points the entire season. No one could do anything against them in the playoffs, either. Ray Lewis and the fellas gave up just 23 points in their four postseason wins, including a 34–7 victory against the Giants in Super Bowl XXXV.

Lewis, the best linebacker in the league at the time, was a guy you definitely respected on the field. And he was surrounded by a great group of players who knew exactly what they were doing.

Tennessee didn't have the same type of players, but they had a great defensive scheme. They'd put eight, nine guys in the box and beat me up. I respected their strategy because they made a commitment and stuck with it.

About the only guy in the league I truly despised was Denver linebacker Bill Romanowski. We didn't play the Broncos in 2000, but I can still remember the time he tackled me, and then grabbed my ankle and tried to roll it over. He specialized in cheap shots.

That time he didn't get me. But when I got up he wouldn't even look at me. He knew what he had tried to do. What a coward.

We lost our first three games, but then won our next five. Because of the extra rest my knee was getting, I was putting up some good numbers. Halfway through the season (we beat the Ravens at their place in the rematch) I had almost 700 yards and we were still in the playoff chase.

Huntley, who barely got any carries, was steaming. Too bad for him.

But then we lost four of our next six games and fell out of contention. We finished 9–7 (third in our division behind Tennessee and Baltimore), but by the end of the year we had become a pretty good team. And our offensive line had really come together.

The missing ingredient was a stable quarterback situation. Once again, Coach Cowher had brought in a new guy. And once again, it backfired.

This time it was Kent Graham. Graham was a veteran guy who came to us from the New York Giants, where he had put up respectable numbers on a part-time basis. Coach Cowher named him the starter and Kordell became the backup again.

Coach Cowher and Kordell had kind of a love-hate relationship. For some reason, Coach would never really commit fully to Kordell. He committed to giving him a chance, a shot at the job, but he never gave him his full 100 percent, "You're-the-guy, let's go" endorsement. And because of that we had no consistent leadership from the quarterback position.

I think if you would have taken a poll of the players, we would have voted for Kordell. Kordell was a friend, but I also thought he gave us the best chance to win ballgames. Graham was a guy who had lost starting jobs in Arizona and New York.

Coach Cowher disagreed. Kordell became Coach Cowher's Plan B, which wasn't fair to Kordell or to the team. Kordell had split time with Tomczak in 1999 and now he had to watch as Graham took the job in 2000.

It always seemed like we were unsettled at quarterback, like we were caught in the middle. Personally, I wish Coach Cowher would have made a decision and stuck with it. If you're going to go with a guy, go with him and *stay* with him. And if you don't like him, go to the next guy and stay with *him*.

I didn't think Graham was better than Kordell. He was an average quarterback who was big (six foot five, 245), but not very mobile. He was like a statue back there. Kordell was smaller, but he could scramble and create problems for a defense.

Our offense at the time wasn't very quarterback-friendly. We didn't throw on first down very often, so that meant when we did throw the ball, it was usually to keep a drive alive on third down. Another problem was our offensive line, which struggled at the beginning of the season. Graham was getting beat up back there.

Coach Cowher eventually replaced Graham (who got hurt in our third game) with Kordell, and Kordell responded well. We won seven of the eleven games he started, including four of the last five. But the move came a little too late.

Part of the blame has to go to Coach Cowher. I'm not sure he ever knew what to do with Kordell. Kordell was such an unusual talent, like a Michael Vick, a Donovan McNabb, or a Randall Cunningham. I think if you asked Coach Cowher now if he made some mistakes with the way he handled Kordell, he would say he did. Sadly, I think it affected Kordell's development as a quarterback.

Had we made the playoffs—the Colts got the last spot in the AFC— I dare say we would have reached the AFC Championship. We had that good of a football team by the end of December. Kordell had earned our confidence. Our defense was ranked seventh in the NFL. And the offensive line was moving people.

Even though we didn't reach the postseason, we were at least able to give Three Rivers Stadium a proper sendoff. After thirty-one years, the place was going to be torn down and replaced by Heinz Field in 2001.

My body was glad it was being torn down. That artificial turf cost me an ankle surgery and a knee surgery. And the facilities were so old. We lifted weights in the same weightroom that Franco Harris had lifted weights in. Nothing ever changed.

But my football soul was going to miss that dump. Three Rivers was one of those cookie-cutter stadiums, but the Steelers fans turned it into an electric place to play. Oh, did that place have character.

Three Rivers was where Harris made the Immaculate Reception. It was where you could find Franco's Army and the Steel Curtain. There was so much history in that place, and I was honored to have played on the same field as those four Super Bowl champions of the 1970s.

The turf was terrible, but the rollaway bleachers at Three Rivers brought the crowd right on top of you. When the place got rocking, you could see whole sections of bleachers bouncing six inches off the ground. You'd hear these huge *boom!* sounds every time the bleachers would smack the ground. *Boom! Boom! Boom!* It was amazing. And loud? Oh, was it loud. It could scare the hell out of the other team.

About forty former Steeler players were there for our December 16 game against the Redskins. We didn't disappoint them or the standing-room-only crowd. We won 24–3, and the place was literally shaking.

After two horrible seasons it was nice to end the year on an upbeat note. No, we didn't make the playoffs, but we were beginning to feel good about ourselves and our chances in 2001. And because we were moving into a new stadium the following August, there was talk that Steelers management might finally spend some money on free agents.

I was one of those unrestricted free agents.

I wanted to stay in Pittsburgh, but I wasn't sure the Steelers wanted me back. They said they did, but I was going on twenty-nine and knew about management's philosophy about older players.

But the Steelers were in a bind. The organization had said they needed the new stadium so it could increase its revenue. If it had more revenue, it could spend more money on free agents and keep its veteran players.

They got their new stadium. Now, with the new stadium scheduled to open in August 2001, the Steelers had to make good on their promise.

So there I was, a marquee franchise guy who had just been voted team MVP by my teammates for the third time. I was active in the community, popular with the fans, and a guy fresh off a 1,341-yard season. But I'm sure the Steelers had to be wondering how long I could keep going.

But the pressure was on them. They could re-sign me, or try to sign another free agent running back, or add a running back through the draft.

As a soon-to-be unrestricted free agent, I would have been able to sign with any team. But when the Steelers offered me a six-year $30 million deal with a $6 million signing bonus, I didn't even test the market. I knew Pittsburgh was my home and where I wanted to end my career. My loyalty was with the Steelers. Plus, I was sure we were close to winning a championship.

In reality, the contract was really meant to last three years.

Nobody, including me, really thought I was going to play through the 2006 season.

The new deal was the culmination of one of the biggest gambles in my career. In a perfect world, I would have had knee surgery going into the 2000 season. But I didn't have the luxury of a perfect world. So I gambled that it was strong enough to get me through the year. It turned out to be the right decision.

After I signed the new contract in March 2001, I underwent surgery to have the knee cleaned up. That way I had the entire off-season to get it strong again.

Time to go to work again. But this time I was going to do it on two healthy knees.

8

Tim Lester lives in Miami now. He's thirty-eight, "but I feel seventy-eight." Such are the residual effects of being an NFL fullback.

Lester, who has a five-month-old son and runs a nonprofit mentoring program for high school students, still talks with Bettis about once a month.

"I played eight years, but six of those years were as his teammate—three with the Rams, three with the Steelers. And he made my eight years the best eight years. He made me feel loved and respected. He always had a way of making people feel that they had a part in what he accomplished, that they shared in his success.

"But to be honest, the first time I actually met him, I didn't like Jerome much. I had been drafted in the tenth round in 1992 as a fullback. During the off-season I was living in LA and I was watching the 1993 draft. I was sitting at home and the Rams took Jerome, this big-name fullback out of Notre Dame. He was coming to take my job. Here I had just barely made it into the NFL and now I was out of there. When they took him, I thought it was over. It had just started, and now it was over.

"But they brought him in as a tailback. I was the fullback.

"When he first came to the Rams, you could tell he was a big, physical back. I was 215, so as his fullback I didn't want him running up my back. So I would get in there as fast as possible and hit somebody. That's what made us so good together. I was smaller and I would get on guys quick.

"Nobody could really arm tackle Jerome. And for a big guy, he had some of the best feet I'd seen for somebody that size. He could make you miss. I've never seen somebody change direction like him. I always tell him that's why he lasted so long, because in his second year in the league he got real smart and started to make people miss.

"To him, it was all about us being successful together. He took me to the Pro Bowl three times. He bought me a Rolex watch. I've still got that Rolex. When he was with the Rams, he bought TVs for his offensive linemen. He treated you in a way that you actually wanted to destroy people on the field for him. You'd go out on that field and hurt somebody for him.

"Most athletes have egos and chips on their shoulders. This guy never had a chip on his shoulder. He was always the same person. He didn't act like he was the Jerome Bettis. He always kind of fit in. I noticed that right away. He was just a guy from Detroit. He treated everybody around him with respect.

"I remember when the Steelers were thinking of trading for him. Coach Hoak asked me what I thought of Jerome as a person. He said the Rams were saying he wasn't a good locker room guy. I told Coach Hoak, 'This guy is the best guy I've ever met. He would never ever be a problem for anybody.'

"I think the Rams were trying to mess his name up, trying to keep him from getting a job. What a joke.

"At the Rams we ran a lot of weak-side lead. I would block the WIL [weak inside linebacker]. We ran that play a lot against Pittsburgh. And that was one of the game films the Steelers looked at before they traded for him.

"When he showed up with the Steelers it was like, 'It's going to be good in Pittsburgh.' It was a great feeling to be back there in the backfield with him. And when we played the Rams that first year, I was kind of rubbing it in. I kept telling him, 'These guys kicked you to the curb. They didn't think you were good enough. They didn't think you could make plays.' Well, he showed those guys he had the breakaway speed.

"I was just watching ESPN Classics *yesterday. They had on the 1991 Notre Dame v. Michigan game and he was playing fullback. I called him and said, 'Man, you were a real fullback. You were up there lead blocking.'*

"I had to call him on that."

✦ ◆ ✦

Two things happened in the 2001 season that I never thought were possible: I became just the fourteenth player in NFL history to rush for more than 10,000 career yards. And I missed a playoff game because one of my legs wouldn't work.

First, the good.

On October 7, on the first play of our third possession against the Bengals, I took a handoff from Kordell, ran off tackle to the left, gained three yards, and then a few moments later, heard the Steelers crowd go berserk. I had just passed the 10,000-yard mark.

It was an incredible moment. There I was, a guy whose own mother didn't want me to play football, whose nearby college (Michigan) didn't recruit me as a running back, whose Notre Dame coach said he didn't think I'd be this good, whose Rams coach benched and traded me . . . and now I had 10,000 yards?

I couldn't believe it either. For the longest time I had never thought Yard No. 1 was possible, much less Yard No. 10,000. The NFL had never been an aspiration of mine because it seemed so beyond the realm of reality. I couldn't even imagine it. But when it happened—and it was only fitting that the game was in Pittsburgh—it surpassed my wildest dreams.

Gale Sayers didn't gain 10,000 yards. Neither did Earl Campbell, Jim Taylor, or Larry Csonka. And they're all in the Hall of Fame.

What makes 10,000 yards such a milestone is that it takes both talent *and* longevity. I think longevity is just as important as talent because of the physical demands of the position. That's why running backs don't last very long in the NFL. Lester always said that if you run the ball thirty times in a game, you'll get hit ninety times. Now multiply that over the course of a season, over the course of a career, and you'll know why running backs don't last long in the NFL.

In my case, I carried the ball 3,479 times during my regular season career (that's not counting preseason games, playoff games, practices, and scrimmages). Using Lester's formula, I got hit 10,437 times.

At first, none of the officials in our game against Cincy realized I had broken the 10,000-yard barrier. But after the next play, referee Larry Nemmers went over to the sidelines, got the ball, handed it to me, and then patted me on the shoulder pads. As the crowd roared, I raised the ball above my head for everyone to see. I wanted them to know that they, along with all my teammates and coaches, had helped me get those yards. By the way, that particular ball now has a place of honor in my house.

When the game got started again, I commenced to blitzkrieg the Bengals to the tune of 153 yards. We won that game. In fact, we won eight of our first ten games and were feeling pretty good about our chances.

Coach Cowher had brought in free agent quarterback Tommy Maddox during the off-season, but Kordell beat him out for the job. When that happened, Coach finally committed to Kordell, and Kordell responded with one of the best years of his career.

Meanwhile, Hines and second-year receiver Plaxico Burress (he was our No. 1 pick in 2000) were catching everything thrown their way. Our offensive line had picked up right where it left off at the end of the 2000 season. And our defense was great. We were rolling.

As for me, my knees felt great. In fact, aside from the usual bumps and bruises, my body was holding up well. It was important to me to show my worth after signing my big contract. And that's what I did during the first half of that season. I was putting up the kind of numbers that could get me my first rushing title.

But then came one of those freak injuries every player dreads.

During our December 2 win against the Minnesota Vikings, we ran a trick play where Kordell got under center, then walked down the right side of the line of scrimmage and started yelling at our receivers, like he was giving them last-second instructions. As the defense watched Kordell yell the supposed new play, our center snapped the ball directly to me. I ran around the left end and just as I was headed out of bounds a Vikings defender tried to sling me to the ground. As he did, I tried to throw him off me. My body was in a weird, contorted position when I heard *pop!* One pop. That was all she wrote.

I didn't know it at the time, but I had torn 30 percent of my groin muscle from the bone. At first, the pain was intense. But once it settled down I thought I could go back in. I tried, but the longer I played the more it hurt. Something was seriously wrong.

This was a rough one because time and rest were the only things that could heal that type of injury. But I didn't have the luxury of time. The playoffs started in January and no way was I going to miss the post-season.

The killer is that I was so dialed in at the time. I had 1,072 yards and was leading the league in rushing when I got hurt. With five regular season games left to play, I would have finished somewhere between 1,400 and 1,600 yards for the season.

Instead, I sat. I had no choice.

While I was on the sideline, we won four of those last five games and finished 13–3 for the season. Ray Lewis and the Ravens were our opponents in the divisional playoffs.

As I warmed up for the Ravens game I still felt a little twinge. It wasn't terrible, but just to be on the safe side I went to our team doctor, Dr. James Bradley, and asked him if he would give me a painkilling shot. So he gave me the shot. No problem.

I went back out to the field and as I was walking, I caught my cleats on the grass and kind of tripped. "That's the weirdest thing," I said to myself. Then I tried to jog a little bit and I tripped again. And then again.

Something wasn't right. So I decided I better get in the locker room and sit down for a few minutes. I was feeling crazy and I didn't know what was going on.

At Heinz Field you have to walk up some steps to get to the Steelers locker room. As I made my way up those first few steps my left leg went out on me and I crashed to the ground.

"What the hell?" I thought.

Somehow I got up those stairs, but with each passing second my leg was becoming less and less functional. When I saw Dr. Bradley in the training room I told him it felt like my whole leg was going to sleep.

Suddenly I saw the panic in Dr. Bradley's eyes and he started to tear up.

"Doc, what's wrong?" I said.

"Jerome, the medication must have struck your femoral nerve. Your whole leg is going numb."

I couldn't believe it. "How long will it be numb?"

"Eight hours," he said.

Eight hours meant I couldn't play in the game. Eight hours meant my season could be done if the Ravens beat us. It was the sickest feeling I've ever had.

I started crying like a baby. Dr. Bradley started crying like a baby.

We couldn't help it. He kept telling me how sorry he was, and I kept thinking, "It's a playoff game—one of the biggest games of my life— and this happens to me?"

It was an accident, of course. When he gave me the shot in the groin—at the place where I told him to put the needle—the medicine bled down into the femoral nerve. Gravity.

After our crying session, Dr. Bradley had to break the news to Coach Cowher.

"Will we have him back by the start of the second half?" Coach Cowher said.

"Hopefully we'll have him back by tonight," said Dr. Bradley.

It didn't take long for the news to spread through the locker room. I could hear the whispers as my teammates told one another what had happened. So one by one my guys started making their way to the training room and gave me a little nod or a pat on the back. I couldn't get up—by then my leg was completely numb—so I just nodded back and tried to hold back the tears.

Coach Cowher called everybody up to the middle of the locker room and gave one of the best speeches I've ever heard.

"When a teammate is down," he said, "you have to pick him up. Jerome wants to be out there with you guys, but he can't this time. So you have to go out there and take care of business for him."

I couldn't help it; I broke into tears again. In fact, the whole team got caught up in it. It was such an emotional moment, such a compelling speech. You could almost feel the energy in the room as Coach finished talking to the team.

And then they went out and destroyed Baltimore, 27–10. I watched the whole thing on TV in the locker room. I was so proud of them. We were moving on to the AFC Championship against the Patriots.

I wish there were a happier ending to this story, but New England beat us, 24–17. This time I didn't let anybody get near my leg with a needle. But early in the game I got tackled and hurt the groin again. I knew I couldn't run, but I gutted it out as long as I could.

I scored on a one-yard TD run in the third quarter to cut New England's lead to 21–10, and then Amos Zereoue scored a few minutes later to bring us within four points. But that's as close as we got.

Afterward, there was a lot of talk and criticism of Coach Cowher's decision to play me. I had only gained 8 yards on nine carries. But my thinking is this: Go with the horse that got you there. And Coach Cowher obviously believed in the same philosophy.

I have to admit, I was beginning to wonder if I'd ever get a chance to plant a kiss on the Super Bowl trophy, or know what it was like to ride in a victory parade, or feel the weight of a championship ring on my finger. The Steelers and I were 0–2 in AFC Championship games, even though both games were at home and we were favored each time. At some point I started to look at the calendar and wonder if it was meant to be.

I didn't want to end my career without at least playing in a Super Bowl. That's what happened to Barry Sanders, Eric Dickerson, O. J. Simpson, and Earl Campbell. They put up incredible yardage numbers, but in the end, they never got a chance to play in a title game. That doesn't diminish what they accomplished during their careers, but football is a team game. I wanted to win something as a team. I hadn't done it in high school, in college, or in the NFL—yet. And I was running out of time.

I turned thirty during the off-season—and I knew how the Steelers felt about players once they turned thirty. My age was getting closer and closer to my jersey number. And the toll of 10,876 career rushing yards was beginning to show.

Don't get me wrong: it wasn't like I was washed up. If I hadn't torn my groin in 2001, I probably would have won the rushing title that year over Kansas City's Priest Holmes. And I was only 477 yards from becoming the tenth-leading rusher of all time. But the first thing I had to do was make sure the groin tear was completely healed.

So I rested it. And rested it. And then rested it some more. No question the coaches weren't thrilled with my rehab timetable, but I wasn't going to take any chances. To be productive, I had to be healthy. And I couldn't be healthy if I rushed back from the groin injury.

I'm not a "Why me?" kind of person. Whenever I got hurt, I tried to play hurt. And if I couldn't play hurt, then I did what I could to help the teammate who took my place. I learned a long time ago that feeling sorry for yourself doesn't accomplish a thing. And if I needed any reminders, I got them when I was invited by Commissoner Tagliabue to visit U.S. military personnel during a four-day trip to several of our bases in Germany.

The trip was part of an NFL/USO tour that featured me, Eddie

George, and Commissioner Tagliabue. I brought Jahmal and my brother, John, who was born in Germany when my father was in the service over there.

We went to Baumholder Military Base, which has the largest concentration of combat soldiers outside the United States and is called the Home of Champions (I liked that). The 1st Armored Division's 2nd Brigade is headquartered there, so I got a chance to ride in an Abrams M1A2 tank. My middle name is Abram, so The Bus and the 69-ton, 1,500-horsepower tank had a little bit in common. I only wish I could have worn some of the tank's depleted uranium armor. It would have cut down on football injuries.

And for anybody who is wondering, I didn't have any problem fitting through the turret hatch.

We also visited the Hanau Military Community and then the Landstuhl Regional Medical Center, which is the largest American hospital outside the States. Landstuhl is about a five-hour medevac flight from Iraq and is the place where U.S. soldiers and personnel are treated for wounds, illnesses, or injuries suffered while serving in Iraq, Kuwait, or Afghanistan. I saw those brave people and all of a sudden my torn groin muscle didn't seem like such a big deal.

This was serious stuff. The clocks on the hospital's Web site only feature four places: Washington, D.C., Germany, Baghdad, and Kabul. So everything revolves around taking care of those soldiers.

I was honored to meet the troops. It was one of the first times I got to see how powerful of a public platform the NFL provides. The servicemen and servicewomen were so passionate about their favorite NFL teams and I saw a few Terrible Towels being waved. Here I was, a little kid from inner-city Detroit, and I was in Germany talking to the troops, doing my very little part to inspire them. But really, they inspired me.

Sometimes I hear broadcasters talk about a football player making a "courageous" run or catch. Sorry, but courage is what these servicepeople do: put their lives on the line for a country they love and believe in. I got an opportunity to see firsthand the sacrifices these soldiers make. So the very least I could do was to pat as many backs, shake as many hands, and tell as many soldiers as I could that I appreciated everything they did, that their efforts weren't forgotten, and that everybody in the States owed them thanks.

I really enjoyed that trip because I got to meet hundreds and hundreds of soldiers, and because it helped put things in perspective. Football was important—after all, it was my profession—but, in the end, it was just football. It wasn't life or death.

That doesn't mean a championship was any less important to me. But I was a different person from the teenager who ran with the ABP, the Aurora Boulevard Posse. I was different from the freshman who showed up on the Notre Dame campus in 1990. I was different from the guy who got traded from the Rams to the Steelers in 1996.

Life is a series of decisions, some big, most of them small. Somewhere along the way, I decided I had a responsibility as a role model to help make a difference. If you play professional sports, you become a role model, whether you want to or not. If I was going to be a role model, then why not excel at it? That's what my parents taught me.

Little by little, I had become more involved in community service. It started at Notre Dame, but by 2002 it was a huge part of my life. My charities helped donate thousands of football cleats to Detroit high schools. Our Cyber Bus program taught underprivileged kids how to use a computer. And if you could see the kids' faces when we give each of them their very own computers to keep . . .

Raising money is an important part of the process, but I've found that participating in the charities themselves is what makes the difference. I've said it before: You have to get your hands dirty when you do community service. It's wonderful to write a check for a charity, but it's even better to contribute your time and effort. That's when you see the greatest results.

I've been fortunate enough to receive all kinds of awards during my career, but one of my cherished trophies doesn't have anything to do with how many yards I gained. During the 2002 off-season, I was presented with the Walter Payton NFL Man of the Year Award, which recognizes a player's off-field contributions to the community. It was quite an honor, but the truth is, every one of my charities is a labor of love for me.

When I reported to training camp, I was going on my tenth NFL season and there wasn't any doubt in my mind that the 2002 Steelers were going to be the best team I had played on. We had twenty starters com-

ing back from a thirteen-win team. Kordell was fresh from the Pro
Bowl. I was healthy. And little by little, the Steelers had added some
important parts to our roster, such as rookie utility man Antwaan
Randle El.

I could tell Antwaan would be a special player. He made some plays
in the preseason that wowed me. He was impressive. We knew he'd be
great on punt returns and kickoff returns, and he did not disappoint.

For the first time in three or four years we were starting to retool our
roster. Not only did we have starters who could do the job, but now we
were getting backups who could step in and perform. In the '98 and '99
seasons, we didn't have that. But now we had experience, depth, and incentive.

And then it all fell apart.

To begin with, we lost our first two games of the season, including
the season opener to those Patriots.

Then, in our third game, I got benched during the second half for
Fuamatu-Ma'afala. In the same second half, Coach also pulled Kordell
from the lineup and replaced him with Maddox. Suddenly we had ourselves a running back *and* quarterback controversy.

I got back in the lineup the following game against New Orleans,
but we lost to drop to 1–3. Kordell was out as our starter and Maddox
was in.

Nothing against Tommy, but I always had my doubts that he won the
job fair and square. Kordell was coming off a Pro Bowl year and was
going into the last year of his contract. The Steelers wanted to renegotiate his contract before he became a free agent, but Kordell was probably going to be too rich for their blood.

Anybody who tells you money isn't a factor in personnel decisions
doesn't know the NFL. I can't prove it, but in my heart I really believe
that Kordell was set up for failure that season. You've got a guy who
just took you to the AFC Championship, had one of his best years
ever . . . and you're going to give him the quick hook three games into
the season? You bench your Pro Bowl quarterback for a guy who had
been out of football for years, who hadn't started an NFL game in ten
seasons? That just doesn't happen by accident.

I think they pulled Kordell partly because they didn't want to pay
him a big salary and signing bonus. It was cheaper for them if he didn't
have success. If he recovered and had a huge year, then the public sen-

timent would be, "Hey, you've got to re-sign him for whatever it costs." I'm telling you, it was a monetary decision. The Steelers had no interest in paying Kordell his market value.

The other part of the equation was Tommy. I think the Steelers felt that Tommy gave the offense a different dimension because he was an accurate pocket passer. With the addition of Randle El, they felt like they could exploit teams with three-receiver packages.

And Tommy turned out to be just what they had hoped for. I mean, he was a gunslinger. He threw the ball around all year and did a tremendous job. But he was an unproven commodity.

We beat Cincinnati (I loved running against them—109 yards and two touchdowns), but then on a Monday night, with the nation watching, I hurt my knee against the Colts on the first play of the second half. Yep, that left knee again. How depressing.

This time I sprained the medial collateral ligament, missed the next two games, dressed but didn't play the following week, and saw very little action when I did come back against the Titans in mid-November.

The injury helped usher in a new era for the Steelers offense. We became primarily a throwing offense, partly out of necessity and partly because of Tommy, our wide receivers, and Zereoue, who was extremely fast, but really small (five eight, 205). With me out of the lineup, there wasn't a power running back to equalize the situation. The well-known Steelers' physical style of play disappeared a bit.

When I did come back, I had to wear a knee brace. There isn't a running back alive who wants to wear a knee brace, but I didn't have any choice. As it was, I was going to need surgery at the end of the season. If I wanted to finish out the 2002 season, I needed that brace to help stabilize the knee.

During my time out of the lineup I started to hear the rumblings from the media and fans.

He's getting old . . . He's only been healthy for five of the last fifteen games . . . He can't take the hits anymore.

I could take them. But I couldn't take them if my knee wasn't right. Nobody, young or old, could take those hits without two good knees. But patience was in short supply, especially with us scratching along with a 5–3–1 record.

The situation got worse for me as the playoffs approached. The knee wasn't close to 100 percent, but I was ready to give them what I could.

I mean, it was the postseason—you press on and do whatever you can do. Plus, Fu was injured and Zereoue was dinged up.

But as we prepared for the Wild Card game against the Browns it became obvious that I wasn't in the offensive plans. I was told privately that Amos was going to be the starter and I'd have to take a backseat.

For the first time in my playoff career, I was relegated to cheerleader duty because Coach Cowher didn't think I could do the job. That hurt.

Yeah, I was banged up, but I was healthy enough to handle more than the one carry they gave me in the win against the Browns. And I was healthy enough to carry the ball more than the three carries I got in the overtime loss to Tennessee in the Divisional Playoff.

I'll go to my grave believing that our reliance on a passing attack rather than a consistent running game is what hurt us the most that season. When you can't run the ball (we only had 89 rushing yards against the Browns and just 67 against the Titans) you can't control the clock and the tempo of the game. You become one dimensional, predictable.

Tommy did a great job leading us back from a seventeen-point deficit against the Browns, but at some point in the playoffs you have to win a game on the ground. We couldn't do that.

As if the Titans weren't tough enough to beat, we also had to deal with referee Ron Blum.

Blum is the guy who made one of the most terrible calls in the history of NFL playoff football. He threw a flag on Dewayne Washington for running into the kicker—even though he clipped Titans kicker Joe Nedney's ankle *after* Nedney missed a 31-yard overtime field goal by a mile. It was like this: Nedney kicked . . . Nedney missed . . . Washington bumped into his ankle . . . Nedney pretended to be hurt and collapsed to the ground . . . Blum threw the flag.

The Titans got another chance from 26 yards and this time Nedney made the game winner.

What a joke. Coach Cowher was so mad that he chased down Blum and screamed in his ear as they left the field. I guarantee you Blum had to towel off his ear after that tirade. But Blum was going by the letter of the rule, which was that Washington made "solid contact" with Nedney and knocked him down.

Yeah, he made contact, barely, and after the kick had already missed. Nedney himself said after the game that he should have gone into acting.

Maybe we would have ended up losing the game anyway, but it was terrible that Blum's bogus call is what decided who advanced to the AFC Championship.

Again, what was supposed to be a great season for us turned into another early postseason elimination. And because of my knee injury, I only ended up with 666 yards. It was the first time in my seven seasons with the Steelers that I didn't reach 1,000 yards or lead the team in rushing.

Then came another bombshell.

Three days after our season ended, Coach Cowher met with the local media and, without even being asked, volunteered that Kordell and I might not be back for the 2003 season. I knew Kordell was probably going to move on, but I didn't think they'd push me out the door too.

I still had four years left on my contract, but the Steelers were looking at ways to shake things up. If that meant releasing me so they'd have extra salary cap room, then the Steelers were going to consider it. And if I did come back, Coach Cowher made it clear to the media that I might be put into a different role. Translation: backup.

When the reporters asked me about what Coach said, I told them I planned to retire as a Steeler.

"I still think I have some football left in me," I said. "My whole career I've had to prove myself, so I don't see this year being any different."

High school. College. Pros. It never changed. As an NFL rookie you had to prove you could establish yourself. And as a ten-year veteran you had to prove you deserved to stay. That's how it works.

Nobody said it was fair. Two years earlier in training camp I had manipulated the business situation to my advantage. Now the Steelers were manipulating the situation to their advantage.

Of course, the Steelers couldn't release me just yet. If they did, then the remaining $4 million of my signing bonus would count against the salary cap. So they had to wait until June 1 to make a decision. That gave me time to have surgery on my knee (in February, Dr. Bradley removed a small piece of cartilage that had worked its way into my knee joint), rehab with Bob Kersee, and be ready for training camp—either with the Steelers or with another team.

As expected, Kordell became a free agent and signed a two-year $5 million deal with the Chicago Bears. And thus ended the "Slash" era in Pittsburgh.

Steelers fans were hard on Kordell, and sometimes they had a right to feel that way. But when Kordell was on, we were as good as anybody in the league. When he wasn't, we were average. He could win a game for us—and you can't say that about a lot of quarterbacks in the league.

The reality is that Kordell never really got an opportunity to develop as a quarterback. He became a jack of all trades, a master of none.

With Kordell you always ask yourself, "What if?" What if there had been a long-term commitment made to him by the coaching staff? What if he hadn't played wide receiver his rookie year and instead had concentrated on learning how to be an NFL quarterback? What if they had found an offensive coordinator who could have designed an offense to benefit Kordell? Poor Kordell had five different offensive coordinators—Ron Ehrhardt, Chan Gailey, Ray Sherman, Kevin Gilbride, and Mike Mularkey—in eight years.

And still, he was good enough to get us to the playoffs and to two AFC Championships. He was good enough to go 46–30 as a starter. Only Terry Bradshaw has thrown for more yards as a Steeler. And Kordell is still the thirteenth-leading rusher in team history.

Again, nothing against Tommy—he did a good job for us in 2002— but he was making $725,000 a year. The average salary for an NFL quarterback was almost $5.5 million. Even our backup quarterback, Charlie Batch, was making more money than Tommy. So do the math. I saw the situation develop with Kordell and the Steelers. I knew why they did what they did.

So Kordell, who was thirty (that magic number again), went to Chicago and it turned out to be a big mistake. I chewed him out about that one.

He had signed a short-term deal, figuring he'd play well and then cash a huge long-term contract. But the Bears were terrible. Terrible! Kordell was no help, but guess what? The guy who played quarterback after him didn't do any better.

As for me, the surgery had gone well and I was still confident I was going to be around. It wasn't like I was walking on eggshells about my future. I was thirty-one, but I could still play. Emmitt Smith, Tony Dorsett, and Walter Payton all had 1,200-plus-yards seasons when they were thirty-one.

When I reported to Steelers headquarters for my April weigh-in (yeah, I had a weight clause in my contract), I was down about ten pounds from the previous season. There were rumblings from some people within the organization that my weight was one of the reasons I had suffered so many injuries in the previous few years.

I wasn't fat, I was big. There's a difference. Plus, I don't remember hearing anybody question my weight when I was racking up those 1,000-yard seasons. The reality of the situation is this: Sometimes the body isn't meant to be twisted, pulled, and tackled a certain way. I could have weighed 215, and the same thing would have held true.

Earlier that month, there was also talk the Steelers might use their first-round pick on a running back. The media kept talking about Larry Johnson of Penn State.

Hey, if they wanted to draft a running back, that was fine with me. But our real need was at safety. And sure enough on draft day, the Steelers traded up to the sixteenth pick and took USC safety Troy Polamalu. Kansas City used our twenty-seventh pick to take Johnson. The Steelers didn't take a running back (Georgia fullback J. T. Wall) until the seventh round, so that should tell you something.

I knew I was going to have to fight for my starting position. Coach Cowher said there were "no guarantees" and that there were going to be some "very competitive situations" going into training camp. That meant Amos, Fu, and me would be playing for the same starting spot.

At least, that's what I thought it meant.

Instead, I later learned that Coach had basically made his decision in May to replace me with Amos. I showed up at camp thinking it was going to be an open competition, but in reality, the choice had already been made. He made it official the week of our third preseason game.

Coach Cowher had told *Post-Gazette* columnist Ron Cook in April that it looked like I had something to prove. But it's hard to prove something if you're not given a fair shake.

When Coach made the decision, he said it was based on a gut feeling. A gut feeling? I would have hoped I'd get the benefit of the doubt on gut feelings.

Maybe he was worried about my knee. Even though the surgery had been successful, the knee wasn't completely stable. I had to wear that damn knee brace from the start of training camp to the end of the season.

Still, I had to be a professional about the situation. So when the reporters asked me about being demoted, I said that I had been on the positive side of a lot of Coach Cowher's decisions, but now I was on the negative side. I didn't agree with the decision, but I accepted it. Now my job was to change his mind.

But the truth is, there was no competition for the job. That's what hurt me the most about the situation. It was like they were humoring me. They had already decided that they liked the offense they had at the end of the 2002 season: three wide receivers; a pocket-passer quarterback; a small, fast tailback who would supposedly allow them to strike from anywhere on the field. It was all about up-tempo, pass-the-ball offense.

Our offensive line had been built to run the ball, to wear down the opposition. So as a result of this philosophy change, we didn't spend our usual amount of time in training camp working on the running game. Instead, we were throwing the ball a lot. Pass, pass, pass.

That worked great until the actual regular season started. We beat the Ravens in the opener, but then got crushed during the first half of our schedule. Everybody was defending us against the pass, so when we tried to run the ball . . . nothing. We couldn't run it because we hadn't put the work into the running game during training camp. You just can't say, "OK, now we're going to flip the switch on our running attack."

The same team the experts picked to win the AFC North and make another run at the Super Bowl was 2–4 after six games. We were in shock. We had so much talent, but were playing like we didn't have a clue. And it only got worse.

Big and little things were killing us. For example, Amos wasn't exactly the hardest-working guy in practice. So I went to him and tried to offer some advice.

"Amos," I said, "what you have to understand is that you're the starter, and every day you have to show the coaches why they made the right decision. And I'll tell you why: Because every single day I'm trying to show them they made the wrong decision."

Had I been a selfish player, I would have kept that to myself. But because I never got the help when I was a young guy coming up, I felt that it was important to remind him about not getting complacent.

Amos listened, but he didn't take it to heart. He didn't understand the significance of getting that advice from a competitor. I warned him that I was coming to get his job. But he didn't work any harder and, subsequently, I got my starting position back.

By then our running game was among the worst in the league. We had lost our identity as a physical team. I take that back: Our offense had lost its identity as a physical attack, but our defense was showing signs of life.

Polamalu wasn't close to being a star yet, but you could see the potential. I remember when he first came to Pittsburgh. Some of the veterans were sizing him up and, to be honest, he wasn't the biggest guy in the world—five ten, 205 pounds or so (about ten pounds of it hair). There were a lot of expectations on him, especially after we had traded up to get him.

But Troy was quiet, *really* quiet. Rookies are like children—they're supposed to be seen, not heard. But Troy was extraordinarily quiet. He was whisper quiet.

Of course, he wasn't quiet when he hit you. No question you knew he was around then. But he struggled to understand our defense, and it wasn't until the latter part of the season that he started to figure it out. But once he figured it out, you could tell we had drafted the right guy.

We only won six games, so there weren't too many memorable moments. I led the team in rushing with 811 yards, which shows you how much we struggled to run the ball. Need more proof? We didn't have a 100-yard rusher until our December 7 game against Oakland. I gained 106 yards, which moved me past Thurman Thomas and into ninth place on the NFL's all-time rushing list.

I didn't know what to expect that day, but before the game tight end Mark Bruener and I were getting our ankles taped and he said, "You're going to cross the century mark today."

What made the day so gratifying, aside from the win, was the respect my teammates gave me. Bruener and my offensive linemen—Faneca, Jeff Hartings, Oliver Ross, Kendall Simmons, and Keydrick Vincent— started clapping and pumping their fists when the new career numbers were flashed on the Heinz Field scoreboard. And you should have heard them in the huddle when they found out I only needed 4 more yards to reach 100 for the game.

"You better run hard," they said.

So I ran hard and gained 5 yards.

Afterward, everybody was talking like I was deceased. Cook wrote in the *Post-Gazette* the next day: "This was probably Bettis' last big moment in Pittsburgh. Chances are less than 50–50 that the Steelers will bring him back next season. Even if he agrees to a pay cut and does come back, there's no guarantee he'll have enough left for another 100-yard day."

Surprise! I had 115 yards two games later against San Diego and ended the season with 54 yards against the Ravens at Baltimore—good enough to overtake the legendary Jim Brown at No. 6 on the all-time rushing list.

But I could understand why Cook wrote what he wrote and why some of my teammates weren't sure if I'd be back in 2004. Remember, when we did the original deal, nobody was sure I'd still be playing in 2004.

But I wasn't ready to quit just yet. I had 12,353 yards and just about all the individual honors I'd ever want. But I was missing one thing.

A championship ring.

9

Ben Roethlisberger is ten years younger than Bettis. They came from markedly different backrounds. They were the products of different football generations. They didn't even play the same position. And yet, no two players on the Steelers roster seemed to look out for each other like Roethlisberger and Bettis.

Bettis has scar marks older than Roethlisberger's high school yearbooks, but guess who was the first guy to make a rookie quarterback feel at home?

Roethlisberger takes it from here.

"I had known a lot about Jerome; everyone did. I was kind of in awe. He was this super icon of a football player.

"Right after the draft they had one of those mini-camps at our facility. I was standing there with two playbooks and some notebooks in my hands when he walks right up to me. He opens up my notebook to the first page and writes down his phone numbers. He says, 'This is my home number, this is my cell number. If you ever need anything, give me a call. Anything you want to buy, I've bought. Anywhere you want to go, I've gone. So if you need help with something, let me know.'

"When he walked away I was like, 'Wow, I can't believe that just happened.' I was so in awe. I even told my parents about it.

"I didn't call him right away, but eventually I did. At first, you're so scared and nervous. But with him, it's easy to get over that.

"People always said that me and Jerome had a special relationship. It just seemed like when we were around each other, we were laughing, joking around. It was almost like a combination of a big brother–little brother, father-son relationship.

"Now when the draft comes, I try to get the cell phone or home numbers of some of the players. I did that when we got Heath Miller and Santonio Holmes. I try to do what Bussie did and just say, 'If you ever need anything, call me.' "

Coach Cowher didn't waste any time when we met during the off-season to discuss my future with the Steelers. He said the team was going to draft a running back or sign one via free agency. Unlike the situation in 2003, this time he was totally up-front with me about my status. I appreciated the honesty. I didn't have any problem with them wanting to bring in another tailback. I probably would have done the same thing if I were them.

Then the Steelers asked me to take a pay cut, from the $3.75 million I was supposed to receive in 2004, to a more manageable $1 million (plus incentives). It wasn't a difficult decision: I took the pay cut. If I hadn't, the Steelers would have released me.

I was thirty-two, but I knew I was still capable of getting the job done. I also knew that from a long-term financial and post-career standpoint, I was better off staying in Pittsburgh. I was worth more in a Steelers helmet than I was in any other team's helmet. I was very conscious of that value and of my relationship with the Pittsburgh community. Plus—and it's a pretty simple reason—I liked it there. I liked the people. I liked the city. I liked my team.

I wasn't the only one who restructured his deal. Joey Porter and offensive tackle Marvel Smith also reworked their contracts. The Steelers were trying to create as much salary cap room as possible for when the free agent signing period began in early March (they also cut veterans Mark Bruener, Dewayne Washington, and Amos Zereoue during the off-season). The difference is, Joey and Marvel were guaranteed starting jobs, I wasn't.

About a week after I agreed to the pay cut, the Steelers signed free agent tailback Duce Staley to a four-year $14 million contract. So they had their starter.

Still, from a football standpoint, I was convinced nobody understood the Steelers rushing offense better than I did. I knew all the ins and outs. Deep down I knew I could work my way around a football field with the best of them, even in a diminished role and at a reduced rate.

Nobody likes to be told they aren't the No. 1 option anymore. But I had been through this before. So nothing they could say was going to shake me or break me. I had been to this dance before and had come out on top.

For all intents and purposes, this was my going-away present from the Steelers. It was like, "Hey, give him this million dollars for all the work he's done and how he's represented the franchise. We're not going to ask him to do much this year. He's going to be a reserve and this is his bonus for being a loyal and faithful Steeler."

The domino effect of Staley's signing was that the Steelers could then use the No. 11 overall pick on a quarterback. So they drafted big Ben Roethlisberger from Miami of Ohio. And after the draft, they signed a little-known free agent who had barely played at North Carolina: Willie Parker.

During training camp, word leaked that the Miami Dolphins had approached the Steelers about a trade. This was after Ricky Williams had violated the NFL's substance-abuse policy and then announced his retirement about a month before the season started. Dolphins coach Dave Wannstedt needed running back help. And he needed it fast.

But the Steelers passed on the possible offer, which told me two things: 1) People in the NFL didn't think I was washed up, and 2) I still had value to the Steelers. Otherwise, they would have traded me in a minute. They had Duce, but management wanted insurance. So I became Duce's $1-million insurance policy.

I wasn't upset when I heard the potential deal fell through. Even though Wannstedt was looking for a fifteen-carry-a-game veteran, I knew once I got there people would want the Bettis of 2001, not the Bettis of 2004. They'd want a guy who could tote it thirty times a game. I probably could have toted it that much, but it would have been my last year in the league because that many carries would have killed me. At that stage of my career, it was better for my quality of life to stay where I was.

I could tell during the off-season, when I was grinding it out in my workouts with Kersee in hot, humid St. Louis, that my left knee felt incredibly good. It was so strong and stable that I didn't need to wear a knee brace anymore. I hated that brace. You look like damaged goods when you wear one of those things.

Still, with all the money the Steelers had spent on Duce, it was obvious the starting job was his. My job was to do everything I could to get him ready for the season. And to be ready if he got injured.

Duce came into training camp with an incredible attitude. He was nice enough to acknowledge my career, my accomplishments, and everything I stood for. He said he was looking forward to working with me and would do whatever was necessary to help the Steelers win games. I was impressed. Here's a veteran who knew he had the job, but he still took time to embrace me as a teammate and to offer his respect. That was big. And it was a lesson that Amos never learned when he was with the Steelers.

You would think there might have been some tension between Duce and me, but there was none. I had the utmost respect for his game, and he had a similar respect for my game. We actually developed a friendship, and I did everything I could to bring him up to speed on the nuances of our offense. He was an easygoing guy, a pro's pro.

Meanwhile, I wasn't doing too bad myself. In fact, the coaches' eyes were bulging out when they saw the way I was moving on the field. During one of our practices, I made an incredible cut during a goal-line play and Coach Cowher couldn't believe it.

"You're gonna run goal-line," he said, meaning that I'd be on the field for any short-yardage or goal-line situations. Then he told our beat reporters that this was the best I had looked in the last three years. And he was right.

Coach Cowher kept his promise. Duce got the start in our season opener against the Oakland Raiders (where Amos had signed after the Steelers released him), but I got the touchdowns—three of them, to be exact. It was the strangest statistical box score I'd ever had: 5 carries, 1 yard, 3 touchdowns.

The strangeness continued the following week when Ben was forced into the starting lineup after Tommy hurt his right elbow during the third quarter of our game at Baltimore. We didn't have any choice. Charlie Batch had been placed on injured reserve during training camp because of a leg injury.

Ben made some mistakes (two interceptions), but he also made some plays (two touchdown throws). We lost the game, though, and there were a lot of questions about the rest of our season.

So now Ben was our quarterback. I liked the kid, but nobody knew how he'd react under pressure. He was a rookie quarterback, and rookie quarterbacks usually get you beat. His last start had been almost eleven months earlier against the University of Louisville in the GMAC Bowl. Facing the Dolphins at their place was going to be a lot harder than beating Louisville in Mobile, Alabama.

I remember when I first saw him in training camp: big kid, big feet—size 14 shoe. He had a strong arm and he ran around a lot. But that's normal for rookie QBs because they usually don't know who the hell to throw the ball to. They've got that glassy, confused look in their eyes. They make their first read, but if the first read breaks down, they're lost, so they run. At the time, I didn't know running the ball was part of his game.

The truth is, when Tommy got hurt it was like the whole team said to itself, "Damn, here we go." Everybody was down in the dumps, especially when the news came back that he'd miss at least six weeks. Under normal circumstances, Ben would have spent the year on the bench. We were a veteran team primed for a postseason run. But that was before Tommy got hurt.

A reporter asked Faneca if he was excited about Ben becoming the starter. And Alan said no, he wasn't excited about it at all. With a rookie quarterback, opposing defenses were going to crowd the box and dare Ben to beat them with the pass. They were going to blitz. They were going to try to freak him out. Why would anybody be excited about that scenario?

Alan took some grief for the comments, but he spoke the truth. We figured the season was over for us. No way were we going to win with a rookie QB. You could chisel that in stone.

A rookie quarterback doesn't know what the hell is going on. In Ben's case, he had just gotten to camp five or six weeks earlier. He didn't really know the plays, much less the defenses he was going to see. So we were just being realistic when it came to Ben leading our team. It wasn't personal; we just didn't think any rookie quarterback could handle that type of situation.

Turns out we were wrong.

Ben, I apologize for doubting you.

In his first career NFL start he had to overcome the weather, the hostile crowd, the Dolphins, and his nerves. We won the game, 13–3, thanks to a scoring drive he led late in the fourth quarter.

The next week we beat Cincinnati and Duce gained 123 yards, while I put up some more funny numbers: 6 carries, 9 yards, 2 touchdowns. But leading up to that game, some of the reporters started to ask why I was getting all the touchdowns when Duce was doing all the work? To them, it was like Duce built a house all by himself, but I was the one who got to live in it.

Anyway, after I scored my second touchdown of the game I started hearing boos. It took a few moments, but then I realized Steeler fans—*at my home stadium*—were booing me for scoring a touchdown. I was so angry that you could have grilled a hamburger on my forehead.

These people thought I was taking away Duce's thunder, when all I was really doing was my job. I hadn't asked for the short-yardage scoring role; Coach Cowher *told* me to do it, so I did it to the best of my ability. And considering all the things I had done throughout my Steelers career, I felt I didn't deserve those boos.

What was supposed to be a positive situation—Duce starts, I come in on short-yardage downs—had turned into a negative thing. I was very upset about the criticism, and I said so publicly. That, along with several newspaper stories explaining my role on the team, helped end the booing. But it should have never come to that.

Meanwhile, we were winning games and Ben was making believers of us all. By the time we played Philadelphia in early November, Ben was 5–0 as a starter and we were 6–1 as a team. As every week went by—and every win came—his confidence grew, as did ours in him.

This was no ordinary rookie. He was making plays and winning games, which is something you don't see on a regular basis from a lot of veteran quarterbacks, much less from a rookie quarterback. He even helped end New England's NFL-record, 21-game winning streak by completing 18 of 24 passes for 196 yards and two touchdowns in our October 31 victory against the Patriots.

During our bye week leading up to that game, I had appeared on CBS' *The NFL Today*. I said I hoped the Patriots were still unbeaten when they came to Pittsburgh. No big deal.

But Patriots linebacker Willie McGinest thought it was a big deal and took a shot at me. "I thought Duce Staley was their running back," he told reporters. "I didn't even know Bettis still played for the Steelers."

Think he knew after the game? We beat New England and I had 65 yards on fifteen carries. McGinest had one tackle.

Everything was going great until just a few days before our game against the Eagles. During Friday's practice, Duce tweaked his hamstring while running a screen play. The doctors said he was 50–50 for Sunday, but with a little rest between then and the game, who knows? Duce wanted to play. The Eagles were his former team and they entered the game with an unbeaten record. So you know he had some incentive to put on a show for them.

But on Sunday, while I was driving to Heinz Field, I got a phone call from Duce.

"J.B.," he said, "I can't go today."

I felt bad for Duce because this game was so important to him.

"Don't worry, I got your back," I said. "I'll make sure we take care of business."

By the time I pulled into the stadium parking lot I was beginning to feel that adrenaline rush. It was showtime. I couldn't wait.

When I walked into the locker room, Coach Hoak was waiting for me.

"Duce can't go," he said. "You're going to start, but Verron is going to get a couple of series. He's going to play."

Nothing against Verron Haynes, but I couldn't believe what I had just heard. Coach Hoak was basically telling me the coaching staff didn't think I could do the job for the whole game. They already had their contingency plan, Verron, in place, and they weren't shy about telling me.

I was infuriated because after eight-plus years of carrying the load for the Steelers, my own coaches didn't think I was capable of doing that for at least one more game.

I was fired up for that game. I mean, I ran with some *anger*. Coach Cowher and Coach Hoak wanted proof? How about me going berserk for 149 yards and thirty-three carries against the Eagles?

We beat Philly, 27–3, and they pulled me late in the game. That's when they let Verron have a bite to eat, but only after the game was decided. He had spelled me for a play here and there, but I had a point to make that day, and I made it. In fact, after the game I told Coach Cowher, "That's the reason you kept me."

Then I gave him more reasons: 149 yards in the win against Philly (and you had to go back to 2000 to find a thirty-three-carry game for me), 103 in the win at Cleveland, 129 in the win at Cincinnati, 100 yards in the win against Washington. Four starts, four 100-yard games, four victories.

The win at Cleveland was memorable because Jim Brown, one of the guys I really admired, came over to me during warm-ups, shook my hand, and said he liked the way I played the game. That's like Picasso telling you he likes the way you hold a paintbrush. I was honored that he was there for the game.

And the game at Cincy is where I passed Tony Dorsett and moved into fifth place on the all-time rushing list. To pass Dorsett, who had played for my favorite childhood team, was another big honor for me.

I was in a pretty good mood after that Washington game. But two days later came the shocking news that my alma mater had embarrassed itself by firing Tyrone Willingham as its head coach.

I still get upset just thinking about it. There's no question Tyrone got the rawest deal ever of any head football coach at Notre Dame. For the first time in the history of the program, they fired a coach after only three years. That means Tyrone had the shortest tenure of any noninterim Irish coach in seventy years. Unlike the coaches before him, he wasn't allowed to finish out his contract.

It was a sad situation. It was also the first time in my career that I was ashamed of having gone to Notre Dame.

I was ashamed because of the hypocrisy and double standard used by the men who made the decision to fire Tyrone. I'll never understand why some of the worst Notre Dame football coaches were given the chance to finish out their five-year contracts, but Tyrone—who was the Coach of the Year in 2002, who had the same number of wins after three seasons as Bob Davie did, and who had more wins in his first season than the guy who succeeded him, Charlie Weis—is the one who got fired.

Notre Dame also didn't distinguish itself with all the shady business that went down before the firing, the controversy after the firing, and the confusion about the search for a new coach. It was so ridiculous. If you're going to give a coach the quick hook based partly on the opportunity to get Urban Meyer, then you damn well better get Urban Meyer. But they got outsmarted and outmaneuvered by the Florida athletic director. They should have had their man locked up before they made a move.

I'm not saying Ty was the perfect coach. In a way, he was the wrong coach for that time. That's because you've got two kinds of coaches: coaches who build programs and coaches who maintain programs.

Ty would have been better following a guy like Coach Holtz. Coach Holtz was a builder of programs. Ty is a maintainer of programs. He's got a no-nonsense, disciplined style that is perfect for keeping a program stable and successful.

But to build a program you've got to have a little different type of demeanor. You've got to be able to convince players that the old way didn't work, that you've got to blow everything up, and that the new way will work better. So that's going to take a guy who probably is more fiery, more confrontational, more willing to get in a player's face. I'm not saying Ty can't do that, but it isn't his natural demeanor. He's more calm, cool, and controlled.

But even if you weren't a Ty supporter—and I was, and still am—the man at least deserved to see one of his recruiting classes become seniors. Davie got that courtesy. Gerry Faust got that courtesy. Charlie Weis is going to get that courtesy. That's all a coach wants: the chance to win or lose with his own guys. Ty never got the chance to coach his own seniors.

Meanwhile, Weis, who we faced when he was the Patriots' offensive coordinator, is having a lot of success with guys that Ty recruited. Based on how Charlie has done during his first two seasons at Notre Dame, you can argue that letting Ty go turned out to be the right move. And maybe those people are right. But it still doesn't change the fact that Notre Dame treated Tyrone Willingham shamefully and with disrespect. And I say that as a person who proudly endowed a Notre Dame academic scholarship for students from inner-city Detroit, LA, and St. Louis.

In my opinion, race was a part of the equation. There's no question in my mind it played a part in what happened. Here's Tyrone, an African-American at the largest, highest profile university in the country. It was a delicate decision to hire him in the first place (he was the first black head coach in any sport to be hired by the university), but Notre Dame did so and received acclaim and accolades for the bold move. And Ty rewarded that trust with a 10–3 record in his first year.

But ultimately it became apparent that Ty was on a shorter leash than his white predecessors. The proof is indisputable: He wasn't given close to the same amount of time to build a program as those white coaches before him. This is just simple fact. All the other coaches were given at least five years. Ty wasn't.

Don't get me wrong. I've got nothing against Charlie. I love Charlie and the job he's done. I've had a chance to meet him and he's a great guy. I think he's a great fit for the university.

My anger is directed toward the people who made the decision to fire Ty. As an African-American who attended Notre Dame and loves what it stands for, I'll always be embarrassed by that decision.

OK, that felt good to get that off my chest.

Remember what I said about rookies having to establish themselves? In my mind, Ben established himself in that win against Washington. When I stepped into the huddle, I no longer saw the glassy-eyed, dazed look of Training Camp Ben. Now I saw a totally different person. I saw and heard confidence in the way he called a play. He was a rookie, sure, but he was a damn good rookie.

He was sacked eight times at Cincy, but he didn't fall apart. He completed only nine passes against the Redskins, but he didn't throw any interceptions. And the week after the Washington game, he had a near-perfect performance (158.0 passer rating—158.3 is the best you can have) while leading us to a one-point win at Jacksonville. He was doing so well that Dick's Sporting Goods stores in Pittsburgh started selling an "official" Ben Roethlisberger T-shirt.

One of the main reasons Ben had been successful was our running game. We had ditched the pass-oriented philosophy of 2003 and gone back to what the Steelers did best: run the ball. Our ball-control offense shortened games and took some of the pressure off Ben. We were the second-best rushing team in the NFL, compared to next-to-last in 2003.

As for my role, I went back to the bullpen when Duce returned to the starting lineup against the Jaguars. And I was there the following game against the New York Jets, when New York's Curtis Martin bumped me from fifth to sixth on the career rushing list. Martin got fifth place; we got the win.

But then Duce's hamstring injury flared up again and I got the start against the New York Giants. Thirty-six carries and 140 yards later, we picked up another victory.

We just kept winning and winning. We became the first Steelers team, including those four Pittsburgh Super Bowl teams from the seventies, to win twelve in a row. *Post-Gazette* columnist Gene Collier asked me if it was the best Steelers team ever. I told him it was the best team I'd been on, but it hadn't done near enough to compare with the championship Pittsburgh teams stocked with Hall of Famers.

I started against the Ravens (twenty-seven carries, 117 yards—my first 100-yard game against those guys since 1997) and temporarily moved ahead of Martin and permanently ahead of Eric Dickerson as the fourth-leading rusher in NFL history. Moving into third place was out of the question. I had 13,294 yards and No. 3 Barry Sanders had 15,269 yards. Sorry, but The Bus didn't have that much gas left in the tank.

In fact, just to be on the safe side, I didn't play at Buffalo in our final regular season game because of a sprained ankle. The decision might have cost me a 1,000-yard season (I finished with 941 yards and a career-high thirteen touchdowns), but it also gave me two weeks to rest for our first playoff game.

Everything had worked out perfectly. Ben got to sit out the Bills game so his bruised ribs could heal. A lot of veterans also played sparingly against Buffalo, which meant a lot of the reserves got some valuable time. And with the league's best record (15–1), we had the home-field advantage throughout the playoffs. You couldn't have asked for a better postseason setup.

One of those reserves who had played against Buffalo was the rookie Willie Parker. Willie hadn't seen much action during the season, but he introduced himself to the NFL that day against the Bills with a nineteen-carry, 102-yard game.

As far back as training camp, I had been impressed with Willie. I've seen free agent running backs come and go, but he was different. Most free agent running backs come into camp and you can tell right away that they can't make the transition physically from college to the pros.

Willie wasn't like that. He was physical enough, and he was plenty fast enough, but he was also raw. He had the natural talent, but he just needed the work. For a guy who basically didn't play in college, he looked really good.

We played the Jets in the Divisional Playoff and barely squeaked by, 20–17. If Jets kicker Doug Brien hadn't missed each of his two field goal attempts in the final 2:02 of regulation, who knows if we could have tied the game? Instead, we got a reprieve and beat them in overtime.

The reprieve only lasted one week. The Patriots crushed us at home in the AFC Championship game, 41–27.

I wanted to cry. In fact, I did cry. Ben and I were both crying on the sidelines after the game.

Ben had had a terrible game. His very first pass had been intercepted, and he ended up throwing two more to kill drives. We had more first downs, more net yards, more plays, more rushing yards, more passing yards, and more time of possession than the Patriots. But they had zero interceptions, zero fumbles lost (to our one), and they took advantage of almost every mistake we made.

My best and probably last chance at a Super Bowl was gone. My career was probably finished.

As we were both boo-hooing, Ben pleaded with me, "J.B., just stay with me one more year. Give me one more year and I promise I'll get you to the Super Bowl."

Ben was distraught, so I knew this was the emotions of the moment coming out. He was a young guy just sick about the game and he was talking. He was blaming himself for the loss and he wanted to make it up to me and everybody else. Hey, I had been in that situation in the past, so I knew what he was going through.

> *"I remember sitting by him on the bench. For him to be so disappointed . . . I had tears in my eyes just sitting there thinking I had let him down. That's when I said, 'Jerome, if you give me another chance, I promise I'll do better. I'll do everything I can to get you to a Super Bowl.'*
>
> *"I can't really recall the last time I ever cried. And I do think some of it was just me feeling bad about the way I played. But I really wanted to do better for him."*
>
> —Ben Roethlisberger

But Ben's promise didn't really resonate with me. I had too many other things on my mind.

When I got home that night I had a conversation with myself. The best team I had ever been a part of couldn't reach the Super Bowl. And we hadn't reached it in 1997 or 2001. So as I sat there, it became obvious that me and Super Bowls were never meant to be together. It wasn't in God's plans and you know what? I was sort of OK with that.

Slowly but surely I began to make peace with the situation. I had to, otherwise I wouldn't have been able to live my day-to-day life. I didn't want to be one of those bitter, What-if? people. Those kind of people go crazy. Those kind of people jump out of windows.

And even though it had been an emotional time right after the game, this latest loss didn't hurt nearly as bad as the ones in '97 and '01. That had to be a sign, right?

So the reality was this: I was going to walk away from the game without ever having played in a Super Bowl or having won a championship.

Opening kickoff of a Super Bowl—all you see are the camera flashes. The place just explodes in light. I always got goose bumps thinking about those cameras being aimed at me and my team on that field one day. In fact, I always told myself that I would never go to a Super Bowl until I played in one.

Well, I had to break that promise during the 2001 season, when the Patriots beat the Rams in Super XXXVI at the Superdome in New Orleans. I had to be there for a Visa appearance, but I purposely made sure not to arrive at the stadium suite until after kickoff. I didn't want to see somebody else's flashing lights. They weren't mine, so I didn't want to see them.

I always used to ask myself, "Is having seen the lights better than never having seen them at all?" And my answer was always, "I wish I would have just seen the lights one time for my team. Just seen them flashing *one* time."

So on the night of January 23, 2005, I went to sleep thinking that I had just played my last game. I had asked myself the question, "Am I done?" And the answer was yes . . . probably.

The next morning we had our final team meeting at the Steelers' headquarters in the UPMC Sports Performance Complex. Coach Cowher always had one of these meetings after our last game.

This time I asked him if I could talk to the team after he was done speaking.

"Guys," I said, "I want to thank every player here for being a great teammate to me. I want to thank the coaches for giving me an opportunity. And if this was the last game I played, I'm glad I played it with you guys. It meant a lot to me to call you my teammates and to call you my friends."

There wasn't a dry eye in the house, including mine. I was crying so much, I'm not sure how I got the words out. It was such an emotional moment for me.

Before I left, Coach Cowher asked me what I was thinking in terms of returning for the 2005 season. I told him I wasn't sure, though, in truth, I had basically made up my mind.

"Well, take your time," he said. "I just want you to know that we want you back."

His saying that meant something to me. So did a conversation I had with Howie Long late in the season. He had come to town to present me with a Tough Man award and a new truck. We started talking and he asked me if I was thinking about calling it quits. I told him I was.

"If you still love the game and want to play, then play," he said. "If you don't, you'll never forgive yourself."

Howie's advice made sense. And with Coach Cowher saying he wanted me back, and to take my time, I started to reconsider my preliminary decision.

I had left Steelers headquarters that day thinking it was 90–10, I was retiring. But then I got home, turned on the news, and there was an interview with Hines after our team meeting. Hines was crying like a newborn, saying that the team wanted to win a Super Bowl for me, that I deserved one, that I meant a lot to them.

Man, when Hines said that, it sent a chill down my spine. It was such a touching gesture on his part.

A day or so later I left Pittsburgh for Atlanta. That's where my fiancée, Trameka, was about to give birth to our first child. It was the perfect way to distance myself from the Steelers situation and focus on my family.

Trameka and I had met in 2000, and it wasn't exactly love at first sight when I introduced myself to her. For her, it was more like, "Get out of my sight."

I was vacationing in South Beach and a friend and I decided to make an appearance at a local party. That's when I saw Trameka. I tried to put my smooth moves on her. I said some things that were a little bit flirtatious and pretty silly. Needless to say, I didn't charm her. She walked away.

I happened to see Trameka the next day, so I walked up to her and said, "I really screwed up. I apologize for being so rude." And then I left. I knew we'd probably never see each other again, but I thought I owed her an apology for my slightly risqué comments the night before.

About seven or eight months later, I was in Atlanta doing a photo shoot for Coca-Cola. That night I was at a club when I ran into a friend who said she wanted to introduce me to someone. So I met her friend, but it didn't go well.

"I've met you before," she said, "but I don't think it was very pleasant what you said to me."

"Well, I think I would remember meeting you," I said.

"In Miami," she said.

Oh, no. My jaw nearly bounced off the floor. It was Trameka.

I composed myself and then came up with an idea: I would pretend the first meeting had never taken place. So I said, "How you doing? My name is Jerome."

It worked. In fact, I even got a little smile out of Trameka. Reintroducing myself—this time without the smooth moves—got us off on a better foot. It was the beginning of a five-year courtship.

One of the things that initially impressed me about Trameka was that she walked away from me during the party at South Beach. She's very strong willed, very organized. She knows what she wants—and there's no question she didn't want any part of me or my smooth moves the first time we met.

Our relationship slowly grew to the point where I found myself confiding in her more and more. But there were ups and downs. Going out with a professional athlete isn't the same as going out with a CPA. I lived in two worlds: the everyday world and the NFL world. And sometimes those two worlds didn't fit together very well.

At first, it was hard for Trameka to understand why I spent so much time with my teammates off the field. She didn't understand that an NFL team is a strange, forced mixture of personalities, backgrounds, and ages. As a team leader, I had to help everybody on the roster find a common ground that went beyond winning or losing a ballgame. We had to trust and believe in one another. We had to fight for one another. And through this shared experience of bleeding together, sweating together, laughing together, and competing together we would become a real team.

So if that meant hanging out with the offensive linemen one night, or spending quality video time with the younger running backs after practice, or making myself available to any player who just wanted to shoot the bull, then that's what I did. Trameka had a rough time under-standing my role early on, but eventually she did.

I was always honest with Trameka. I told her I already had a wife, and it was football. Football and I had been married for a long time and I wasn't ready for an NFL divorce. Yet.

Trameka wasn't crazy about the situation, but she accepted that foot-ball was my life. I loved her, but I told her I couldn't commit to some-thing as important as marriage until I was done playing football. Football was not only my first wife, it was my only wife. But once foot-ball was finished, I'd be ready for my next wife.

I finally popped the question at the annual Carson Scholars Fund benefit in Pittsburgh. The event was held at the Level Club Lounge in the Strip District of town. The benefit took place on the upper level of the the nightclub, and the lower level was where I arranged to spring my surprise.

During the benefit I asked Trameka to come downstairs to the lower level club. The place was empty except for me, her, and a deejay I had hired to play our favorite song. When the deejay cued up the music, I asked Trameka if she'd dance with me. And in the middle of the dance, I dropped to one knee and asked if she would marry me.

Trameka had tears in her eyes and, lucky for me, she didn't leave me on the hook. She immediately said yes to my marriage proposal. I slipped the engagement ring on her finger (I had done some pre-engagement scouting work) and just like that, it was official.

We welcomed our daughter, Jada, into the world on January 28, 2005, just five days after the AFC Championship defeat. She was seven weeks premature, so she couldn't come home from the hospital for about ten days. But what an incredible moment. I was in the delivery room when she was born. In fact, I snipped the umbilical cord. Let me tell you, I had a better appreciation for Trameka—and all women, for that matter—who endure the pain of childbirth. She was tough.

It was just amazing to know that I was a father. You can never un-derstand a parents' love for their children until you become a parent yourself. Looking down at this baby girl—my daughter—was a life-changing experience for me. She was my responsibility. I had a family

now. It was a totally different situation. Football was no longer the pri-
mary focus of my life.

The moment I saw Jada, it was like all of the negative feelings I had
about our season and the playoff loss temporarily vanished. I felt reju-
venated. Her arrival really boosted my spirits and turned one of the
worst times of my life into one of the best moments almost overnight.
She was such a blessing.

Of course, I immediately called my mom and dad with the news. I told
them they had a healthy baby granddaughter. And then I called Jahmal.

"Man, she's here," I said. "I've got a beautiful daughter, man."

"Did you stand at the bottom, man?" he said. "Did you catch?"

"Yeah, I caught," I said.

"Then you did it," he said. "You caught and cut."

*"That was a crazy time. Jada wasn't supposed to come for an-
other six weeks or so. We had so many business commitments.
And Lou Oppenheim and I were looking at TV deals for Jerome.
ESPN and CBS were interested, but they weren't going to make a
commitment until he announced his retirement.*

*"I was 80 to 90 percent sure he was done. And if he would have
had a TV opportunity come up after the 2004 season, he wouldn't
have played again. He wouldn't have played."*

—*Jahmal Dokes*

We finally brought her home on a Tuesday and that same day I got a
phone call from the NFL office. They told me Corey Dillon had a broken
rib and wouldn't be able to play in the Pro Bowl. Since I was the first al-
ternate, they wanted to know if I would take his place on the roster.

My daughter had just come home. The last thing I could do was
leave for Hawaii and play in the Pro Bowl. I told the guy no, but just to
be polite, I said that I would talk it over with Trameka.

"Baby, you won't believe this," I said to her. "The NFL just called
and asked me to go to the Pro Bowl."

"And what did you tell them?" she said.

"I said no, but told them to call me back in an hour after I talked to you."

"Well, you know, if this is your last opportunity because you're done
playing—or even if you're not done—you probably won't ever get another
chance to go to a Pro Bowl again. You should go. I'll take care of Jada."

THE BUS ◆ 159

I was like, wow. I would have never expected that reaction. But the more I thought about it—and the more Trameka insisted that I go—the more intrigued I became.

"How many running backs in their twelfth year get to play in a Pro Bowl?" she said.

"I don't know."

"Go look it up," she said.

Well, I wasn't going to look it up, but she had made her point. It was a rare opportunity and honor, so, with her blessings, I told the league to add me to the AFC roster.

What I didn't realize at the time was that eight other Steelers— Hines, Faneca, Polamalu, Joey, Marvel, Aaron Smith, Jeff Hartings, and James Farrior—were also on the Pro Bowl roster. And those guys brought over other Steelers teammates, just like I had brought Lester over when I had made the team earlier in my career.

There were so many Steelers personnel and coaches there that Mr. Rooney threw a dinner for us in Honolulu. During that dinner—actually, during the entire week—those twenty or so guys just bombarded me with pressure to come back for another season. Every time I saw Larry Foote, he said, "Bussie, you've got to come back. You've just got to come back." Clark Haggans would tell me, "Man, you can't leave. You can't go."

And these were the guys on defense. Faneca would slip in his little comments all the time, and Hartings would hit me with all these philosophical questions and theories. He would say, "You said earlier that you would at least think about coming back, so that means the door isn't closed, right? So where are your thoughts now?"

After a week of the constant questions, they had worn me down to a nub. They had me isolated in Honolulu, so that helped their cause. Plus, I was genuinely moved by their efforts.

On the plane back to Atlanta I was probably 60–40 in favor of returning for the 2005 season. That was a complete turnaround from when I was on the plane to Hawaii.

But I still hadn't made up my mind. Maybe that's why Hines was relentless whenever I talked to him.

"A lot of guys really didn't want to ask him if he was coming back. Not me.

"His birthday is in the middle of February and mine is in early

March. So we met in Vegas to sort of celebrate. We were playing blackjack and I kept saying, 'I know you got another year . . . I know you got another year.'

"He started getting annoyed by it. But I was like a little brother to him. So I kept saying, 'You got another year.' "

—*Hines Ward*

There was no Big Moment when I decided to come back. One day I just said to myself, "OK, I want to do this. I want to take one more shot at it."

Trameka's insistence that I go to the Pro Bowl might have been the difference. If I hadn't gone to Hawaii and been around those guys during that week, I'm not sure I would have returned to the Steelers. I would have been home with my bride-to-be, with my baby daughter, and beginning to make that off-season transition from football player to family man. Being home would have shifted my priorities, probably to the point where I could have walked away from the game. So that Pro Bowl trip probably sealed the deal for me. It made a humongous difference.

It also helped that Super Bowl XL was going to be played in my hometown, Detroit. There were no guarantees we'd even reach the Super Bowl, but the thought crossed my mind that it would be a shame if the Steelers made it to Ford Field and I wasn't there with them.

I finally told Trameka that I probably was going to play in 2005.

"Oh, you know you're going to play," she said playfully.

"Yeah," I said, "I'm gonna play."

"After the season I asked him if he was coming back. He said, 'Mom, you know what? I don't know. If I had to answer them right now, it would be no. My body is hurting. It's starting to take its toll on me. I don't feel that I'm effective out there. I don't think I want to go to camp.'

"I had been silently praying for him to retire, and now he was starting to feel that way. I wanted him to retire.

"If he had had the ring, he would have been gone. That ring meant the world to him. Whenever he talks about how important a ring was, believe it—that's gospel. But I guess I didn't understand the ring issue, how deeply he wanted that ring."

—*Gladys Bettis*

Fourth Quarter

✦ 10 ✦

Willie Parker was a no-name, will-never-make-it-on-the-roster longshot when the Steelers signed him as a free agent in 2004. For no particular reason other than his University of North Carolina coaches didn't think he was good enough, Parker had a grand total of forty-eight carries during his senior year. Not one of those carries came on Senior Day.

In 2005, he gained more yards with the Steelers—1,202—than he did during his entire four-year career at Carolina. Several years earlier, as he sat on the bench for his Senior Day game, Parker had written on his wristband, "I'm gonna make it."

He did. With a little assist from Bettis.

"When I actually first reported to mini-camp with the other free agents and draft picks, I was saying, 'Where's Jerome? Where's Jerome?' I wanted to see Jerome Bettis. I wanted to see some of the bigger names and faces. But on the first day, nothing.

"The next day we were walking down the road from the Steelers' headquarters to the UPMC training center when we saw someone fly by in a Ferrari down the road. Someone said, 'Who's that?' I said, 'It had to be Jerome.'

"When we did meet him, he was kind and polite. He introduced himself, said he was looking forward to working with all of us. Later on down the line, he explained to me what happened with him and Cleveland Gary. He kind of raised me, taught me. He said that one day I had to teach the younger players.

"During practices I could tell he was kind of studying me. He had never seen me play before, so he was sort of analyzing my game. He started to point out my weaknesses and my strengths. He threw darts at me. He threw darts at me for the longest time. He didn't want to give me praise at first.

"We'd be at practice and he'd tell me I was running the ball too fast, that I wasn't reading my Three Technique. A Three Technique is basically the running back reading what the defensive tackle is doing. He would ask me, 'What made you do what you just did?'

"I didn't know. I was just free-balling out there.

"He said, 'Young buck, that's not how it's supposed to be. You're making plays. It's not bad, mind you. But that 10-yard run can be a 30-yard run. You and me, we're going to watch some tape after practice.' So he would take me in and get some cut-ups, and we'd watch tape together, just him and me.

"I didn't play much in college. But that's the thing about Jerome. He's such a wonderful guy to take an interest in someone like me. Maybe he saw something in me. He'd say, 'You mean to tell me you didn't play at UNC? How many yards did you have? What was the problem?'

"He didn't have to do any of this. I ended up starting and he could have easily just let me be. He could have let me play the way I played, and not corrected me. Instead, he kind of took me under his wing. Sometimes when I'd make a mistake, he used to get mad and say, 'I ain't helping you out anymore. Don't ask me for anything.'

"But he was always there for everything.

"When I was growing up I was stuck on Barry Sanders and Emmitt Smith. I'd get the remote and watch them every Sunday. I thought they were the best. But being around Jerome really changed how I thought. Jerome was a great running back. He's got the quickest feet I've ever seen on a big guy. I always told him that I wished I would have been watching him a little earlier in my life.

"Jerome worked so hard all the time. One time I asked him what motivated him. He said, 'The will to be great.' "

✦   ✦   ✦

It was early July, it was equator hot, and I was soaked in sweat after one of my killer training sessions at a St. Louis high school track with Kersee. That's when I realized I might have made a terrible mistake.

"What in the freakin' world are you doing?" I said to myself between sprints. "What are you doing on this track? You're supposed to be retired."

That's the problem with sticking your foot in the retirement waters and then pulling it out at the last minute. My mind started to get used to the idea of calling it a career, but then it had to readjust to the reality of one final season.

This was my first encounter with buyer's remorse, but it wasn't my last. During training camp, Duce hurt his knee and had to undergo surgery. So it looked like he wasn't going to be ready for the season opener. That meant I would be the starter. That was fine. I'd been the relief pitcher before. No problem.

But in our next-to-last preseason game, I took a counter step to fake a run and that's when I felt a pop. At first it felt like somebody had hit me in the leg or like the referee had thrown the penalty flag at my right calf. But then the pain arrived and I fell to the ground.

As I lay on the turf, a single thought entered my mind: "Oh, my goodness, I just tore my Achilles'." If so, I was done.

But the training staff came out on the field, looked me over and said it was my calf, not my Achilles'. That was close. So they helped get me on my feet and I limped to the sidelines.

Buyer's Remorse Instance No. 2 came when I was sitting on the bench, my leg propped up and the calf hurting like hell. I said to myself, "Man, you got no business here in the first damn place. Your ass should be at home. Your body is starting to break down. Look at you. This is exactly what you didn't want to have happen."

The next day I got the news: I was out anywhere from three to six weeks.

This Farewell Tour Season was already a disaster. But you know what? I was in it for the long haul. I had taken another pay cut and I was committed to my teammates and coaches. But I have to admit, part of me was saying, "You stupid."

Even though I couldn't play, I still had plenty to do, such as helping the new No. 1 tailback. See, we were without Duce, without me, and our replacement was a guy who had a total of one career NFL starts.

We were going to have to depend on Willie Everette Parker, aka, Fast Willie.

I was frustrated about my injury, but there wasn't much I could do about the recovery time. What I could do was tutor Willie. My role suddenly changed from player to player/coach. After all, Coach Hoak could only give Willie so much information. But I could give Willie a veteran player's insight into our offense, into opposing defenses, and into the nuances of playing the position. Willie was a gifted runner, but it takes more than physical talent to succeed in our league.

Plus, I had a vested interest in seeing Willie succeed. If he flopped, then we were going to have problems winning games. And I hadn't come back in 2005 so we could finish 7–9. I needed him to perform well until the calvalry—Duce and I—arrived.

We opened the season at Heinz Field against Tennessee, and it was the first time, not counting when my leg was completely numb, that I didn't watch the opening kickoff from our sidelines. Instead, I decided to give myself a different vantage point. So I went upstairs to the stadium suite I leased each season for my family and tried to watch the game with them.

I couldn't do it. I tried, I really did. I thought going up there would be a good way of coming to terms with my inevitable retirement. I knew eventually I was going to have to become comfortable with watching a game from somewhere other than on the field. But I wasn't ready for the future yet. It felt so weird to be up there, to be so far away from my teammates. So I watched the first few series of the game and then I took off. I had to go back to the sidelines. Call it separation anxiety, whatever, but I needed to be near the action and near my teammates.

Willie went bananas against the Titans. He had 161 yards and a touchdown in the 34–7 blowout. I knew Willie was pretty good, but he surprised me with how well he played. And even though Tennessee had one of the worst defenses in the league, Willie made some moves that would have broken ankles against anybody.

The next week at Houston he put up another 100-plus-yard game and scored a TD in the 27–7 victory. We were 2–0, but we hadn't exactly played the cream of the NFL crop.

I thought about giving it a go against the Texans. I went out on the field and did my pregame warm-ups, but I could still feel a bite in my calf. It felt better than the week before, I still felt something there. I wasn't ready yet.

During the warm-ups I did my usual once-around-the-field pregame jog. As I jogged, I could see and hear all the Steelers fans in the crowd going nuts. They were applauding and shouting encouragement, and it made me feel good about my football legacy.

Here I was at Reliant Stadium in Houston, and there were thousands of Steelers fans, some of them wearing my No. 36 jersey. I don't know how else to say it, I was just so proud.

First of all, it's ridiculous how many Steelers fans there are in the world. They're the best fans because they're loyal and they're everywhere.

I've been in the city square of Turin, Italy, doing an interview on NBC's *Today Show*, and sure enough, someone in the crowd started waving a freakin' Terrible Towel. In *Italy*. Nobody in the crowd could have known I was going to be on the show that day, but there they were, Terrible Towels. I can't explain it.

That's when I realized that it isn't just Steelers City; it's Steelers Nation. Maybe even Steelers World.

I've seen those Terrible Towels everywhere. And I've seen people all around the country wearing my jersey. To me—and I take this stuff seriously—it's the fans' ultimate compliment to a player. After all, they can go into a store and choose from ten or twenty jersey numbers. But if they paid their hard-earned money to buy *my* jersey, there had to be a reason.

Maybe it means they liked the way I played or represented myself. I've always been very appreciative that they wanted my name and number on their backs. And I've always remembered that I have to do my part to keep them wearing my jersey number. Those jerseys represent a belief in me and what I stand for.

I probably could have worn one of my own jerseys for our next game against New England, the franchise that had eliminated the Steelers from the playoffs in 1996, 2001, and 2004. But Coach Cowher put me on the inactive list because we had a bye the following week. "You can get two more weeks off and I can have you totally healthy going into San Diego," he said.

I hated to sit, but he was probably right. Willie had been playing well, and my calf wasn't 100 percent yet.

We lost, 23–20, because we tried all this dipsy-doodle, yipsy-do garbage that almost never works against good teams like the Patriots. It was frustrating because New England had become our nemesis and they had now beaten us two straight games at our place. And each time I thought we were the better team.

But that's how it goes. We played poorly and they beat us. Can't whine about it.

During our bye week, I flew to New York to take part in a Habitat for Humanity project at Rockefeller Plaza—or, Humanity Plaza, as it was called that week. This was a little more than a month after Hurricane Katrina had devastated the Gulf Coast, so Habitat for Humanity, with help from NBC's *Today Show* and Warner Music Group, set up a work area on the plaza where professionals and volunteers helped build actual homes to be delivered to needy families in the Gulf Coast region. I'm not exactly Bob Vila, but I was glad to do what I could. So I helped frame a house with some Boston Celitcs players and one or two of the team's owners.

While I was in New York, my television agent, Lou Oppenheim, arranged a meeting with Ken Schanzer, the president of NBC Sports. NBC was going to broadcast NFL games beginning in 2006 and I was interested in discussing the possibility of a job on their Sunday night studio show.

Ken asked me if I was retiring after the season and I said that barring some unforeseeable change of heart, 2005 was going to be my last year. Then I told him I'd love to take a stab at a television career. He said that if there were a short list, I'd be at the top of it, and he'd get back to me later in the year.

But that job was for 2006. In 2005, I had other priorities.

Finally, on October 10, I made my season debut: a Monday night game at San Diego. I loved Monday Night Football because it was the only game of the day and everybody was watching. Plus, I'd been on the shelf for a while, so I was pumped up.

Shortly before kickoff, Coach Cowher said, "We're going to put you in early, so be ready."

True to his word, he stuck me in the lineup early and I broke off a couple of decent runs. But late in the game, and with us trailing, 22–21, Ben hurt his left knee and had to leave the game. The way he went down, well, I thought he could be done for the year.

Batch took Ben's spot and we started grinding away. There wasn't any confusion about our philosophy: with Ben out we were going to run the ball.

The problem was, this was Game No. 4, but I was in Game No. 1 shape. I had already been in way too many plays for my first game and I was sucking wind. I had practiced during the week, but there's no way you can simulate actual game tempo in practice.

Didn't matter. They kept giving me the ball. Bettis. Bettis. Bettis. I kept churning out the first downs, but the whole time I was thinking, "Oh, my goodness, I can't breathe. How can they leave me in here like this?"

But they did, so I had to give myself a pep talk. I said to myself, "Your quarterback went down. You've got to get some tough yards against one of the best rushing defenses in the league. If ever your team needed you, this is that time. Show your worth."

Show your worth. That was a phrase I had always used for some self-encouragement. Show them how a professional does his job. Show them why you were meant to play football. Most tailbacks run to daylight. But Howie Long once said I run "to darkness . . . to impact." And he was right.

So I churned and pounded for those dark yards. It wasn't sexy; those kind of yards never are. But we moved 40 yards in eleven plays to get into field goal range. And then, with just six seconds left in regulation, Jeff Reed kicked a 40-yard field goal to beat the Chargers.

I would have jumped for joy, but my legs were as heavy as beer kegs. My lungs were screaming. I was happy, but exhausted after seventeen carries and 54 hard-earned yards.

Months later, long after the season was finished, I was on a flight and saw Clarence Shelmon, the running backs coach for the Chargers. He paid me a wonderful compliment when he said the San Diego coaches had secretly hoped my calf injury would cause me to miss that game against the Chargers. Then he added that he appreciated my professionalism and the standard that I had set.

Here was a guy who was coaching one of the best running backs in the NFL, LaDainian Tomlinson, and he took the time to offer those kind words to me. Any compliment is nice, but when it comes from opposing coaches and players, it means even more.

Four games into the season we were 3–1 and in decent early position for the playoffs. But then we somehow lost to Jacksonville in overtime at our place. An ugly, ugly game.

Tommy replaced Ben in the starting lineup, but it wasn't a day for passing the ball. The wind was blowing as strong as I've ever seen in a stadium. It was howling so much that if you threw a ball straight, the wind would push it at least 5 yards to the left. Miserable conditions.

The Jaguars were a tough team and we were having trouble running the ball. We were having trouble passing the ball, too, but so were they.

We took the kickoff in overtime and Quincy Morgan returned it 74 yards to the Jaguars' 26. All we had to do was run it three times, kick a field goal and, boom, we'd go home with a win.

Well, this was Bussie Time. This was when Coach Cowher would usually call on me to get the tough yards. So I waited, and waited, and waited some more for him to send me into the game. I was standing right next to him, just waiting for the word. I waited so long that I actually started to move off the sideline and toward the field, looking at him the whole time, waiting for him to say, "Go, go, go." Instead, he said, "Whoa, whoa, whoa."

What? This was my time to do what I do. This is when I got the tough yards and moved the ball into better field goal position.

But Coach Cowher didn't motion for me to go into the game. He motioned for Willie.

I couldn't believe it. These sort of situations were my specialty, but now the specialist was on the sideline wondering what the hell was going on.

Willie fumbled the ball, but got it back for a short loss. Then he gained a few yards on second down. Then Tommy fumbled the ball away to the Jaguars on third down.

Our defense held, but then Tommy threw an interception that Rashean Mathis returned for a game-winning TD. We had lost an important game (the Jaguars now owned the Wild Card tiebreaker if we finished the season with idential records), and we had lost it because of some poor decision making.

I was livid after the defeat. You can't give away games in the NFL and expect to reach the playoffs. And if you're going to have me on the team, then at least use me for what I do best.

I was a game-closer and that situation was tailor-made for me. It was *the* kind of moment for me. I mean, if Coach Cowher wasn't going to use me in that situation, then when was he ever going to put me into a game?

I was so upset that I purposely kept my postgame comments to the media at a mininum. Win or lose . . . good or poor performance, I would always make myself available to the media after a game. You can't just talk to them when you're a hero. You've got to talk to them when things don't go your way too.

But in this case, I didn't want to say something publicly that I'd regret. So when the reporters asked me why I hadn't played in crunch time, I said something like, "That's a very good question. I would like the answer to that myself."

But the more I thought about it, the more upset I became. Even Willie came up to me after the game and asked why I had been left on the sidelines. And I couldn't answer him. I could not understand for the life of me why things had happened the way they did.

As my anger increased, I decided it was time to find Coach Hoak and ask him, rather bluntly, I might add, why I hadn't played.

"We blew it," he said. "You were supposed to be in the game."

I appreciated his honesty, but I also knew the decision to keep me on the sidelines had been made by Coach Cowher. Maybe Coach Hoak had wanted me in the game, but when push came to shove, Coach Cowher was the guy who chose Willie over me.

The next day I had a meeting with Coach Cowher. I asked him why he had kept me on the sidelines and he said he was sorry, that he forgot, that he was mad at the assistants for not reminding him. But his explanation didn't make any sense. There was no way he "forgot" to put me into the lineup. I was standing right next to him. It was a critical part of the game and we're talking about a veteran coach. He didn't forget anything.

If I had been in that game, we would have never fumbled the ball away. I can't guarantee you that Reed would have made the game-winning kick in that wind, but I can guarantee you I would have run downhill three consecutive times and we would have been closer for the field goal attempt.

Never in the ten seasons I had played for Coach Cowher had I felt betrayed like this. Through it all we had always had a great relationship because we were able to talk to each other about almost anything. He didn't have to hold back any punches, so to speak. And through dialogue, we were always able to get to the truth of the issues. If I had a concern about or issue with something, I knew I could voice it with him, that we'd solve it and then move forward.

But not this time.

I'm a creature of logic and I was having a hard time finding the logic in his decision. Hmmm. Maybe he wanted to give Willie that opportunity. But that wasn't Coach Cowher's mentality in those kind of situations.

I went through every possible scenario, but none made sense. In the end, it was, "My coaches were supposed to tell me, but they didn't," which was the football equivalent of, "The dog ate my homework."

There wasn't necessarily a rift between Coach Cowher and me, but the decision had hurt me. At least I got a chance to talk to him, get it off my chest and move on. I'm not the kind of guy to hold grudges. I said what I had to say, and he did the same. I didn't agree with or understand his decision, but there were still eleven games left in the regular season.

We played 5–1 Cincinnati the following week and the Bengals and their fans were talking about it being their biggest game in ten years . . . yada, yada, yada. Well, we went down there and smacked them silly. Ben had returned to the lineup and we beat them, 27–16.

But late in the game, one of their rookie linebackers dove at me and hit me flush in the quadriceps muscle. He hit me so flush that it vertically split the quad muscle. I had to leave the game after thirteen carries.

Great. Another injury. First the calf injury in training camp. And now I had to deal with a torn quad muscle. The last thing I wanted was a season where I suffered injury after injury after injury.

I'd had injuries in the past and usually figured out a way to deal with the pain. Whether those injuries were actually healed or not was another story, but I played.

In the NFL there are some injuries that absolutely keep you out of games: torn ACLs, broken legs . . . those sort of things. But a vertical tear in my quad muscle wasn't one of those kind of injuries. At least, it shouldn't have been.

Our next game was against Baltimore on a Monday night. That gave my quad muscle almost eight full days to recover. Problem was, it didn't get better. Whenever I tried to tighten the muscle, it felt like a knife was stuck in there.

By the time Sunday rolled around I knew I was in deep trouble. I was hurting bad and my quad wasn't making any progress. The one thing I had always dreaded in my career—not being able to physically recover in time for a game—was happening to me. All the signs were telling me, "You are done, man."

In the past I could get an injury to cooperate with me. I could get it to OK status. Not good, not bad, but OK.

But this didn't feel OK. It hurt. A lot. And because it was muscle, and because it was located near the femoral nerve, I didn't even think about getting a painkilling injection.

But I played. Early in the game I took a handoff from Ben, somebody broke through the line and—bam!—the guy hit me right on the quad. I might as well have had a target on it. My leg suddenly felt like a wet spaghetti noodle.

I got up and tried not to let anybody know how bad it hurt. But I was done. I couldn't go on. I went to the sidelines and just knew I was in huge trouble.

Willie did a nice job for us. Hines made an incredible catch over Ravens defensive back Chris McAlister. And by the time they needed me late in the game, the pain in my quad had quieted to the point where I could deal with it.

Once again it came down to a final drive where we needed to pound out yards and get close enough for a game-winning field goal. But this time Coach Cowher didn't call on Willie; he called on me.

After making such an issue of my situation after the Jacksonville game, I knew I couldn't tell Coach Cowher no. This was maybe his way of apologizing, of letting me prove him wrong. The difference was, I didn't have a quad injury when we played the Jaguars. But if I didn't go in the game, I might not get another opportunity to show they could depend on me.

So we started pounding it out. We covered 60 yards on that final drive and at one point I carried the ball four straight times for 18 of those yards. I was running on pure adrenaline. The pain in my quad was excruciating, but no way was I going to come out of that game.

We moved the ball into Reed's range and he kicked a 37-yarder with 1:36 to give us a 20–19 win. And I had made my point to Coach Cowher.

What nobody knew, except for team trainer John Norwig, is that I had an audition with NBC the next day, our off day. NBC's Ken Schanzer had arranged the audition in New York and I had agreed to be there.

Under normal circumstances, I would have had to report to the Steelers' headquarters Tuesday morning for treatment on my quad. But John was a good friend and I trusted him. I told him I needed a favor and I was very honest about my situation. I said I had the audition with NBC, that it was important to me, and that I needed him to cover for me.

Had John said no, that I was required to be there for the treatment, I wouldn't have gone to the audition. But John looked out for me and he didn't say a word to anyone about my trip.

By the time the game ended and I got home from Heinz Field, it was already past 2:00 A.M. I had to be at the airport a little after 7:00 A.M. But I was still jacked up from the game. My nerves were still going 100 miles per hour and I couldn't fall asleep right away. Plus, my spaghetti noodle leg was on fire from the pain.

When the alarm rang that morning, I was hurting. Trameka kept trying to get me out of bed, but I was struggling to move and to pry my eyes open. But I had made a commitment, so I got up, got to the airport, and flew to New York.

I first met with my television agent, Lou Oppenheim, in his Manhattan office and we discussed a game plan for the audition. I had no idea what the NBC people were going to want me to do, so I had spent some time researching each team in the league.

At about one o'clock I arrived all suited up at 30 Rock for the audition with Bob Costas and Cris Collinsworth. Not too much was at stake—only a chance at network television. And I was doing it on fumes.

Bob was the moderator. Cris and I were the analysts. We discussed some of the highlights from Sunday's games and then, out of the blue, Bob asked me my opinion on the Brett Favre situation. At the time, there was a lot of debate about Favre's future: Should he come back in 2006, and how should the Packers handle the situation?

Well, here was a subject I knew a little something about. So, speaking from experience, I said that Favre was the ultimate competitor and that he wasn't going to bow out on his own. So if this was truly a rebuilding year for the team, then the Packers had to cut their losses. They had to explain to Favre why it was best they parted ways, and then thank him for his amazing career in Green Bay. The Packers had taken Cal's Aaron Rodgers in the first round of the '05 draft, so if he was the quarterbacking future of the franchise—and you weren't going to be competitive anyway (and the Packers weren't going to be)—then you had to start developing the kid. You couldn't allow Favre to dictate that situation because Brett would always want to keep playing. That's how competitors think. So if you were serious about the rebuilding process, you had to let Favre go.

I think the candor of my answer surprised a few people in that studio. First of all, I had been in a similar situation, but here I was taking a hard line against Brett. Plus, I'm a friend of Brett's. During the off-season I had played in his golf tournament in Mississippi.

But NBC wasn't asking me what I thought about Brett's golf game or how I valued his friendship. They were asking me for a professional opinion on Brett's relationship with the Packers. So I couldn't hold back; just like I don't think Brett would have held back had he been in my position.

Brett was sort of holding the Packers' organization hostage. Of course, the Packers were letting him do it, so you can't entirely blame Brett for the situation.

Had the Steelers told me it was time to look for another team after the '04 season, I would have said, "Thanks, but no thanks." I would have walked off into the sunset. I didn't want to play for anyone else. And I definitely didn't want to do what Emmitt Smith had done, which was define his career as a Cowboy, but then spend his last two seasons in the league as an Arizona Cardinal, where he had no chance to be successful. I'd heard about too many great players—Franco Harris, Joe Namath, O. J. Simpson—who had done the same thing and regretted it. In fact, Franco and I talked about that very subject. He had left the Steelers in 1984 to finish his career with the Seattle Seahawks. The Seahawks paid him a lot of money, but it just wasn't the same. He gained just 170 yards that season and then retired.

I felt good about the audition, and Cris and Bob thought it went well too. But it wasn't like anybody offered me a job. The whole experience was a little bit like playing in a ballgame. Anxiety . . . big build up . . . play the game . . . exhaustion. I was on reserve power anyway, so by the time I left the studio, flew back to Pittsburgh, and drove home, I had zero energy. I disappeared into my pillow that night.

I got up at the crack of dawn the next day and reported to the training room. Norwig took a look at the quad and knew we were in trouble. It was tender to the touch and the only real solution was rest. So after a brief discussion, we decided I'd have to sit out the next game.

I never liked missing games, and I was definitely disappointed about not playing that week against Brett and the Packers at Lambeau Field. Pittsburgh is a bigger city than Green Bay, but they share the same level of passion about their football teams. If you go anywhere in the country, you'll find Packers fans and Steelers fans. And if you have success with the Packers or the Steelers, those fans will love you for life.

I consider myself an NFL history buff. So I always liked playing in a place like Lambeau Field. The place actually reminded me of Notre Dame Stadium. In fact, the same people who renovated Notre Dame Stadium in 1997 also renovated Lambeau Field in 2003. The only difference is, we didn't have a Lambeau Leap at Notre Dame.

At the same time I was ruled out of the Packers game, Duce saw his first action of the season. We needed him too, since Willie had to leave the game in the third quarter with a sprained ankle and Ben was out after having arthroscopic surgery on his right knee. Duce ended up with 76 yards and a touchdown in the win. You couldn't help but be happy for the guy, as well as for Charlie, who made his first start since 2001.

We beat Cleveland the next week to move to 7–2. Hines became the Steelers' career leader in receptions, Duce got his first start of the season, and I scored my eighty-fourth career TD. The bad news: Ben was still out, and wasn't expected back for at least one more game; Charlie injured his hand late in the first half and was out for a while, and we had to face the Ravens in Baltimore.

The Ravens blitzed the hell out of us and Tommy got sacked six times. The game went to overtime and their kicker, Matt Stover, beat us with a 44–yarder.

With three losses in our conference, we couldn't afford any more defeats. So we went to Indianapolis for a Monday night game against the undefeated Colts with a definite sense of urgency. And we got absolutely pummeled, 26–7.

The coaches had decided to try a tag-team running back attack. Willie would be the first- and second-down guy. Duce would be the third-down guy. I would be the short-yardage guy. And if Willie needed a quick rest, I'd go in for him.

It was a disaster.

On the Colts' very first play, Manning hit Marvin Harrison for an 80-yard touchdown. The place just erupted. It was like a concussion bomb went off in the RCA Dome. I had never been in a louder stadium. You couldn't hear yourself scream.

Ben, who was making his first start after missing three games, stepped to the line of scrimmage and yelled the snap count, but we couldn't hear him. We couldn't hear anything—not "hut, hut," not audibles . . . nothing.

The NFL has a rule about piping in artificial noise during a game, but I could swear they do it anyway at Indy. You can hear it. They don't even try to hide it. The fans are going nuts, and then all of a sudden the noise gets even louder. We couldn't handle it.

Worse yet, we didn't have a silent count ready to go. Well, we had one, but we hadn't worked on it during practice. So the Colts just teed off on us and we finished with less than 200 yards total offense.

So we got trounced, dropped to 7–4, and fell behind Cincinnati in the division standings.

After the game, Coach Cowher came into the locker room and made a promise.

"I hope we get another opportunity to see these guys," he said. "Because if we do, it's going to be a whole different story. We've got something for their ass. Now let's get the hell out of here."

The only way we were going to see Indy again was if we made the playoffs. But if we didn't beat the Bengals the next week we were probably out of the postseason mix.

But to be honest, I wasn't too worried about Cincinnati. The Bengals? We were going to be fine. We'd beaten them six out of the last seven times, and thirteen out of the last nineteen times. The Bengals hadn't beaten us in a meaningful game since, well, ever.

Seriously, the Bengals hadn't finished above .500 since I was a freshman at Notre Dame. No way were they going to come into our house, with the playoffs on the line, and beat us. I mean, it was *Cincinnati*. There's a reason why Myron Cope and Steelers fans called them the, "Bungles." We weren't going to lose to Cincinnati.

We lost to Cincinnati.

They came in and it was a freakin' air attack. They were bombing us. We were bombing them. CNN should have covered the game.

Ben threw for almost 400 yards and three touchdowns. Carson Palmer, who was becoming one of the best quarterbacks in the league, threw for three touchdowns. They made some huge plays and beat us 38–31. Now we had lost three games in a row and were two games behind the Bengals in the standings.

Uh, oh, we were in trouble. Panic set in. Nobody on our team thought we were going to lose that game. There was no Plan B because we thought Plan A—beat the Bengals—was infallible.

We were 7–5 and all I could do was sit in the locker room after the game and say to myself, "I came back for *this*?"

We had a good team, but we were at the very edge of playoff elimination. I couldn't believe it. We only had four games left and after looking at the standings and the tiebreaker scenarios, I didn't like our chances.

When we assembled the next day for our usual Monday team meeting, Coach Cowher said he wanted us to grade ourselves on our individual performances. The coaches usually looked at the film and then issued grades. But this time they left it up to us.

It was a really smart move on Coach Cowher's part because when you lose three in a row and your playoff hopes are slipping away, the natural tendency is to start pointing fingers at each other. Now we had to judge ourselves before we started judging others. I thought it was the perfect idea at the perfect time.

Coach Cowher said something else that really stuck with me in the aftermath of the Bengals loss.

"The playoffs," he said, "start now."

Needless to say, we weren't favored to beat the Chicago Bears when they came to town on December 11. They were 9–3. We had lost three in a row for the first time since 2003. They had the NFL's No. 1 defense. We had just given up thirty-eight points. It was desperation time.

Willie started the game and did pretty well until the snow started coming down. Then the field got wet and mushy, and Willie started to slip and slide a little bit. A bad field almost always negates speed, especially when you're trying to get around the corner.

The Steelers needed a mudder. Well, I'm a mudder. My mudder's a mudder. It runs in the family.

I only had one carry in the first half. It covered one yard for a touchdown and gave us a 14–7 lead.

As the snow kept coming down, and the field got sloppier, and the visibility at times was reduced to about 30 or 40 yards, Coach Cowher decided we needed to keep pounding the ball. So he put me in the game early in the second half and said, "Hey, go to work."

The Bears had a tough defense, but they were small up front. They depended on their speed and quickness, but the field conditions took care of that. So their defensive linemen became sitting ducks for our O-line. We got hat on hat and just started pushing them all over the place, like they were on skates.

Meanwhile, they kept feeding me the ball and it was like old times. Everybody knew what was coming, but the Bears couldn't stop it.

Late in the third quarter, on a second-and-goal situation, we ran a little run play where I go between our right guard and tackle. It wasn't anything fancy.

At about the 4-yard line I ducked a shoulder into Bears safety Mike Green and sort of plowed him out of the way. Then I saw Bears linebacker Brian Urlacher waiting for me.

I didn't have time to try to dodge him. And you know what? I didn't want to. This was going to be Bears linebacker v. Steelers running back, power v. power, history v. history. It was sort of a symbolic moment when all the tradition of one great franchise met all the tradition of another great franchise.

Urlacher v. Bettis. It was one of those confrontations that you loved as a player.

So Urlacher got low and prepared for the hit. But I got a little lower, took advantage of my leverage, and we collided at the 3-yard line like two freight trains. Three yards later the mudder was in the end zone, with Urlacher along for the ride.

If there was a turning point in our season, the 21–9 win against the Bears was probably it. We dominated them. We controlled the ball for more than thirty-seven minutes.

I had one carry and 1 yard in the first half . . . sixteen carries and 100 yards in the second half. Willie was on the sidelines yelling, "He's got his snow tires on! He's got his snow tires on! Ride The Bus!" Even some of our defensive starters had left their seats on the bench to watch.

Sports Illustrated's Peter King, a guy I've known for a long time, wrote that it was one of the ten best games of my career. Considering the circumstances, he might be right.

After the game I made sure to find Urlacher on the field. I think he's a great player and I wanted to shake his hand. I also wanted a memento because I respected him and his game.

"Hey, man," I said, "let's exchange shoes."

So I sent our equipment manager over to the Bears' locker room with a pair of my cleats, and their guy gave me a pair of Urlacher's cleats. I'd done that with a handful of other players I really respected, guys such as Terrell Davis, Junior Seau, and Drew Brees. Now those shoes are displayed at my house.

We had three regular season games left, but in reality everything was a one-and-done situation for us. Coach Cowher was right: our playoffs had started with the Bears win.

We beat the Vikings, 18–3, and this time we were prepared for playing in a dome. The Metrodome wasn't half as loud as the RCA Dome, but we had spent the practice week working on a silent count. We ended up using our silent count system during that whole game. One of the reasons we did it: just in case we played at Indy again.

Six days later we punished the Browns, 41–0. It was our most complete game of the year. And I couldn't have been prouder of Willie, who became the first Steelers running back, other than me or Barry Foster, to rush for 1,000 yards since 1992.

Everything was gelling for us at the perfect time. Our defense had given up just twelve points in our last three games, and there was a feeling on the team that we were pretty damn good. When we beat Detroit at home on New Year's Day, it completed a four-game must-win stretch that put us into the playoffs as the AFC's lowest-seeded team, No. 6.

Six . . . sixtieth, we didn't care. We just wanted to keep playing. Name the place and the time, and we'd be there.

The game against the Lions was a very, very sentimental experience for me. I was playing against my hometown team, but more importantly, I was playing in front of my adopted hometown, Pittsburgh.

No matter what happened, this was going to be the final time I'd run out of the Heinz Field tunnel. It would be the eighty-first and last time I'd play in Pittsburgh. If we lost, I was done. If we won, all of our playoff games would be on the road. So I wanted to savor every second of it.

Before the game I jogged around the field and acknowledged the crowd. Those fans had meant so much to me and our team. But I didn't get emotional until we assembled in the tunnel a few minutes before kickoff.

As I stood there, I tried to take mental snapshots of my surroundings. I wanted to remember everything about that final game at Heinz Field.

Willie was the starting tailback, but Coach Cowher did a real nice thing: He had the PA announcer introduce me as the twelfth man on offense, which meant I got to run out of that tunnel by myself. It was one of those moments I'll never forget—and never want to. My goose bumps had goose bumps. Everything was in slow motion and I couldn't hear a thing, couldn't feel a thing. I'm not sure my feet touched the ground.

I only had ten carries that New Year's Day, but I made sure every one of them counted. I scored three times and gained 41 yards.

Meanwhile, you should have seen the celebration going on in the stadium suite I had at Heinz Field. There were about thirty-five family and friends crammed into the suite, and it was the only one with the windows open on a cold Pittsburgh day. After my first touchdown (a fourth-and-goal run from the 1-yard line late in the first quarter), I looked up at the suite and saw everybody whooping it up. I always looked up there after a score at home.

Little did I know that my brother, John, had said that if I scored again, he'd take his shirt off. Better yet, most of the other guys in the suite said they'd do the same thing.

Sure enough, I scored late in the second quarter and apparently every man in the suite took off his shirt, except my father, my TV agent Lou Oppenheim, and a few others. But they were just getting started.

At halftime, my brother had arranged a champagne toast in the suite in honor of my last regular season game. Even Pittsburgh Mayor-elect Bob O'Connor (who, sadly, would die nine months later of brain cancer) stopped by for the little ceremony. I was told later that there were a lot of misty eyes after John's heartfelt words. I wish I could have been there to clink a glass with them. And I really wish I would have been there when my father, Mr. Conservative, said he'd take off *his* shirt if I scored a third time.

Well, I tied my single-game scoring high early in the third quarter on a 4-yard touchdown run. And when I looked up at the suite, I was shocked to see all those bare-chested men, including my father, going crazy. I even have the photos to prove it.

During a timeout late in the game, the stadium big screen showed a highlight video of my career. When it was done, Coach Cowher pulled me out of the game and the crowd started yelling, "One-more-year! One-more-year!"

I wanted to yell back, "Thank you!"

After the game some of my teammates wanted me to pose for photos with them. Others wanted me to autograph their game programs. Ben said he wanted my last game jersey. Willie even wore a Bettis throwback Rams jersey.

So I posed and signed. I would have done anything for those guys.

Incredibly enough, we had won four in a row to get into the postseason. Now we had to win four in a row to get a Super Bowl ring—and we'd have to win all four on the road.

People talk about the home-field advantage, but we *liked* playing on the road. We looked forward to it, as opposed to most teams who looked at their schedules and counted the days until they could get back home.

Coach Cowher used to tell us over and over, "It's us against the world." That's never more true than when you're on the road. But we believed in each other so much that being on the road didn't bother us. If anything, it brought us closer together. We actually couldn't wait to get on the road. We'd get a good night's sleep, concentrate entirely on football, and then go out there and kick butt. That was our mentality and it worked. Going into the playoffs, we had won six of our eight regular season road games.

Waiting for us in the Wild Card game was none other than the Cincinnati Bengals. And we were *really* looking forward to that rematch. We owed those guys big time.

Not only had the Bengals beaten us at home, but Coach Cowher showed us some video footage of Cincinnati wide receiver T. J. Houshmandzadeh cleaning his cleats before the December 4 game at Heinz Field. He was cleaning off his shoes with Terrible Towels. And there was also footage of Bengals receiver Chad Johnson using a towel as a food bib.

That wasn't a smart thing for them to do. We were already pissed about losing that game, but then to use our Terrible Towels as shoe wipes and bibs? And in front of the cameras? As Jimmy Johnson later said in a Miller Lite commercial: "Du-umb."

On the Bengals' second play of the game, Palmer hit Chris Henry on a 66-yard pass down the right sideline. I was thinking, "Here we go again—bombs away, just like the last time we played."

But then I saw Palmer on the ground. Our defensive end, Kimo von Oelhoffen, had hit Palmer on the play and it was obvious Carson was seriously hurt. It wasn't until later that we learned he had suffered torn knee ligaments on the play.

It was sad watching him leave the field. You never want to see a guy go down like that, especially a guy like Carson, who, after Peyton Manning, was the best quarterback in the NFL. Plus, you always want to beat a team at its best. Without Carson, the Bengals weren't at their best.

But even with Carson out of the game, we trailed, 10–0, at the end of the first quarter, and 17–7 late in the second quarter. But then we went crazy and scored 24 unanswered points. Final score: Us 31, Them 17.

When it was over, Ben came up to me in the locker room and stuck a football in my stomach.

"Here's the game ball from the last snap," he said. "I've got two more to give you."

Huh? Then I remembered Ben's promise about getting me to the Super Bowl. One down, two to go.

In a weird way, the playoffs set up pretty well for us. We had played every AFC playoff team during the regular season, except the Denver Broncos. Now with the Bengals gone, Coach Cowher's November 28 wish came true.

Remember? He had said that he wanted to play the Colts again. *"Because if we do, it's going to be a whole different story."*

I just didn't know the story was going to need a miracle ending.

✦ 11 ✦

January 15, 2006
AFC Divisional Playoff
Pittsburgh Steelers v. Indianapolis Colts
RCA Dome
Indianapolis, Ind.

Twenty-one seconds were left in regulation. Colts kicker Mike Vanderjagt jogged onto the field for the game-tying field goal attempt. Up in the WBGG radio booth, color analyst Tunch Ilkin reduced the storyline for his listeners to its most essential point.

> *Ilkin: Well, you know what, nobody is going to be rooting harder for Vanderjagt to miss this field goal than Jerome Bettis. It's always the guy in a situation like this, it's really, really tough.*
> *Play-by-play announcer Bill Hillgrove: He's not missed a field goal at home in the playoffs in six tries. And he's fourteen of fourteen in extra points.*
> *Ilkin: Yeah, the law of averages says he misses this one.*
> *Hillgrove: We got a low snap. The ball is down. Vanderjagt's kick is on the way. That kick is long enough, high enough and it's . . . no good!*
> *Ilkin: He missed it!*
> *Hillgrove: It's no good! It's no good!*

Ilkin: Oh, man. Call back the travel agent. Remake those reservations. We're going to Denver!

He missed it? He really missed it?

When Vanderjagt kicked it I could tell it was going right. But it was like my mind couldn't comprehend what my eyes were seeing. I was thinking, "It's up . . . it could be . . ." But then I looked at the refs and they were signaling that it was no good.

I couldn't believe it. Nobody could. And Vanderjagt didn't just miss it; he *missed* it. It wasn't even close.

Somehow we had pulled it out, which meant my mom could come out of the bathroom at the RCA Dome. That's where she had hidden and prayed during those last couple of minutes of the game. It also meant that I got another football.

"This is the second one," said Ben, handing me the ball after the game.

It wasn't until we got back to Pittsburgh and I did an appearance on Dan Patrick's ESPN radio show that I heard about the Steelers fan, Terry O'Neill, who had the heart attack right after my fumble. He apparently was a huge fan of mine, but had had a history of heart problems. Thank goodness for those two firemen who got his heart going again.

The guy was such a Steelers fan that when he regained consciousness, the first thing he supposedly asked the doctors and nurses was, "Did we win?" I don't know if the story is true, but it sounds like something a Steelers fan would say. The guy later told reporters that he was more upset that my career might have ended on that play than he was that we might lose the game.

When I was on the show with Patrick, the producers actually put O'Neill on the air, too. I wished him a speedy recovery, but I told him he might not want to watch the AFC Championship—just to be on the safe side.

We were headed to Denver for the AFC Championship against the Broncos, who had upset the Patriots. We hadn't played the Broncos since 2003, but the more I watched them on film that week, the more certain I was that we'd beat them. There was no question that we were going to tear them up.

The Broncos had this little blitz package they liked to run. They'd bring everybody up to the line of scrimmage and unleash the dogs. Against the Patriots, that blitz had caused all kinds of blocking problems and Tom Brady made some uncharacteristic mistakes.

But our coaches came up with a great way to attack their blitz package. In fact, we were praying they'd run that blitz. Because if they did, we had plays that were going to eat them up.

What we basically wanted to do was to put a wide receiver in motion or in the slot and force the Broncos to hesitate on their blitzes. Sometimes the slot man would block the blitzing free safety. Other times we'd use a second tight end to do it. And with the blitzes, that also would mean a lot of man-to-man coverage, which was to our advantage. It was a great scheme on our coaches' part.

The night before the game, in a ballroom at our team hotel in a Denver suburb, Coach Cowher let Kimo von Oelhoffen and me talk to the team. My speech was short and sweet.

"Nobody has to do more than their jobs," I said. "If you do your job, we win this football game. Nobody has to have an incredible game in order for us to win. All I ask is that everybody give 110 percent and have fun. If you do that, no matter what happens, I'll shake your hand, give you a hug, and thank you for everything. Just get me home. If you get me back to Detroit, dinner at my mom's house is on me."

There were a lot of misty eyes that night, including mine. People need to understand that a football team is like a band of brothers. These were my brothers, and I was asking them to do one last thing for me.

I dare say we ate 'em alive. We were up, 24–3, at halftime and won, 34–17. After thirteen long seasons, I was going to the Super Bowl, where we would face the Seattle Seahawks.

Eddie George, one of my best friends, was on the sidelines for our game against the Broncos. After the game he gave me a hug and said, "Now you get to see the lights."

Those lights. He had seen them in Super Bowl XXXIV. Now it was my turn.

As I walked off the field, Ben handed me the game ball.

"This is the third one," he said, laughing. "I promised to get you there, not win it."

Ben played great, completing 21 of 29 passes for 275 yards and two touchdowns. I scored on our bread and butter play, Counter 38 Power. Our defense forced four turnovers. The only pisser was that my asthma was worse than normal because of the altitude, and we didn't get to celebrate on their field on a beautiful, sunny Denver day. When we had lost AFC Championship games in the past, the opposing team was able to celebrate and receive the conference trophy on our field, which was a humiliating experience for us.

But this time the NFL made us go into the visiting locker room for the trophy presentation. But I wasn't too upset, especially when I got to hold that Lamar Hunt Trophy. It was the sweetest thing in the world, especially with us becoming the first No. 6 seed to reach the Super Bowl.

Later, after almost everyone had left the locker room, Broncos safety John Lynch came in. John and I went way back to our Notre Dame–Stanford days. He's the guy who had caused me to fumble when we played back in the day. So we had a fifteen-year history.

John, a seven-time Pro Bowler who had won a Super Bowl ring with Tampa Bay, gave me a little hug and said, "I'm proud of you. I'm happy for you. Congratulations on a great career. You deserve to go to the Super Bowl."

The last hugs I got were from my mother and father, who were waiting just inside the stadium tunnel. The whole scene was hilarious because Steelers fans (I'm telling you—they're everywhere) were chanting, "Miss-us Bett-is."

When I hugged her, I said something like, "We're coming home."

But even before she congratulated me on the win, she said, "What's this about a dinner?"

Needless to say, I had to do some serious negotiating with her.

Once we got back to Pittsburgh, I finally had to confront the R-word: Retirement.

Everybody assumed that I would definitely call it quits after the 2005 season, but I had played it coy with our local beat reporters. I didn't do that to be a jerk, but because I wasn't 100 percent sure I was going to retire. I was 99 percent sure, but that remaining 1 percent was hard to ignore. And I had learned my lesson back at Notre Dame about speaking too soon.

As far back as December 24, when we played the Browns in Cleveland, I had almost knocked on chairman Dan Rooney's office door and told him I was going to call it quits. But then we beat the Browns and I thought I'd wait until after the Chicago game. Because if we lost to the Bears, then our season was basically over and I could make my retirement official.

But then we beat the Bears and, well, I didn't tell him because I wanted to leave the window open just a little bit for a 2006 return.

Beginning with that Cleveland game, Trameka would ask me, "Well, did you talk to him?" And I'd say no.

The next week: "Well, did you talk to him?" And I'd say no again.

The week of the Lions game: "When you going to talk to him?" And I said that I might as well wait a little bit.

"Whatcha waiting for?" she said. "You sure you want to do it?"

"Uh, yeah," I said.

But it was a very unsure yeah. Because in the back of my mind I wasn't totally ready to close the door on my career. If I closed the door, it was closed for good. The logical part of my brain knew I was done. But the emotional part was still clinging to that 1 percent.

So I didn't visit Mr. Rooney after the Lions game. Or after the playoff win against the Bengals. Or after the playoff win against the Colts. But after the win against the Broncos I decided it was time to talk. Almost.

Our charter flight got back to Pittsburgh Sunday night. On Monday, Trameka said, "You should talk to him today."

"No, no, no, I'm going to talk to him Tuesday," I said.

But Tuesday came and went and I didn't knock on that office door.

On Wednesday morning, Trameka woke me up and laid down the law.

"Listen, you need to figure out what you want to do," she said. "If you want to play, then play."

I loved the *idea* of playing again, but in my heart I knew the Super Bowl would be my last game. So I drove to the Steelers headquarters, went to Mr. Rooney's door, and took a deep breath.

Mr. Rooney isn't a physically imposing man. He wears glasses, has a head of silver hair, and walks with a slight hunch. But he's been part of the Steelers' organization since 1955, is a member of the Pro Football Hall of Fame, and has been involved in just about every important decision made by the NFL during the last thirty years. He's a kind, gracious man who has spent his entire life in Pittsburgh. His opinion mattered to me.

"Mr. Rooney," I said, "I appreciate the opportunity you gave me. I want to thank you for believing in people, as opposed to believing in numbers. Because if you believed in numbers, I would have been gone a long time ago. Your belief in people is the reason why I'm still here and why I was able to finish my career here. I just want to thank you for that, and for all the great memories we had."

He said some very nice things to me—that he appreciated my contributions to the organization and to the community—but he never tried to talk me out of my decision. He respected the decision, and maybe he knew it was time, too.

When I was done talking to Mr. Rooney, I went next door and gave his oldest son, Art Rooney II, the team president, the same news. Now only four people in the world knew I was definitely retiring, win or lose, after the Super Bowl: me, Trameka, and the Rooneys.

As I walked out of Art Rooney II's office, I was overwhelmed by a feeling of relief. Now I would be able to concentrate on . . . Super Bowl tickets?

I had always heard about players complaining about having to find Super Bowl tickets for friends and family. And I always thought, "I'd give anything to have that problem." Well, those players were right: It *was* a pain.

I was getting phone calls up the ying-yang about tickets. But I told my mother that nobody could get in my ticket lottery unless they had come to see me play in Pittsburgh at least three times that season. That eliminated a lot of people from contention. If you had been loyal and made those trips to Pittsburgh, then I was going to be loyal to you by sticking your name in my Super Bowl raffle.

I made one exception to the three-game rule. My high school coach, Bob Dozier, was getting a ticket, no matter what. I made arrangements to fly him from his home in El Paso, Texas, to Detroit for the game.

Not counting a couple of NFL preseason games played outside the country, my mother and father had been to every game I'd ever played. So I thought it was only right that I rent a Ford Field suite (thank you, NFL) for the Super Bowl. The $85,000 rental fee was more than the $73,000 I had earned in playoff shares during the 2005 postseason (you get $17K for the Wild Card win, $19K for the Divisional win,

$37K for the AFC Championship win), but it was the least I could do for my family.

The Ford Field suite came with twenty tickets. I got another eight tickets from owning a stadium suite at Heinz Field. But I still needed four more tickets, so I bought two from Donovan McNabb and two from a former teammate, Mike Schneck.

I thought I had everything under control until I checked my messages on my cell phone.

"Jerome, this is Coach Holtz. I need fourteen tickets for the Super Bowl. Call me back."

What? Fourteen? I nearly fainted. But it turned out Coach Holtz was just messing with me. He got me good, too.

I knew once I got to Detroit it was going to be complete madness. So Jahmal and I devised a game plan to limit my cell phone access. The minute the Steelers' charter flight landed at Detroit Metro, my regular cell would go dark. Then Jahmal would give me a new cell phone and number that I'd use for Super Bowl week. That way nobody could get in touch with me. I didn't want to be antisocial. I just didn't need any more distractions.

We were scheduled to leave Pittsburgh for Detroit on Monday, January 30. When I got to the private airport hangar for our pre-flight security check with the TSA people, I noticed one of my teammates wearing a throwback Notre Dame jersey. Not just any throwback, but *my* green No. 6 jersey. What were the odds of that?

Pretty good, it turns out. Joey Porter had organized the whole thing. He had a whole garbage bag full of green Notre Dame throwback jerseys with my old number.

In honor of my return to my hometown, Joey had arranged for all the guys on defense and a lot of guys on offense to wear the jerseys for the trip to Detroit. I was speechless. Those jerseys weren't cheap. They cost about $300 apiece and Joey had about twenty of them in the bag.

The defensive guys had done this sort of thing in the past to honor the coaches, but never a player. Like when we played the Lions late in the season, the defense wore Dick LeBeau throwback jerseys from when he was an All-Pro cornerback with Detroit. And when we played Cleveland at home, they wore throwback jerseys from Coach Cowher's days with the Browns. So for them to do this for a player—an offensive player, no less—was an incredible gesture.

I was actually presented with one of the jerseys. I didn't get to keep it though. Duce took it and had me sign it for him.

Not long before we landed in Detroit, Troy Polamalu sort of called me over to talk. Troy was a USC man, and as everyone knows, USC and Notre Dame have played each other since 1926 (by the way, we lead the series by double digits).

"What's up?" I said.

"I just want you to know that I would never ever wear a Notre Dame jersey," he said. "But the fact that I'm wearing this says a lot about the person you are and the respect I have for you."

Troy is a really nice guy, but he's on the quiet side. So when he said that, I knew he was serious.

I went back to my seat and a few minutes later I felt another tap on my shoulder. This time it was linebacker Larry Foote, a Michigan man.

"Man, you're lucky this is you we're talking about," he said. "Otherwise, I don't wear nothing Notre Dame."

So guys broke their allegiances to their universities for one day, just in honor of me. And it was a pretty neat thing to turn on the TV later that day and see footage of the guys wearing their Bettis throwbacks as they exited the plane.

I was treated like a king that week. On Tuesday morning it seemed like hundreds, maybe thousands of reporters and cameramen were at Ford Field for the annual Media Day interviews with both teams. Each session lasted a few hours and for some guys it was a pain in the neck. Not for me. I loved it.

A reporter asked me if I was sick of answering so many questions.

"Sick of it?" I said. "I've been looking forward to this my whole career. Every year I'd see guys up on those podiums and I'd say, 'I need to be up there. That should be me.' So I want every question to be asked, every minute to be used. Am I upset about questions? Is this a bother? No way. This is an honor."

About an hour later, Detroit Mayor Kwame Kilpatrick presented me with a key to the city, making me only the fourth person during his tenure to receive such a key. The City Council declared it Jerome Bettis Week, and Gov. Jennifer Granholm issued a proclamation declaring Wednesday Jerome Bettis Day.

I also did a Campbell's Chunky Soup appearance with my mother and Donovan McNabb and his mother, Wilma. I had to do an HBO interview, as well as my own show for KDKA. It got so hectic that I actually had to sneak up to *Post-Gazette* columnist Ron Cook's hotel room (he was following me around for the day for a story), to iron and steam my dress shirt, and then take a fifteen-minute catnap.

Mayor Kilpatrick also arranged for me to have a police escort wherever I went. Nothing like a police escort to make you feel special and get you through Detroit traffic.

With Coach Cowher's permission, we loaded forty players on a bus and drove to my mother and father's house for Wednesday dinner. My mom (with an assist from my sister, aunts, and family friends) was in her glory, cooking for all the guys. She even baked a yellow cake in the shape of a bus. It was so much fun watching her that night. It was as if my mom and dad were part of the team—and in a way, they were.

After dinner a bunch of us shot up to Auburn Hills to watch the Pistons play. I was amazed that the place erupted into cheers when the arena TV camera caught me and a few of the guys taking our courtside seats for the game. I'd come a long way from the ABP.

As much as I appreciated all the love, there was another reason why I didn't mind doing all the interviews and acting like the unofficial mayor of Detroit. My thought process was this: If I could keep all the focus and cameras on me—a guy who wasn't going to play a whole lot in the game—it would take some of the pressure off my second-year quarterback and my second-year tailback. The less pressure on them, the more those guys could go to work and prepare for the game. Plus, this was my thirteenth year in the league. I could handle all the festivities and it wouldn't throw my game off. I hadn't played in a Super Bowl, but I'd been to the rodeo a few times.

I had some help too. Joey and Seahawks tight end Jerramy Stevens got into a little verbal warfare, and the media jumped on that.

The only slightly unpleasant time I had all week was at our practices, which were at the Silverdome, site of my coin-flip controversy on Thanksgiving Day in 1998. Coach Cowher was nice enough to remind the media of the coin-flip flap.

I didn't mention it to the reporters on Media Day, but there was no way we were going to lose to Seattle. The Seahawks had a great coach in Mike Holmgren and they were a good team. But we figured we had the advantage over them defensively. We didn't think they'd be able to run the ball like they had during the regular season and the playoffs.

Some people had said Seahawks tailback Shaun Alexander, who led the NFL in rushing in '05, wasn't a physical runner. Sorry, but that wasn't true. If you looked at his track record, he played at Alabama and in the Southeastern Conference. That isn't a soft program or a soft conference. He came from a power-running program, but he was drafted by a team that featured a more finesse-style of running attack. So he somehow got the unfair label of being a finesse runner.

No, we were confident because we thought our personnel and our more physical defense would win that battle. Plus, our confidence level was through the hotel roof. We were so comfortable going on the road to win games that Coach Cowher decided we were going to wear our white jerseys rather than the home black.

On Thursday night, after my charity bowling event raised more than $155,000 for my The Bus Stops Here Foundation, I went underground. No more media interviews. No more ceremonies. No more nothing except football.

By Saturday, we were ready to play the game. My personal barber, Dave Williams, came to my hotel room and gave me a haircut. All in all, it was a pretty low-key night. I was a little restless, but I didn't have any problems falling asleep.

On Sunday morning I just sat in bed and watched the NFL Network. It was showing each of the previous thirty-nine Super Bowls, including the only one I had ever attended as a fan. After my junior season at Notre Dame I went to Super Bowl XXVII in Pasadena, the one between the Cowboys and the Buffalo Bills. It just so happened that the NFL Network was showing that game, so I started to have little flashbacks from that day.

Later in the morning, Hines knocked on the door and wanted to know if I wanted to play cards. So we played cards. And then dominos. We were just BS-ing, screwing around. Here we were, a handful of hours from playing in the biggest game of our lives, and there was no pressure. We were loose, having fun until we boarded the bus for Ford Field.

Thanks to Duce, I had my Super Bowl wardrobe ready to go. Back in November, Duce had decided he was going to buy me a suit to wear to my last game at Heinz Field. So when we were in Indianapolis for our regular season game against the Colts, his tailor came to Indy for our first fitting. Later we got measured for everything in Pittsburgh.

I picked out a three-piece suit, a hat, an overcoat, and some shoes. Joey found out about it, so he ordered a suit too. But instead of wearing our new suits to the last home game, we decided we'd wear them if we reached the Super Bowl. So on February 5, 2006, I suited up, slipped on my overcoat, and put on my hat—all courtesy of Duce. I felt good. It was time to play a football game.

You ever see those movies where everybody is sitting on the team bus staring straight ahead in silence before a big game? That wasn't us. We were anxious, but we weren't uptight. We were having a ball, just yappin' it up on the ride from the team hotel to the stadium. It was usually quieter, but this time we were laughing and chopping it up. You wouldn't have thought we were a team going to play in a Super Bowl.

It wasn't until we got to Ford Field that it started to feel real. That's when everything started to come into focus.

We had three hours to kill before kickoff, so we just sat around until it was time for us running backs to start our pregame ritual. As usual, I led the running backs out for our customary—and my last ever—jog around the field. But this time when my feet touched the turf, a feeling came over me like, "Wow, at last . . . I'm here." I saw a Super Bowl XL banner and I said to myself, "I made it. I finally get a chance to see those lights."

We did our once-around the field and then went back into the locker room to get ready to come out as a team. While we were in there, Joey said to find him when we got down to the stadium tunnel. So a little while later, after I followed my fullback Dan Kreider from the locker room door to the edge of the tunnel (another one of my longtime pregame rituals), Joey pulled me aside.

"Look, this is your day," he said. "When they call us out, we want you to go out there first. You show 'em what's coming, and we'll be right behind you."

So when I got the signal, I sprinted out of the tunnel as if I were being timed in the 40. I didn't see anything but Terrible Towels and those lights. It was like a home game with all those Towels.

Someone told me later that a lot of the past Super Bowl MVPs were lined up on the field, but I didn't see them. I didn't see anything except those towels being waved and the flashes popping off.

✦ ✦ ✦

Our game plan was simple: hold them to no more than 17 points, score at least 21 points of our own. That was it in a nutshell. We always felt if we could put 17 points on the board, we could win any football game we played. And we knew their offense—even though it was the No. 1 offense in the league—was not going to score 17 points against our defense.

From what we had seen on film of the Seahawks, we definitely thought we were the better team. But on their opening drive they moved the ball from their 18-yard line to almost midfield before we forced them to punt. And when Matt Hasselbeck threw a 16-yard TD pass late in their first quarter, I thought we were in for a full-fledged dogfight.

But wide receiver Darrell Jackson was called for offensive pass interference on the play, so that wiped the touchdown off the board. They settled for a field goal, and even though we didn't have a first down in the first quarter, we only trailed by three.

Ben gave us a 7–3 lead late in the second quarter when he just squeezed over the goal line on a little 1-yard run. I played the part of his blocking fullback. And then Willie added to the lead on the second play of the third quarter with a 75-yard scoring run that was the longest in Super Bowl history.

Willie did all the running on that play, but I'd like to take a tiny bit of credit for helping him out.

Earlier in the game, he tried to force a run to the outside, instead of just being patient and cutting it up inside where the open crease was. I got some Polaroid photos of the Seahawks' alignment and showed them to Willie.

"I can see their game plan," I said. "They're waiting for you on the edges. See how the safeties are coming down?"

Willie nodded.

"OK, then no more east-west running," I said. "C'mon, north south, north south. You're reverting back to your rookie year. You're gonna break a big one."

Sure enough, the safeties inched down, Willie made the adjustment, scored on the play, and gave us a 14–3 lead. When he came back to the sideline after the touchdown, I was whooping it up. I just looked at him and winked. You know, one of those, "I told you so" winks.

We had the lead, but Seattle cut it to 14–10 and that's how it stayed until midway through the fourth quarter. Those guys wouldn't go away.

With 9:04 left in the game, Whisenhunt sent in a gadget play. I wasn't in the game at the time, but I was standing right next to Mark Whipple, our quarterbacks coach, when I heard the play call: Zero Strong Z Short Fake Toss 39 X Reverse Pass. We had run a screen pass to Antwaan Randle El out of the same formation a couple of plays earlier and gained 7 yards. That was the setup. Now we were going for the kill.

I hated the call. When I heard it, I sort of groaned and had a look of disgust. Coach Whipple saw my reaction, but didn't say anything. All I could think of was that 1997 AFC Championship, when we had tried a gimmick play and it cost us the game. So I was against doing anything in a big game that went against what you normally did in those situations. Do what you do best, that was my motto.

Ben took the handoff, pitched the ball to Willie, who then handed it off to Antwaan, the former college quarterback, who then threw a perfect pass to a wide open Hines at about the Seattle 5-yard line. Hines could have baby-stepped in for the touchdown.

As Hines scored the touchdown, Coach Whip gave me a look like, "Well? Did it work?" And I just looked back at him sheepishly and said, "Yeah, I know."

For all intents and purposes, that was the ballgame. We had our pregame goal of 21 points. And we held Seattle to below 17. It might not have been the most artistic Super Bowl win of all time, but it sure looked like a work of art to me.

I finished with fourteen carries for 43 yards, but I didn't care about those numbers. The only numbers that mattered to me were the ones on the Ford Field scoreboard: Pittsburgh 21, Seattle 10.

Had it been five years earlier in my career, it would have been important to me to score a touchdown in the game. Five years earlier I would have been one of the centerpieces of the team. But in 2005, at that stage of my career, scoring a touchdown in Super Bowl XL wasn't important. A championship was all that mattered.

I must have set a Super Bowl postgame record for Bear Hugs Given and Received. What had started on July 28 in Latrobe, Pennsylvania, had ended more than a half-year later on a downtown Detroit stadium located just six miles from the house I grew up in.

Hines was named the Super Bowl MVP and no question he deserved it. Five catches for 123 yards and a touchdown. One carry for 18 yards.

His usual knock-you-on-your-ass blocking. Yeah, they picked the right guy.

Hines always played with a chip on his shoulder pads. That's what helped make him great. He doesn't have an ACL in his left knee. He wasn't a first-round draft pick. And the Steelers always seemed to bring in new receivers each year. But Hines believed in himself and became a working man's star. I was so happy when they named him the MVP.

The Super Bowl MVP is always the guy who does those, "I'm going to Disney World!" commercials on the field right after the game. It's been that way since Phil Simms did the first one in 1987.

But this time Hines looked into the cameras and said, "I'm going to Disney World! And I'm taking The Bus!"

Can you believe it? I didn't even win the MVP, but Hines and Disney still wanted me to come along. For them to include me in that spot, and for Hines to share that moment with me, was a tremendous honor.

Crazy, huh? Nine hours earlier we were just two guys playing cards and dominos in a Detroit hotel room. Now Hines was the MVP (he did his postgame interviews holding the keys to his new Cadillac Escalade in his still-taped hands) and I was about to meet the love of my football life.

After the game, a stage was set up on the field and Commissioner Tagliabue presented the Lombardi Trophy to Mr. Rooney, whose father Art—everybody called him The Chief until the day he died in 1988—had founded the team in 1933. Mr. Rooney was now seventy-three, and he had seen the Steelers win five Super Bowls in his time. But this was the franchise's first championship since the 1979 season, when the Steelers beat my old team, the Rams. So the One-for-the-Thumb Super Bowl win had to mean a lot to him.

It also meant a lot to Coach Cowher, who had been labeled as a guy who couldn't win the big game, the so-called Best Coach Never to Have Won a Championship. Entering the 2005 season he was one for five in AFC Championships and zero for one in Super Bowls.

Don't people understand how hard it is to even *get* to five conference championship games? The man had more wins than any NFL coach since 1992, and yet when we struggled in '98 and '99, a lot of fans wanted to see him fired.

Coach Cowher and I had had our disagreements over the years, but they were few and far between. I didn't always agree with his decisions or methods, but I never doubted his ability as a coach or as a leader. I understood that those decisions were made in the best interests of the team—even if that didn't always mean what was best for Jerome Bettis.

He was a grinder, just like me, just like a lot of guys on our team. He had had to follow the legendary Chuck Noll and those four Super Bowl championships, which wasn't easy. But he survived. From the time he was hired in 1992, to the time we stood on the Ford Field turf as Super Bowl champs, there had been ninety-four head coaching changes in the league. That's the definition of a grinder (and of loyalty on the Rooneys' part).

He was my coach, but he was also my friend. And our friendship had been built on mutual trust and going through the football wars together.

After they presented the Lombardi Trophy to Mr. Rooney and Coach Cowher, the emcee asked me if this was my last game. It was the perfect moment to officially announce my retirement, so I told all those Steelers fans who were still waving their towels, and the worldwide television audience that, yes, this was it, I was retiring as a player.

Right after I said it, Coach Cowher kind of leaned toward me and said, "You could have talked to me about it."

We laughed about it, but the truth is, I purposely left him out of the loop when I informed the Rooneys that week after the Denver win. If I had told him, "Coach, I'm done, I'm retiring. The Super Bowl will be my last game," he might have done something out of the ordinary for me in the Super Bowl game plan. I didn't want that to even be a consideration for him. I didn't want my role to be any different just because it was my final game. So I didn't tell him.

One of the best moments of my life came when they handed me the Lombardi Trophy. It's the one thing made by Tiffany and Co. that you can't buy, no matter how many millions of dollars you have. The trophy is made out of sterling silver and weighs seven pounds—not that it mattered. It could have weighed 700 pounds, and I still would have raised it in the air for my teammates and our fans to see. At that moment, I had the strength of a thousand men.

It felt incredible to hold it, to see my reflection in that polished silver. I looked at that trophy and said to myself, "You have eluded me all of these years. Finally, I have you. Come here and give me a kiss."

So I planted a wet one on Vince's trophy. It was a kiss thirteen years in the making.

After the presentation, we all made our way to the locker room. Ben was waiting with a football in his hand. He had kept his promise, and for that I'm forever grateful.

"I told him, 'Thanks for everything you've done. I promised one last game ball and here it is. I love you.'

"When I gave him that last ball, that was a special moment. He just gave me a hug, and with tears in his eyes he said, 'Thank you.' "

—Ben Roethlisberger

Ben took a picture of the two of us in front of the Lombardi Trophy. Then we had the team photographer take a picture of the two of us kissing the trophy.

A little later I saw Mr. Rooney and his brother, Art Jr., holding up the Lombardi Trophy. With everybody in such a great mood, I figured this would be my one chance to talk to Mr. Rooney about our Super Bowl rings.

The way I figured it, the other players in the room might get another crack at a championship, but this was it for me. So I had to make sure the ring design was the right stuff.

"Mr. Rooney, I don't know the process that goes into designing the Super Bowl rings, but I was wondering who's going to make those decisions with you?" I said. "Is there a committee to help you design it?"

"I'll you what, Jerome," he said. "It will be me and you."

My heart started pounding harder.

"Are you saying what I think you're saying?"

"Yes, Jerome, we'll design it together."

"OK, Mr. Rooney."

It was crazy in the locker room. Guys were passing the trophy around. We were taking photos. A lot of guys wanted me to pose with them. It was my pleasure.

"I never asked him for anything after the game. But, uh, I actually stole something of his. He had these special T-shirts made just for him. This one was a black shirt with little 'Bus 36' designs

on it. He always used to talk about those shirts before the game. He'd say, 'This means so much to me.'

"After the Super Bowl, I didn't ask . . . I just took the shirt. It was all sweaty. He wore it all the time.

"He doesn't know that I took it. I don't wear it when I play. But before every game, I hold up that shirt and look at it. It's kind of an inspiration."

—*Willie Parker*

Jahmal brought my daughter into the locker room to see me. Jada was only a little over a year old, so she didn't understand why Daddy was smiling so much as he held her. One day I'll explain it to her.

I got pulled out of the locker room to do some media interviews. My family and Coach Dozier were out there and we had a group hug. I gave my mother a kiss and said, "Momma, I did it. Momma, I got it."

A few minutes later they took me across the street to make an appearance on *The Jimmy Kimmel Show*, which took forever. By the time I got back to the locker room, there was only one player left: Antwaan.

As I walked in, Antwaan was walking out. It was kind of a poignant moment because we all knew Antwaan was a free agent and that he would almost certainly sign a huge contract with another team. And he did: a six-year $31-million deal with the Redskins that included $10 million in bonuses.

Maybe it was fitting that I was the last player in the locker room. I stood there for a few minutes with Jahmal, my financial advisor Odell Winn, and *Sports Illustrated*'s Peter King and Michael Silver. Just before I walked out the door, I stopped, turned around and took a mental snapshot of the place. This was going to be my last time in a locker room, so I wanted to give it one more long look. I stood there for a few moments and then raised my hands and literally waved goodbye.

That was it. Amazingly, I was leaving as the fifth-leading rusher in NFL history. And best of all, I had seen those lights. My playing career was done.

✦ 12 ✦

The late afternoon practice complete, Bill Cowher walks toward the edge of the Saint Vincent College football fields and says hello to several Benedictine priests. About a dozen media members wait nearby for a brief post-practice update.

Since 1966 the 200-acre campus, located about 35 miles east of Pittsburgh, has been the home of the Steelers' training camp. The players' dorm, built with the help of the Steelers organization, is named, appropriately enough, Rooney Hall. And the four-week tour of duty here on a foothill of the Allegheny mountains actually has a name: Camp Cowher.

It is early August 2006. A few days ago, about 20,000 fans attended a Pittsburgh practice session. Twenty thousand . . . for a practice. They were there to see their world-champion Steelers. But for the first time in ten years, they wouldn't see Jerome Bettis—at least, not in person. His oversized image is still visible on the side of a nearby semi-truck trailer that houses a traveling Steelers exhibition, but that's it for Bussie sightings.

Roethlisberger, less than two months removed from a near-fatal motorcycle accident, practiced today, but watched the last fifteen minutes from the sidelines. Ward, nursing a leg injury, spent part of his practice time taking pictures with a camera he borrowed from one of the photographers.

The movie, Invincible, *is about to make its debut and Cowher tells re-*

porters that Vince Papale (the inspiration for the football film) and he were both cut at the same time by the Philadelphia Eagles in 1979.

"Coach Dick Vermeil, when he first came in, he ran a tough camp," says Cowher of the former Eagles coach.

Cowher runs a tough camp too. Except now he does it without the familiar sight of No. 36. In fact, nobody wears Bettis's number on the Steelers' roster. It hasn't been officially retired, but the equipment manager knows better than to issue it to anybody.

"It's different," Cowher says. "Not to hear his laugh, not to hear him talking . . ."

An eleven-year-old girl in glasses, waving a Terrible Towel and wearing a Polamalu jersey, yells for Cowher to autograph something. A mother holds up her infant son, wearing a tiny Steelers jersey, and asks if Cowher will sign the child's back.

Cowher glances toward the crowd. He'll be there in a minute. First, he wants to talk about his retired running back.

"Jerome Bettis was always a guy you could count on. It got to the point where I could look in his eyes and know how much of him I was going to get in a game. You knew he was going to give you whatever he could. But there were times when he only had so much to give.

"I felt a lot of times there was a part of me in him. I probably lived vicariously through him at times. At the end of the game, when he was running the ball, he was able to control a game almost by himself. I thought that was like a part of me out there.

"I think the one thing with him is that I always remained 'Coach,' and he was always the player. And I could never make him any guarantees. The last few years, every year, I couldn't guarantee him a roster spot. I couldn't guarantee him a role. I made him have to earn it. We talked about his weight. I respected the fact that he understood the process. And through it all we had a very professional relationship, but we also had a very special one that wasn't talked about, a relationship that was based on fairness. There was so much respect between the two of us. I think I respected his approach to the game more than anything else.

"You look at today's game and age, and here's a guy who took a cut in pay, took a reduced role, and yet he'll end up in the Hall of Fame. That to me speaks volumes about the guy, and the individual he really is.

"We all kind of knew that 2005 was his last run. It was a storybook ending for a very classy individual who sacrificed a lot, who was self-less in his approach to the game, and who was a tremendous role model, not just for kids, but for other football players.

"He's a very, very special person. His unselfishness, his humility, his approach to the game and his respect for the game is something that's very unique. I put him in the elite class.

"When the [Super Bowl] was over, I didn't have a chance to see a lot of players. I didn't even see them in the locker room because every-body was whisked away to interviews and those sort of things. But I don't think that's a bad thing, because the memory you'll have is the memory of everything that led up to that game. And to me that was the essence of the Super Bowl. It was not the game, it was the journey. To me, what we were able to accomplish and overcome in those last eight weeks—the challenges, the adversities, the circumstances—is what made it a very, very special season."

Orlando for a Disney World visit. Pittsburgh for our victory parade (some Pittsburgh companies extended their employees' lunch hours just so they could watch the festivities; schools and banks had high ab-sentee rates that day). Tampa for a Home Shopping Network commit-ment. Los Angeles for an appearance on *The Tonight Show*. The post–Super Bowl/retirement gig was crazy and chaotic—and I loved every minute of it.

When I did *The Tonight Show*, Jay Leno asked me if I had any re-grets.

"Yeah, I've got one," I said. "You know, if I had to do it all over again, I'd probably have had a job already planned before I retired."

That got a big hoot from the audience and, as it turned out, helped seal the deal with NBC Sports. I guess Dick Ebersol, the chairman of NBC Sports, saw the interview with Leno and liked what I had to say.

Not long after the Leno appearance, NBC offered me one of its stu-dio analyst jobs for *Football Night in America*. I couldn't say yes fast enough. But I did notice the Steelers opened the regular season on a Thursday night at home. So before I had worked day one for NBC, I had to ask Mr. Ebersol a favor: Would it be OK if I attended the September 7 Miami-Pittsburgh game at Heinz?

OK? Mr. Ebersol said NBC was doing that game and he *wanted* me there. So everything was perfect.

Then the network flew me, my mother and father, and my fiancée Trameka to Turin, Italy, where NBC was broadcasting the Winter Olympics. That's where they made the formal announcement about me joining the network.

A few weeks after I got back from Italy, Mr. Rooney called me in Atlanta.

"I need you to fly to Pittsburgh," he said. "I think I've got something you'll like. I want you to come and see it and tell me what you think."

So I flew to Pittsburgh and Mr. Rooney showed me the design for our Super Bowl rings. I don't know how to say this tactfully, but it was horrible.

I now had the daunting task of convincing Mr. Rooney that his initial design was awful and that we needed to go back to the drawing board. The problem was that the ring design looked very similar to the one from the 1979 championship, except that the 2005 version had a bigger diamond in the middle. Sheesh, it was awful.

So I delicately asked Mr. Rooney what other options we had. About the same time, Ben stopped by Mr. Rooney's office to say hello. This wasn't by accident. I had seen Ben earlier in the day and told him that I might need his help to "encourage" Mr. Rooney to consider other ring designs. I figured the more firepower, the better.

To Mr. Rooney's credit he agreed to look at some other designs by the Jostens ring people and to consider some suggestions from Ben and me. I dare say we ended up with a great ring: five small diamond-studded Lombardi Trophies forming a semi-circle around the Steelers team logo on the face of the ring. Classy and elegant.

We were presented with the rings at a June 4, 2006, private ceremony at Heinz Field. I can't help but stare at my ring with a sense of pride and wonder. I know it's only a ring, but it represents so many things to me. It's my most prized material possession.

In late April I flew to South Bend to serve as an honorary coach for Notre Dame's Blue-Gold spring game. Like I've said, my disappointment over Tyrone Willingham's firing never had anything to do with Charlie Weis. In fact, after we lost to the Patriots in the 2004 AFC

Championship, I had made it a point to find Charlie on the field. At the time, he was already juggling the New England job and the Notre Dame job. But I told him if there was anything I could do for him and the Irish football program, to just let me know.

And he did. He asked me to talk to his team before they played the Pitt Panthers at Heinz Field to open the 2005 season, and I was happy (and surprisingly nervous) to do so. And he asked me to join Rocket and Mike and Bob Golic as honorary spring game coaches in 2006. It was an offer I couldn't refuse, mostly because he wouldn't let me.

On June 2, two days before we got our rings, the entire team and assorted members of the Steelers' front office and staff was invited to the White House, where we presented President George W. Bush with an authentic jersey (No. 43) and a signed football.

I guess some of the White House staff weren't real big NFL or Steelers fans. I say that because when we first walked into the East Room, there were name tags Velcro'd to the stage floor to show us where to stand. Coach Cowher's name was spelled *Cower*. That put things in perspective real fast.

Once we were assembled on the stage and risers, there was a brief pause and then a voice came over the East Room loudspeaker. "Ladies and gentlemen," said the emcee, "the President of the United States."

President Bush walked in, and I could have sworn I saw somebody wave a Terrible Towel in the crowd. Steelers people aren't shy about cheering for their team, and this event was no exception.

"It sounds like some people have been drinking some Iron City beer here," said the president.

President Bush acknowledged the dignitaries in the crowd, admitted that he was a Cowboys fan, told us he used to pump iron with Texas alum Casey Hampton, and was looking forward to meeting Joey. Then the president did a very nice thing. He said he appreciated the work I had done through my charitable foundation.

Later, he threw a tight little spiral to Hines, and then he was off to run the country. I shook his hand and he said, "God bless. Thank you."

No matter what one's political views are, it's an honor to meet the president and to see the White House. One of my favorite sights during the tour was to see a painting of Martin Luther King prominently displayed on one of the White House walls. One of my favorite experiences during our trip to Washington, D.C., was visiting, which we did at Mr. Rooney's request, Walter Reed Army Medical Center. I'll talk with our soldiers anytime, anywhere.

In early July, Trameka and I were married in Jamaica. And as much as I loved kissing that Vince Lombardi Trophy, Trameka's lips are a lot softer.

My brother, John, was my best man, but a lot of the Steelers came to the ceremony. One of the guys I was happiest to see was Ben.

Ten days after our early June visit to the White House, Ben had nearly lost his life in a motorcycle accident in Pittsburgh. He suffered facial injuries, a mild concussion, and lost several teeth when he collided headfirst into a car windshield. Considering he wasn't wearing a helmet at the time, Ben was lucky to be alive.

But he was almost fully recovered when I saw him in Jamaica. He even beat me in golf.

Not long after Trameka and I got home from our honeymoon, my mother called me. I asked her how she was doing. She said fine. I asked her if she needed anything. She said no. But I could tell something was on her mind.

"Is everything OK?" I said.

"Everything's fine," she said. "I was just wondering how you were feeling now that Steelers started training camp today."

"They went to training camp today?" I said.

I had totally forgotten about it, which was a great sign. It meant that I almost had closure. It meant that my body clock wasn't telling me it was time to start getting ready for another season.

Instead, it was time to play a little golf. I was lucky enough to be paired with Tiger Woods during the Buick Open Pro-Am at Warwick Hills Golf and Country Club, which is located just outside of Detroit. It was the first time I had ever met him, and we kind of hit it off.

I think for one of the few times in his life, he wasn't the center of attention. More than a few times the gallery chanted, "Bus! Bus! Bus!" When we got to the seventeenth tee box, Tiger looked at the crowd, then looked at me and said, "How do you do it? How do you handle it?"

We busted out laughing because one of the world's most recognizable people was asking me how I handled the attention. It was hilarious that he would say it, and say it with such a straight face. I was impressed.

I played damn good that day (83, my second-best round of all time) for being paired with the greatest golfer of all time and dealing with those crowds. But I knew better than to ask Tiger for any golf tips. Even though it was a pro-am, he was still working and getting himself prepared for the real tournament. So I let him do his thing. In fact, we mostly talked about football.

At the end of the round, I gave him one of my jerseys and he gave me an autographed flagstick flag. He wrote, "Thanks for a great day. Tiger." I should have had him write, "You beat me again. Damn!"

Total football closure came shortly before kickoff of that September 7 game at Heinz Field. As part of the pregame festivities, an actual bus pulled up near the edge of the field. It's only passenger: me.

When the door opened, I jumped off the bus and did sort of a pro glide onto the field. The crowd went nuts and it was great seeing that sea of yellow and black Terrible Towels and hearing those Steelers fans roar. But this time I was wearing my new uniform: a business suit. I wasn't a player anymore, but you know what? That was OK. I had finally let go. Almost.

I ran to the 50-yard line, but then I couldn't help myself. I reached down, pulled out a handful of that Heinz Field grass, and stuck the turf in my pants pocket. That handful of turf is now prominently displayed in the office at my house.

My time as a Steeler was done. And I had the feeling, even during that summer of 2006, that Coach Cowher was contemplating a change in his life, too. He had won a Super Bowl and had spent a long time in the same organization. I could sense that 2006 would be his last season with the Steelers. I even said so a few months later during our NBC pregame show. As it turned out, Coach Cowher did resign at season's end and, like me, became a broadcaster. I can't get rid of the guy.

It used to take me two months to recover physically after a season. But now I actually get out of bed without it taking ten minutes to work my way off the mattress. And I don't have to sit down on the stairs and slowly slide down the steps anymore. My body isn't 100 percent, and never will be. I'm a little stiff in the morning and my ankles pop every now and then. But I don't have to worry about Jada splitting one of my quad muscles.

As for business, I have some major real estate development projects that are important to me. And I also own Urban Mortgage, a company that specializes in educating and helping urban-based consumers who have either been exploited or neglected by major mortgage companies. My brother, John, is the president of our Detroit branch.

And, of course, there are the Miller Lite "Man Law" commercials that have taken on a life of their own. My father liked those commercials.

I can't tell you how many times people have stopped me and said there ought to be a Man Law about this, or a Man Law about that. The one I get the most is, "There ought to be a Man Law against athletes dancing on TV."

They're talking about the *Dancing with the Stars*, show on ABC. Emmitt Smith, the NFL's all-time leading rusher, won the 2006 installment. But before they asked Emmitt to be on that show, they asked me.

I turned them down. My agent, Lamont Smith, kept telling me, "The show is watched by 38 million people." But that was my point: I didn't want 38 million people watching me dance. I didn't want thirty-eight people watching me dance.

The producers of the show said they'd contribute money to my foundation, but there wasn't enough money in the world to get me to wear green shoes on a dance floor. That's what Emmitt wore—green shoes. And gold shoes. And Ultimate Warrior bands around his arm. And glitter on his arms and head. Come on now.

They kept asking me to do the show, but my answer was, "Absolutely not."

I was at an event with Jerry Rice, arguably the greatest player of all time, and he was making a speech about how more people knew him from his appearances on *Dancing with the Stars* than they did from his days on the football field. It was funny, but it was also kind of sad in a way.

I was doing a commercial in Miami in November 2006 when this little girl—she was eleven—told me she didn't know anything about football. But later on she mentioned Emmitt.

I said, "So you do know something about football."

And she said, "No, Emmitt Smith is the guy who was on *Dancing with the Stars*."

A whole generation of kids know him just from that show? Sorry, but that's not for me.

Phase two of my life means wife, daughter, family, charities, business investments, and TV career. I had a master plan for a lot of those things. My one aching regret is that my father won't be here to enjoy it with me.

On Tuesday, November 28, 2006—I'll never forget the date—Trameka called me on the golf course and told me I needed to come home. She didn't say why, but I could tell by the sound of her voice that something had happened.

About a minute later, I received a call from a police officer asking to speak to my wife about my father. The officer wouldn't give me any details, other than to say he needed to talk to Trameka.

I immediately called my mom, but there was no answer. Then I called my brother.

"Dad's at the hospital," John said. "Dad might be dead."

I made a beeline for the house. Shortly after I got home, Steelers PR man Dave Lockett called and said my father was in bad shape, but nothing had been confirmed. That's when I knew to expect the worst. For Dave to call meant that the Steelers organization had heard something pretty bad.

A little while later my worst fears were realized: My dad had suffered an apparent heart attack while driving home from the gym. He was only sixty-one.

According to the police, my father was able to pull his SUV over to the side of a busy road before the heart attack took his life. His actions, said the police, likely prevented someone from being hurt, possibly fatally, in a car accident.

Several people, including a doctor and nurse, tried to revive my dad at the scene, but it was too late.

The funeral was six days later at Messiah Baptist Church. More than eight hundred people attended the service, which says a lot about how many lives my father touched.

My dad was a great man. He stood for integrity and he believed in doing and saying the right things. He taught me that your actions always speak louder than your words. And my father's actions always spoke loud and clear. He was my hero.

I was so appreciative of the respect paid to my father, and of the outpouring of support from people all around the country, but especially in Detroit and Pittsburgh. Detroit mayor Kwame Kilpatrick spoke eloquently about my father at the service. Former teammates such as Kordell Stewart and Dewayne Washington made the effort to be there. So did Ben, Joey, Clark, James Farrior, Ike Taylor, Deshea Townsend, Casey Hampton, and Charlie Batch. Ben had asked Coach Cowher if he would delay the Steelers' afternoon practice that day so they could visit with my mom and me before the service. A few days later, Coach and the team observed a moment of silence in honor of my father. That meant a lot to me.

Hines was quoted in the Pittsburgh papers as saying my dad was like the team grandpa. In fact, Hines called him Pops. Everyone on the team did. They called my mother Moms and my father Pops. Everybody knew my family on a first-name basis.

But my father developed relationships outside of me. He was a quiet man, but he had a disarming way about him. And he had a great laugh. Like father, like son.

My mother had wanted me to retire after the 2005 season, but my dad wanted me to come back for one more year. He wanted me to take one last run at a Super Bowl. Maybe that's why that championship meant so much to both of us. He knew how much I had wanted to see those lights. Like all fathers, he wanted his son to be happy.

It wasn't supposed to be like this. My father had retired only a couple of years earlier. He used to say he'd like to make the introduction speech if I was fortunate enough to be selected to the Pro Football Hall of Fame. Believe me, if I do make it, he'll be with me in spirit.

My father influenced me in so many ways, and his influence is apparent in almost everything I do: hard work, a commitment to integrity and loyalty, and making the world a little better place. My evolution from Detroit Jerome to the person I am today was made possible by his example.

I started my The Bus Stops Here Foundation in 1997 to help raise money for troubled and underprivileged kids. We also have the Cyber Bus Computer Literacy Program for inner-city kids. If it were up to me, every kid would have a computer.

We run the Friends Forever Scholarship program, as well as Save Children Opportunity Recreation Education (SCORE), which helps fund scholarships, computer systems, and the rebuilding of rec centers and parks. There's also the Bettis Turkey for All program that gives

Thanksgiving turkey dinners to people and families who can't afford to buy their own.

I've established scholarships at Mackenzie High School and done public service announcements about asthma. I think it's the very least I can do. I've been blessed, so why not try to make other peoples' lives a little better?

One of the most heartbreaking letters I ever got was from a family in Mississippi whose house had been destroyed by Hurricane Katrina. One of their few belongings that survived the hurricane was a Jerome Bettis bobblehead doll. They sent me a photo of it and I was speechless. All I could think was, "You folks are going through all of that pain and suffering, and you still have time to be a *fan*?"

I made sure to send them a big care package of Steelers' goodies.

I oversee a couple of football camps, including Reggie McKenzie's camp in Detroit. A few years ago I asked him why he started his charitable foundation. And he said he wanted to try to affect one kid. He thought if he could affect one kid, then he had made a difference.

I told him he had. And that kid was me.

As of early January 2007, I still hadn't filed my retirement papers with the NFL. Don't worry, though, I'm not making a comeback.

I don't miss training camp, or the off-season workouts, or the pain, or the practices. I do miss the games. And no question I miss the camaraderie of being part of a team. I tell people that one day, if I get enough zeroes behind the first few numbers, I'd love to buy an NFL franchise. If I did, Coach Cowher would be one of my first hires, either as the head coach, the general manager, or as an advisor. The man understands coaching, talent evaluation, and the business of the game.

But that's somewhere down the road. Until then, I'm going to try to enjoy life without a helmet. After all those yards and all those hits, I think I've earned it.

ACKNOWLEDGMENTS

When I look back on my younger days, there were a lot of mistakes made but there were also a lot of good decisions made. One of those was to listen to a friend of the family, Jeffery Holmes. Jeff was always there when I needed him whether it was saving me from a backyard party gone bad or running around the track with me to make sure I'd be in shape when I reported to Notre Dame. Another person who helped shape my life then and is still involved in the shaping process is Jahmal Dokes, a high school football teammate turned business manager. I cannot take all the credit for my off-the-field success because Jahmal has been a part of it all, and in some cases, creating it all. It has been great to have a loyal guy like that in my huddle.

I would like to thank Tom Seabron for not only being my financial adviser but for being a mentor and a friend. Early in my professional career I often needed guidance, and being a former NFL player himself, Tom was able to relate and give me good advice, like choosing an agent. Tom introduced me to Lamont Smith and, after a few conversations, I knew I found the right man to represent me. What I did not know was that I had also found a great friend who would play an important role in my player development and also my life development.

I would also like to thank my crew: Odell Winn, Deral Boykin, Al and Frank Costa, Chuck Betters, Chuck Olstoff, and Chuck Sanders each playing an important role in my life—thanks for being lifelong friends! A big thanks goes to Greg Eastman (G-Money) and Leon

Henderson for keeping the money in order, but also for being great friends, and Larry Parker, thank you for a job well done. There are so many other people who have entered my life and helped me in one way or another and to all of you I say thank you!

I have been blessed to have a wonderful, supportive family, one that has shared in my every success and helped lift me up through every failure. My mother is the reason I have life and that is a special bond, one that I could not fully understand until I had a child of my own. She has been there for me every step of my life, cheering me on as well as up if that was needed, and in a lot of ways this is her story, too. My brother and sister have been the best siblings in the world, always happy for their little brother and his success. A special thank-you has to be in order for my wife, Trameka. She has endured so much in so little time, sharing me with the world. I am amazed at how she handles all the responsibilities and the raising of our children, all while I am pulled away from home for work. To Jada and Jerome Jr., Daddy loves you with all of his heart.

Thank you, God, for giving me such a blessed life, beautiful children, an incredible wife, a wonderful family, and the ring!

—Jerome Bettis, 2007

THE BUS STOPS HERE FOUNDATION

When it comes to making a difference, I'm not ashamed to ask for the help of others. If you'd like to contribute to one of our worthy causes, or simply learn more about the Foundation, log on to www.the bus36.com, or write me at The Bus Stops Here Foundation at 10421 West 7 Mile Road, Detroit, MI, 48221. You know why? Because you never know who that one kid could turn out to be.

One day the phone rang in my office at our family home in Wheaton, Illinois. "How would you like to do a book with Jerome Bettis?" said agent extraordinaire Janet Pawson. "It'll be fun."

She was right. Janet Pawson is always right. It was fun, remarkably fun. So I thank Janet for her foresight and wise counsel. I owe her so much more than just a few lines on an acknowledgments page. Thanks also to her able assistant at Headline Media Management, Michelle Hall. And many thanks to Headline Media's Lou Oppenheim.

Doubleday's Bill Thomas and Rebecca Cole deserve special mention for their contributions to this project. Rebecca, in particular, held this book's hand from start to finish. And assistant Brianne Ramagosa attended to the detail work.

Joe Wojciechowski transcribed nearly all twenty-five-hours' worth of taped interviews with Jerome—at top speed, I might add. His suggestions and support were invaluable, and his imitation of Jerome's voice and phrases became frighteningly similar to Bussie's.

Dave Lockett and Burt Lauten of the Pittsburgh Steelers' media relations department were beyond helpful. Whatever the Rooney family is paying them, it isn't enough. Dave and Burt answered every phone call, interview request, and question with good humor and, better yet, with quick and accurate responses. I would have been lost without them. I'd also like to thank the St. Louis Rams' media relations department for its assistance.

John Heisler, a friend and the senior associate athletic director at Notre Dame, was kind enough to provide me with access to assorted research and backround material on Jerome. He also offered a small collection of Jerome-related anecdotes.

The voluminous, thorough, and well-crafted work of *Pittsburgh Post-Gazette* writers Ed Bouchette and Ron Cook was especially helpful during the research of Jerome's career. And Ed's help during my visits to Steelers' training camp and the Steelers' Pittsburgh facility in 2006 was most appreciated. The work of *Sports Illustrated*'s Peter King and Michael Silver, as well as *USA Today*'s Jarrett Bell, the *Los Angeles Times*'s T. J. Simers, and the *St. Louis Post-Dispatch*'s Bernie Miklasz and Jim Thomas was also used while researching this book.

Many thanks to those who provided their considerable time and insights: Gladys Bettis, Lamont Smith, Jahmal Dokes, Hines Ward, Ben Roethlisberger, Willie Parker, Bill Cowher, Dick Hoak, Mel Kiper Jr., Bob Dozier, Lou Holtz, Tim Lester, Bouchette, Lockett, and Heisler, among others. I now understand why Jerome values his lifelong friendship with Dokes. If Jahmal says he'll take care of something, he takes care of it.

Special thanks to Jeffery Holmes, Deral Boykin, Larry Parker, and Tom Seabron.

I would also like to thank Rick Reilly and O. S. Carr for their support and valuable suggestions. And to my wife, Cheryl, I would like to thank her for her love, seemingly inexhaustible patience, and ability not to nod off as I excitedly explained the genius of Counter 38 Power.

And most of all, I would like to thank Jerome Bettis for his honesty, his integrity, his modesty, his humor, his passion and compassion. I can't tell you how many times he told his lovely wife Trameka he was "wrapping up" an interview session, only to tell me a few moments later, "let's keep going . . . let's get this right."

It isn't often you meet someone who exceeds your expectations. Jerome didn't simply exceed them, he redefined them. He is also the first professional athlete I've ever met who repeatedly used the word, "Sheesh."

"It'll be fun," Janet Pawson had said to me in early 2006. I just didn't know it would be this much fun.

—Gene Wojciechowski
January 2007

ABOUT THE AUTHORS

JEROME BETTIS is now a commentator on NBC's *Football Night in America.* He is the founder of The Bus Stops Here Foundation, which works to improve the quality of life for disadvantaged children, and works with the American Lung Foundation to increase asthma awareness. He lives in Atlanta.

 GENE WOJCIECHOWSKI is a senior writer for *ESPN The Magazine* and ESPN.com. He has authored or coauthored eight books, including *Cubs Nation, My Life on a Napkin* (with Rick Majerus), *I Love Being the Enemy* (Reggie Miller), *Nothing But Net* (Bill Walton), and his baseball novel, *About 80 Percent Luck.* He lives in Wheaton, Illinois.